Contents

Abbreviations

ADT	actual disgust trigger
BBFC	British Board of Film Classification
CPPA	Child Pornography Protection Act (US)
EE	ethical egoism
ESA	Entertainment Software Association
EULA	end user licence agreement
MMOG	massively multiplayer online game
MMORPG	massively multiplayer online role-playing game
NE	Aristotle, *Nicomachean Ethics*
NPC	non-player character
PIU	problematic internet use
PDT	potential disgust trigger
POTA	prohibited offline taboo activity
PVL	preference for virtual life
STA	symbolic taboo activity
VE	virtual environment
VR	virtual reality

ONE

Introduction: playing with right and wrong

According to the Entertainment Software Association (ESA), during the period 1996–2009, in the United States alone, the number of video games sold for use on a console or personal computer increased from 73.3 million units to 273.5 million (ESA 2010). For the same period, spending on these games rose from 2.6 billion dollars to 10.5 billion (peaking in 2008 at 11.7 billion dollars). Similarly, in the United Kingdom in 2008, video games were reported to have become the UK's most popular form of entertainment, with sales for that year estimated to be around 4.64 billion pounds (Cellan-Jones 2008). Moreover, in its 2010 report, the ESA claimed that 67 per cent of households in the US owned either a gaming console or a personal computer used to run entertainment software, that the average age of a gamer was thirty-four – with 49 per cent aged between eighteen and forty-nine – and that, on average, adult gamers had been playing video games for twelve years. The ESA report also contained a list of the top twenty console games for 2009 (based on units sold). Ranked number one in the US was *Call of Duty: Modern Warfare 2* (rated "mature"). In fact, Prigg (2009) reports that 4.7 million copies of this game were sold on its opening day in the US and

UK alone, out-selling the previous best video game – *Grand Theft Auto IV* – by some distance. (Prigg also reports that of the 4.7 million sold, the sale of 1.23 million copies in the UK was a record for that country.)

Both the *Grand Theft Auto* and *Call of Duty* series are held to be extremely violent games. *Call of Duty: Modern Warfare 2* is infamous for its civilian massacre scene, and *Grand Theft Auto IV* has courted controversy by permitting the gamer's character to have sex with prostitutes before mugging or even killing them for their money. The possibility for simulated violence of the kind demonstrated by these games (and others), even when restricted to adults – which demographic data from the US and UK show to be a large percentage of the total gaming population (see The Average Gamer 2010) – raises a number of interesting and important moral questions. Within the context of video games, is it appropriate to judge a legitimate action or even a more sustained gaming strategy as either morally good or morally bad? When one bloodies and brutalizes a stranger to the point of death with a kitchen utensil, as it is possible to do in *Manhunt 2* (for example), or when one sexually assaults a defeated female opponent (watching her cry and hearing her anguish) in *Battle Raper*, are these activities morally bad things to engage in? If so, in what sense are they bad and for whom should we be morally concerned? Conversely, within the game *BioShock*, if one chooses *not* to "harvest" the Little Sisters – that is, kill mutant female children – for the extra power one will obtain, but instead elects to spare them, is this a morally commendable act?

Providing a coherent and philosophically astute response to these questions is an important aim of this book, and is without doubt one of its key challenges. After all, what does it mean for *x* to be a morally bad thing? The answer to this question will depend, of course, on what one considers morality to be. In simple terms, if one holds that it is morally good to do one's duty (among other things, let us say that this involves being kind to other people), then it should follow that not doing one's duty is morally bad. However, what if one virtually enacts not doing one's duty (one is "cruel" or, at the very least, not "kind" to a character within a game): is that morally bad also? Alternatively, what if one virtually enacts doing one's duty: is that morally good? If it is, why should this be? After all, in this case, one has not actually done one's duty, only simulated it (the "person" to whom one was "kind" was not a real person, just a gaming character). So if it is not morally good then how can being "cruel" to a gaming character be morally bad? Perhaps the virtual act of doing or not doing one's duty is, in and of itself, an amoral act that only becomes of moral interest if it interferes with one's tendency to do one's duty for real. Thus, one may judge *x* to be amoral in one sense (in and of itself) but immoral in another: morally problematic *if*, and therefore *because*, it interferes with one's tendency to do one's duty and so be moral (something that, if it is the case, would need to be empirically verified).

Others may hold that morality is not about duty, of course, or is about more than this. But whichever system of morality one adopts, the same issue arises: namely, its application to virtual enactments. A large part of this book will therefore be taken up with just this issue: considering the applicability of different moral criteria to virtual activities within video games, and the extent to which a particular moral theory is able to provide the satisfactory and hence justificatory means – where deemed necessary – for the selective prohibition of video game content. In addition, it is ultimately my intention to argue for the importance of psychology rather than morality as a measure of what should be permitted within video games, based on the view that the selective prohibition of content should stem from what gamers are able to cope with, psychologically, rather than what is deemed morally right or wrong, or good or bad. In order to support this argument, however, it is necessary to provide a detailed philosophical assessment of what I shall call the *current state of play* regarding permitted and prohibited video game content (see Ch. 2). Can traditional moral theory (see Chs 3–5, 8, 9 and 10) or even more contemporary moral approaches (Chs 6 and 7) be applied to video games so as to provide a cogent argument for why certain content is or *should* be prohibited? Through a systematic examination of different philosophical arguments, some of which have applied traditional moral theories to video game content (mostly violent), I aim to show how each is ultimately unable to account for the current state of play or provide a cogent reason for why certain content should be prohibited but not others.

In the chapters to come, then, I shall consider the extent to which the moral theories used to provide guidance for our non-gaming activities may legitimately be applied to the world of video games. More traditional theories, such as Hume's sentimentalism (Ch. 3), Kant's deontological approach (Ch. 4), the consequentialism characteristic of utilitarianism (Ch. 5) and social contract theory (Ch. 10), or even the less popular ethical egoism (Ch. 9), will be critically examined to see if they are able to inform our judgements regarding the selective prohibition of video game content. In addition, I shall consider the extent to which selective prohibition should incorporate views regarding the content's symbolic meaning (Chs 6 and 7), or the gamer's moral character and motivation (Chs 8 and 11, respectively), and how these might best be understood within the context of video *games* and video *gamers*. Finally, by drawing on empirical research, I shall consider ways in which gamers morally manage their activities while playing video games, so as to support my argument for psychologically informed, rather than morally based, prohibition (Ch. 12).

The virtual enactments of interest throughout this book are those that represent real-world taboos:[1] namely, actions that are typically both legally and morally proscribed outside the gaming environment. Such activities include discrimination, murder, rape, assault (sexual and physical), torture, incest, paedophilia, necrophilia and bestiality: virtual enactments that Monica Whitty *et al.* (2011) call "symbolic taboo activities" (STAs), a term I shall adopt here. Before discussing the suitability of moral theory to these, however, it is important to clarify certain key terms – namely, video game, gameplay and gamespace – and how these fit within the more general context of virtual reality. It is also important to consider video games within the wider context of fiction and play, and the relationship these constructs have to morality.

DEFINING "VIDEO GAME" AND RELATED TERMS

In defining "video game", it is not my intention to provide a definition that is able to capture all forms of the medium; that is, satisfy what others may argue constitute different types of video game. Instead, I use the term to refer to a *particular* means by which one can enact STAs; in doing so, I borrow heavily from Grant Tavinor (2008) (and occasionally Juul 2005). Like Tavinor, I favour the term "video game" over, say, "computer game" or "electronic game". By "video game", I refer to games played on personal computers (PCs) or consoles such as X-Box 360, PlayStation 1–3 and Wii. PC games may involve one player or a number of players connected through the internet. Console games also include single- or multiplayer options (a multiplayer game is any game involving two or more players). Following Tavinor, I recognize that there are different components to video games: narratology, ludology and the interactive nature of the fiction. I also use the acronym NPC to refer to a non-player character (that is, a virtual gaming character controlled by the game software).

The video games discussed throughout the book contain some form of narrative, as the narratologists maintain. In keeping with ludology, they also have an obvious gaming quality; they are designed and marketed as *games* (rather than, say, training devices) and are therefore meant to be *played* in a way that subscribes to certain rules, explicitly or implicitly found within the gameplay (set by the game mechanics).[2] By "gameplay" I follow Jesper Juul's lead and mean "the pure interactivity of the game" (2005: 19), which is constitutive of the video game content in terms of the representations found therein and the interactions afforded. These in turn are produced through an "interaction between the rules …, the players pursuing a goal, and [their] personal repertoire and preferences" (*ibid.*: 199–200). By "gamespace", I mean simply the virtual environment in which the gameplay is realized.

The terms "virtual environment" and "virtual reality" are often used interchangeably in much of the thinking and literature on the subject of video games, or cyberspace in general. Ralph Schroeder, for example, describes a virtual environment as providing users "with the sensory experience of being in a place other than the one [they] are physically in, and being able to interact with that place" (2006: 439). A further useful distinction is made by Narcis Parés and Roc Parés, who distinguish between virtual environments (VEs), which they define as static structures, and virtual reality (VR), which constitutes the structures of VEs put into action. The two are interrelated in so far as "VR is a real time experience a user can have of a VE" (Parés & Parés 2006: 528). Throughout this book, VR will be restricted to that constitutive of gamespace, and will be used in conjunction with VE, which is taken to represent the medium through which the gamer is able to experience an embodied and interactive VR. Importantly, the gamespace discussed here will *not* refer to an immersive VE: that is, an environment that "surrounds the body, often engulfing the senses" (Biocca 1997: 11), achieved through the use of "immersive technology" such as stereoscopic helmets, data gloves and even body suits.

Finally, video games are interactive fictions: the narrative is wholly or in part fictional (it may be set on a fictitious alien world, for example, or be set in an actual historical context such as the Second World War). (What being fictional entails will be discussed below.) The video game is interactive in so far as the player can to a greater or lesser degree alter the course of the narrative in virtue of actions carried out, including decisions made during the course of the gameplay. What counts as a game, of course, as Wittgenstein famously pointed out, is notoriously difficult to define, and, for him at least, is dependent on activities possessing certain "family resemblances" (1953: §67). That aside, "video game", as I am using the term, fits well within Juul's more general definition:

> A game is a rule-based system with a variable and quantifiable outcome, where different outcomes are assigned different values, the player exerts effort in order to influence the outcome, the player feels emotionally attached to the outcome, and the consequences of the activity are negotiable.   (Juul 2005: 36)

In addition, I include two essential features made explicit by Tavinor (2008): (a) video games are a digital medium, and (b) they are designed, marketed and played as games. More formally, then, X is a video game if and only if:

1. It is an artefact in a digital visual medium.
2. It is intended primarily as an object of entertainment.
3. It is intended to provide such entertainment through the employment of one or both of the following modes of engagement: (a) rule-bound gameplay or (b) interactive fiction.[3]

Point 3 should be understood to incorporate Juul's definition of a game (above).

GAMES, FICTION AND PLAY

Stating that what the player engages in is *just* a game implies, first, that those representations and actions that occur should be understood and therefore judged (by others as well as the players) not only within the context of the specific rules or structure of the game but also, and more fundamentally, within the context of it *being* a game. To call something "a game" is to establish a point of departure or a means of demarcation – some qualitative shift – away from other (non-gaming) activities, especially as a number of games "possess the characteristics of being social conventions that countenance violations, often substantial ones, of social conventions" (Howe 2008: 569). Not only does the reference to *x* being a game explain certain actions – why, for example, in a game of British Bulldog person A is trying to traverse an area of land (move from one side of a room to the other) while persons B, C, D, ... try to grab them and wrestle them to the ground – but it also bestows on the action (i.e. grabbing a person and wrestling them to the ground) an air of legitimacy: it is a conventional violation of a social convention. In addition, those who insist that what the player does is *just* a game seek to relegate the moral importance of the event outside the space of play, thereby trivializing its need for moral scrutiny (see discussion on the amoralist's position in Ch. 2).

At this point, I should like to distinguish "game" from "sport". It is common enough to say "I watched a *game* of football" or even "I *played* football", but there is an important difference between playing games of sport and the games I wish to discuss here (but by no means the only difference). Typically, in video games, the player is represented by an avatar, and is able to interact in accordance with the abilities and skills possessed by that avatar (in conjunction with one's own skill at playing the games in the form of that avatar).[4] In sport, however, one is oneself within the game and one's abilities and skills are conveyed directly; they are not mediated by an avatar (Sando 2010). Even in non-computer games, one typically plays a character of some description; traditional characters for a child being a superhero, or a soldier, or a cowboy/girl (for example). To say that *x* is *just* a game (as I am using the term, in the absence of sport) is to imply that the game incorporates an element of play, *qua* fiction and therefore make-believe.[5] To play a game of football in the make-believe guise of David Beckham, for example, is different from playing football in one's Sunday League team as oneself. The meaning of "It's just a game" that I wish to explore here, then, is that which views the representations and virtual interactions that occur within gamespace as play *qua* fiction and make-believe (as the example of playing football *make-believedly* as David Beckham illustrates), rather than playing football as oneself in one's Sunday League team, which is bereft of this kind of make-believe.[6]

Restricting discussion to games that involve elements of make-believe rather than games *qua* sport is an important means of maintaining focus. However, it is still necessary to unpack the notion of fiction and make-believe further (hereafter, just fiction); for although play may be synonymous with fiction, fiction can be created in the absence of (or not for the purpose of) play. As such, if we hold (for now) that STAs are by their very nature fictional, and therefore indicative of an act of make-believe (although I shall have more to say on this as we progress), and given that STAs are constitutive of the virtual enactment of taboo or otherwise prohibited activities, what is the relationship between STAs (*qua* putative acts of fiction), morality and play? In order to address this question, we need to consider (briefly) the broader issue of fiction and morality, rather than just fiction within play. Is any fiction a legitimate target for moral scrutiny? If it is not, then this must equally apply to play. If, on the other hand, some fiction is open to moral evaluation, then does this necessarily apply to play? Is there something about engaging in play that removes it from our moral gaze? In order to address this question, I shall first consider the morality of fiction more generally before considering some of the more unique qualities of play and whether these protect it from any form of moral challenge.

IMAGINATIVE RESISTANCE: A MORAL APPROACH TO FICTION?

Does the moral accountability of fiction change if it is engendered within the context of play rather than, say, a novel or film or art? To address this question, consider the following extract from the poem by Samuel Taylor Coleridge:

> Like one that on a lonesome road
> Doth walk in fear and dread,
> And having once turned round walks on,
> And turns no more his head;
> Because he knows, a frightful fiend
> Doth close behind him tread.
> (*The Rime of the Ancient Mariner*, pt VI)

Coleridge presents us with a fiction. He invites us to make-believe that someone is walking on a road alone, except for a frightful fiend in close proximity. I have no problem make-believing that this is the case (see also Gendler 2000).[7] Suppose, however, that Coleridge's poem had continued by describing the frightful fiend as a black man, a native of Africa, and, further, proclaimed in poetic terms how this man, in virtue of his race, was inferior: a savage. Moreover, let us say that the concluding verse announced that it was the moral duty of every white man to kill such a frightful fiend.[8] Would I be as willing to make-believe that a black man is inferior to a white man – to me, in effect – as I am to make-believe that someone walks along a lonesome road just ahead of a frightful fiend? Equally, would I be willing to make-believe that it is my moral duty to kill this frightful fiend because of his race? To be clear, I am not contemplating whether or not I should actually believe this, but only whether I should make-believe it. To make-believe is to engage in an imaginative act: to be creative. As Sarah Worth notes:

> When we enter into a fictional world, or let the fictional world enter into our imaginations, we do not "willingly suspend our disbelief." I cannot willingly decide to believe or disbelieve any-thing, any more than I can willingly believe it is snowing outside if all visual or sensory cues tell me otherwise. When engaging with fiction, I do not *suspend a critical faculty*, but rather I *exercise a creative faculty*. I do not actively suspend disbelief – I actively create belief. (2004: 447, original emphasis)

When exercising one's creative faculty and engaging in make-believe, are there some make-beliefs we are less willing or even altogether unwilling to entertain; some forms of fiction that are unimaginable for some individuals to engage with? If so, should this be seen as a marker of the immoral? (See Chs 6 and 7 for discussion on this point.)

In the context of my amendment to Coleridge's poem, how willing should I be to create the belief, and thereby make-believe, that as a white man I am superior to a black man, or any non-white for that matter? Following David Hume ([1757] 1985) and, more recently, Kendall Walton and Michael Tanner (1994), Tamar Szabó Gendler (2000) uses the term "imaginative resistance" (which she borrows from Moran 1994) to describe how we are typically less willing to make-believe the content of, say, my amendment to Coleridge's poem than we are to make-believe that there is a fiend on a lone-some road, or that the Earth is flat, or that in a galaxy far, far away an evil empire has built a Death Star. What Gendler concludes is that it is not that we are unable to make-believe the truth of white supremacy; rather, it is that our general reluctance to do so "is a function of [our] not wanting to take a particular perspective on the world – this [make-believe] world – which [we] do not endorse" (2000: 74).

The *extent* to which we are willing to make-believe a particular world would appear to be dependent on its make-believe values (such as the view that a mother who kills her baby, because she is a girl, does the right thing).[9] While this makes for an interesting psychological and therefore empirical question – as does the reason *why* we are more or less willing to do this (if indeed this is shown to be the case, empirically, rather than just intuitively)

– of interest here is not whether this is the case, but whether exercising our creative faculty, as Worth describes it, in order to produce such make-belief, such fiction, is morally wrong, irrespective of any alleged imaginative resistance, not because of it.

If I create a work of fiction along the lines of the amended Coleridge poem described above, as the author am I morally wrong to do so: to make-believe in this way? I do not actually hold the belief that black people are inferior to whites and should be killed; I have merely created a fictional world in which this make-belief value is endorsed. Equally, as a spectator, if I am willing to "go along" with the make-belief I am reading, or perhaps viewing or even playing, am I morally wrong to do so? Gendler offers an explanation for our alleged imaginative resistance to the make-believe moral praiseworthiness of racism or female infanticide. She argues that moral claims are commonly thought of as categorical in so far as what is held to be morally good or bad (right or wrong) in one world is equally so in all possible worlds. Thus, if it is wrong to murder or rape, be racist or commit infanticide in one world then this should be true of all worlds, including fictional ones. This is generally not the case with other (non-moral) claims: such as the truth of the fact that in *this* fictional world (let us say) some animals can talk, or unicorns exist. In addition, Gendler maintains that for a fictional narrative to appear coherent, perhaps even appealing:

> a great number of things that are held to be true within the fiction must be held to be true outside of it, and vice versa. The moral principles that govern the world in question are generally among these, as are the truths of logic, mathematics, and – in most genres – the laws of physics and psychology and even etiquette.
>
> (2000: 78)

Thus, while it is perfectly coherent to make-believe that one can talk to non-humans (which requires a change to a contingent truth – that only humans possess language), it would nevertheless remain incoherent for this talking non-human to be at the same time all red and all blue, or be the owner of a four-sided triangle (each of which would violate a necessary truth).

Wayne Booth (1988) likewise directs us to distinguish between two components of a fictional narrative: *nonce beliefs* and *fixed norms*. Nonce beliefs are those we are required to hold for the duration of the fiction (e.g. zombies walk the Earth in ever-increasing numbers); they are not intended to be exported from the fictional world –that is, to transcend the fictional and non-fictional domains.[10] However, contained within the fiction are fixed norms, such as being honourable, treating people with respect, good triumphing over evil and so on (see Ch. 8 for a challenge to this view in relation to virtues). These fixed norms provide the backdrop against which we are to judge the exploits of the protagonist (and others); they provide the moral of the story, and are what we are expected to take away from the fiction. They are therefore meant to possess a transcendent quality; for as Steven Malliet (2006) notes when discussing how gamers perceive the realism of video games, Darth Vader is unlikely to be representative of that which is authentic, and so is understood to be part of the fiction, but the estranged relationship he has with his son, Luke Skywalker, might be considered by many to have a level of authenticity that transcends the fictional domain.

Now it may be that the author of the fiction attempts to provoke us by subverting these norms and challenging our traditional moral values. According to Gendler, herein lies a possible explanation for our alleged imaginative resistance to certain moral claims: for "when we encounter fictional truths that concern deviant morality, we cannot assume that their deviance is an indication that the author does not wish them to be exported" (2000: 78). In other words, if the author invites us to make-believe that a lost race of people exist in the depths of the ocean – the Mariana Trench, say – we may well recognize that the truth of this claim is intended to be restricted to that fiction. If we are then asked to make-believe the moral worth of subjugating and brutalizing women, as is the valued practice within this undersea world, then, according to Gendler, we may be resistant to this because (a) it requires us to adopt a perspective we are uncomfortable with, and (b) it may be unclear whether the author of the fiction intends this make-believe truth to remain within the fictional realm only (in the same way that the reader of my amendment to Coleridge's poem may be unclear whether I intend the value espoused by its explicit racism to be exported and so transcend domains).[11]

In contrast to Gendler, however, for Kathleen Stock (2005: 621), the make-believe of moral claims, such as the moral worth of female infanticide, need only occur in a coherent context for imaginative resistance to subside. She presents an example to illustrate this: "John punched Clare compassionately." Resistance to the make-believe truth of this statement is removed if it occurs within the context of John volunteering to punch Clare (presumably as some form of punishment) so as to avoid someone else doing so less compassionately, and therefore bestowing on Clare a worse beating. Of course, all that Gendler and Stock are doing is trying to provide an account of why imaginative resistance occurs.[12] If, for the sake of argument, we accept that it does occur, even if we are undecided about the reason for it, does the fact that someone is resistant to a particular make-belief make this fiction morally wrong? Conversely, if *I* am willing to engage my creative faculty to share in the make-belief, am I guilty of a moral transgression for doing so?[13] It is not apparent why it should be the case, from the fact that we resist a particular fiction, that that fiction is morally wrong. If the act of imaginative resistance is not itself a measure of immorality, is there, then, another way of determining the morality of make-belief?

Traditional works of fiction are typically intended for an audience to judge (Dutton 2006): certainly aesthetically and artistically and perhaps, some might argue, morally (even legally; see the brief discussion on obscenity in Ch. 6). Literary or cinematic fiction, for example, creates a space for the narrative to unfold. The narrative is the work of the author and/or director (depending on the medium); it is their story to tell and, in the telling of it, typically, the author/director invites us to bear witness to the unfolding drama – to the position they have adopted – and in doing so seeks to provoke a reaction (see Lack 2008; Mey 2007). The structure of the narrative, including the images presented, aims at communicating a message, and it is this message that, more often than not, one is asked to bear witness to and judge. It is the ambiguity of this message that Gendler cites as a reason for imaginative resistance. Is it bound to the context of the fictional world or is it meant to transcend domains? It may be that the message is simply "What if …?" That is, what if women were subjugated and brutalized, and what if this were seen as morally unproblematic, or what if we lived in a world where a certain kind of racism were valued? By inviting a response, the author/director is providing the opportunity for the audience to engage with the message. One may not agree with or even like the stance presented within the book or film, but one *expects there to be one* (Nussbaum 1992). If a perspective is not perceived – that is, if the fiction appears to be vacuous – then typically it is judged (rightly or wrongly) to be of poor quality and derided as a bad example of the art form. If there is a message, then one can morally assess it within the domain in which it was intended to be heard. If it is meant to be restricted to the fictional world, then one can assess the moral worth of this make-believe in the *context* in which it is meant to be heard (to comply with Stock's demand, noted above) and judge it accordingly. If, on the other hand, it is understood to be a message created to transcend domains, then one can (and should) judge it within the context of the moral norms of the transcended world: our world (see Chs 6 and 7 for further discussion on this point).

The fictional worlds discussed so far – of art and literature and cinema – exist in a separate space, but what these worlds express is directed outwards towards an expectant audience whose members are invited to examine the message of the make-believe; and perhaps this customary (even required) invitation to judge enables us to morally scrutinize the content and the potential transcendent nature of the make-believe with an air of legitimacy and moral authority. The fictional world of play, on the other hand, is an excluding place by comparison; it turns away from the gaze of the onlooker and is much more selective in who it invites in. Is this difference morally significant?

THE CHARACTERISTICS OF PLAY

In *Homo Ludens*, Johan Huizinga ([1950] 1992) describes play as having three fundamental components or characteristics. First, play must be a voluntary act; it is not something we are obliged to do. We are not bound by a moral ought or sense of duty to engage in playful activities (see Ch. 4). Instead, play is a liberty for us. In addition, play is distinct from "ordinary" or "real" life; it constitutes a separate space in and out of which we step freely and often suddenly. Thus, it is also a temporary space whose duration is indeterminate. Finally, play is secluded; it is invitation only, and requires that all players adhere to its rules (see also Modell 1990). The rules may stand apart from the rules of our ordinary lives (i.e. when playing British Bulldog it is permitted to grab someone and wrestle them to the ground), or they may reflect them (e.g. do not cheat). If the rules are broken then the play ends, just as suddenly as it began when the rules were first introduced.

In their work on play, Monica Whitty and Adrian Carr argue that rules are especially important to creating and maintaining the separation of play from ordinary life:

> Play depends upon rules and other factors related to space and time, but in so doing we can note that an interesting paradox arises. On the one hand, the fundamental essence of play is the freedom, the license to create and be set apart from ordinary life. Yet, on the other hand, for this to be accomplished, constraint is required in the form of rules and other factors related to space and time. Thus, in an interesting twist of logic, freedom is created only through constraint. (2006: 58)

Likewise, Juul has this to say:

> Since play is normally assumed to be a free-form activity devoid of constraints, it appears illogical that we would choose to limit our options by playing games with fixed rules. Why be limited when you can be free? The answer to this is basically that games provide context for action: moving an avatar is much more meaningful in a game environment than in an empty space ... The rules of a game add *meaning* and *enable actions* by setting up *differences* between potential moves and events.
> (2005: 18–19, original emphasis)

Whitty and Carr and Juul agree that the rules and the fiction constitutive of gameplay enable the separation of gamespace from the non-gaming world. Moreover, the rules are applicable only within a given context and so within a designated space in which that context is realized; in fact, they are contingent on it. Equally, the fictional must be juxtaposed against the actual. Because the rules are contingent on a given space and, as Juul would have it, on a given fiction, it could easily be a contingent fact that, within a particular space, STAs are permitted. Equally, the fiction of the space means that what is permitted may in some looser or tighter sense represent the actual world while not equating to it (making the gamespace half-real, to use Juul's term). The rules and the fiction, therefore, make different, through separation, gamespace and the interactions therein from the actual world. This being so, how does this fact influence the way we approach the question of morality within such a separate space?

Despite the need for rules, Huizinga ([1950] 1992: 6) nevertheless asserts that play has "no moral function" and that "valuations of vice and virtue do not apply here"; for "inside the circle of the game the laws and customs of ordinary life no longer count" (*ibid.*: 12). The necessity of rules for the construction of play alongside the inapplicability of morality would seem contradictory, or at least in need of further explanation. At the most fundamental level, all players have to agree one rule: the rule to behave in *some* way *not* constitutive of ordinary life. As Howe (2008: 570; emphasis in original) notes: "Insofar as one plays, one *must* suspend reality, and thus engage in the pretence that is a condition of play". From this accord, the particulars of the play can then be articulated: in terms of those characteristics that make it *this* rather than *that* type of play. These are facilitated by the application of further rules which I will discuss later in terms of agreed status functions (see Chs 4 & 10).

But what is it to pretend in play? More specifically, what is it to pretend to kill someone in play? Clearly, while playing, I do not actually kill anyone (if I did, it would no longer be play but a tragic accident); but neither do I pretend to kill someone in so far as I fool an onlooker or even my play-mates into thinking I have just killed someone. Instead, I engage in an action (in conjunction with my follow players) that *counts as* an action within the conventions of the game I am playing: in this case, *as* killing (Saltz 1991). This action may bear little resemblance to the act it is meant to "count as". To illustrate, as a child, I recall holding my clenched fists out in front of me and shaking them in rhythm to the rat-a-tat sound I made. My play-mate would then oblige by falling to the ground: a "fatal" consequence of my "mowing him down" with my "machine gun". Both actions were understood to follow the conventions of pretend killing and pretend dying. Thus, as Leslie Howe notes, "a play action *is* a play action, and a play action of a particular sort, not because that action has a particular physical shape, but because it has a particular *meaning*" (2008: 572, original emphasis).

What does it mean, then, to press a button on one's game console, or swivel a joystick in a certain direction or direct one's bodily movement in a particular way (if using a Wii console, for example)? What these actions mean is dependent on how they translate to the virtual world, of course, and so how they are interpreted within the video game narrative or gameplay. As Howe attests, it is not the physical action that denotes play, but the meaning of that action within the context in which it occurs. Thus, with the push of a button, the swivel of a joystick or the swipe of my arm I am able to enact an STA within a given environment because my action adheres to the conventions – the rules – of the gameplay. To adhere to the rules *is* to play. One does not play *and* follow the rules; to do one is to do the other. In committing oneself to play, one plays the part one should, and so plays appropriately; and because of this one's actions are meaningful *as* acts of play. Consequently, by adhering to the normativity of play, one realizes a certain sort of realism and a certain sort of seriousness: one is *really* committed to playing the part (see Saltz 1991). But as Howe also attests: "Play is a privileged zone of expression both because of its structure of normative exception and because of its fundamental pose of pretence" (2008: 570). Moreover, the separation of play from ordinary life – its seclusion and the fact that it is invitation only – makes it a different form of fiction to that constitutive of film, books or other art forms. To what extent, then, can one legitimately judge the morality of pretence in the form of play, and therefore in the virtual guise of STAs?

Despite the separation of play from our ordinary life, play cannot exist in a vacuum. In fact, for Georg Simmel (1950), too much separation would make play an irrelevance. Instead, as well as being separate and secluded, play must also remain in touch with the ordinary and the continuous (a connection emphasized by Whitty [2003] and Whitty & Carr [2003, 2005, 2006] in their work on play in virtual worlds). This connection with the ordinary includes morally prohibited acts: the kind of acts that STAs are meant to represent. Given this connection, might this constitute grounds for the legitimate moral assessment of STAs and other virtual acts within gamespace? In the next chapter, I consider this relationship further and formulate the framework around which the moral evaluation of gamespace will take shape.

TWO

To prohibit or not to prohibit, that is the question

The awareness of the fictional character of the experience is not a limit to be overcome by technological development, but a *necessary condition* and an *ethical requirement*.
                    (Pasquinelli 2010: 213, original emphasis)

In this chapter, I outline a possible argument for why virtual enactments within gamespace might require some form of moral appraisal, and therefore why the indignant cry of "It's just a game" is unlikely to deter those who, following this argument, insist that STAs are a legitimate target for moral scrutiny. I begin, however, by considering the amoralist's claim that there is no case to answer: in effect, that there is nothing about the virtual act itself that warrants moral policing. I then move on to the question of what the act *represents*, rather than what it is *per se*, and so consider the extent to which representational meaning constitutes something above and beyond the literal manipulations of pixels, thereby making it worthy of moral scrutiny. After that, I construct a framework of conditions and related questions designed to inform my assessment of different moral theories that have been (or can be) applied to video game content in order to establish how one might go about discriminating between those STAs that should be prohibited and those that should not, if indeed such selectivity is itself morally justifiable.

THE AMORALITY OF PIXELS

In 2010, the video game *God of War III* was said to contain some of the most brutal and intense violence ever depicted in a video game (Dan Chiappini, editor of *Game Spot*).[1] Within the gameplay, the main protagonist, Kratos, is able to engage in a number of violent activities, including pulling a Cyclops's eye from its socket (in a very strenuous and gory spectacle), and slowly ripping the head from the neck of an altogether more human-looking character, Helios. Similar depictions of violence can be found in other games, of course. In *Fallout: New Vegas*, for example, the shooting of a character results in his head exploding and other body parts disintegrating. Although such scenes may not be to the liking of everyone, are they *morally* problematic? In one quite literal sense, all that has occurred in each of these scenes is the manipulation of pixels. As such, there seems to be no moral case to answer. As Christoph Klimmt *et al.* explain:

> Obviously, in violent video games no living creatures are harmed and no real objects are damaged. Dead bodies, blood, and injuries are nothing more than pixels. The non-reality status of video games can therefore be used to explain why moral concerns are not "necessary", applicable, or rational in their context; there simply seems nothing to be "real" in a game that moral concerns could arise from. (2006: 313)

The view Klimmt *et al.* are articulating is essentially an amoralist one. The "non-reality status" of video game content is perhaps akin to one chess piece taking another, or the fate of the "patient" in the family game Operation,[2] neither of which, on the face of it, warrants moral scrutiny. However, both the amoralist's assertion that what the player enacts is just a game and the seeming corollary that game content is therefore beyond the realm of moral obligation and accountability need further consideration.

First and foremost, those who consider that there is a moral case to answer do not restrict their moralizing to the virtual act itself (to the manipulation of pixels). Instead, they concern themselves with what this manipulation *represents*: that is, with whatever the representation (and ensuing interaction) might be taken to mean by the gamer and even her wider society. In addition, they are concerned with how this might affect the gamer's non-gaming interactions. From such a perspective, one *might* be inclined to argue that what the game Operation represents is a very unethical medical procedure, or that chess is representing the defeat, perhaps even death, of an opponent. One might even query the morality of bishops (or the queen) being represented as combatants in such a context. Perhaps such an argument would receive rather short shrift. Yet what it does highlight, I contend, is how the line between acceptable and unacceptable representation can be nebulous. Can we, for example, provide a moral view on how closely (*qua* graphically, literally or even interpretively) a game enactment should represent what it is meant to represent?

To illustrate, suppose instead of playing a computer chess game using virtual representations of the traditional chess pieces, the board contains virtual persons, animals and objects (bishops, castles, knights on horses, etc.). Suppose further that when "taking" an opponent's piece, each figure is rendered ineffective in a violent and gory spectacle.³ A knight taking a pawn (or foot soldier), for example, might be represented by the latter being hacked to death. Alternatively, a knight could be burned alive at the stake when taken by a bishop. The queen could be beheaded or raped to death, and so on.

For some, this new version of chess may cause unease, even a strong sense of revulsion. Perhaps onlookers would be repulsed by its more literal take on the game. But whether engaging with a more traditional chess set or the hypothetical version just introduced, the actions and *what* they represent – namely, eliminating the opposition – remain the same; they differ only with regard to *how* they are represented within the gameplay, either by having pieces "toppled" and removed or in the more graphic way described above. Irrespective of which set is used, the rules and objectives of chess remain the same (Goffman 1972). All that has changed is how one wishes to represent the pieces within the game and the act of having a piece "taken". In fact, it could be argued that what is being proposed here is merely an extension of chess sets already available offline that use more intricately carved medieval or fantasy characters. Graphically representing the act of "taking" an opponent's piece changes nothing within the rules and strategies of the game in the same way that using more intricately carved pieces changes nothing. After all, chess can still be played even with the most rudimentary objects representing each piece. Therefore, both the addition of more intricate pieces and the new graphic proposed here are gratuitous to the *literal* playing of the game. However, an objection to the use of more intricate chess pieces because they are gratuitous might be considered rather weak and, in the end, a matter of taste. Could the same not be said of any objection to the hypothetical chess set: that it is likewise just a matter of taste rather than morality? After all, and to bring us back to the amoralist's objection, it is *just* a game.

With respect to the claim "It's just a game", a proponent of ludology would argue against an exclusive focus on *representation* and narrative and instead argue that in order to understand the true nature of the gamespace – and so provide informed moral assessment – one must take into account the rules of the game, including available strategies, and even social interaction (in the case of multiplayer spaces). In short, one must assess the *representation* within the context in which it occurs and therefore based on the meaning that should be (or is, typically) derived from this context (Malliet 2006).

THE CURRENT STATE OF PLAY WITHIN GAMESPACE

With this last point in mind, it is my contention that questions surrounding the morality of the hypothetical chess game described above should receive rather more attention than the earlier example involving the game Operation, although I consider the underlying query to be essentially the same: namely, the moral status of representations within the context of play.[4] For when considering the content of video games, particularly in relation to the STAs detailed in Chapter 1, the following statement would seem to hold, at least within the UK:

> **S1:** Of *all* the prohibited offline taboo activities (hereafter POTAs), only *some* of these are likewise prohibited as STAs.

By "prohibited" I mean that, in the case of POTAs, they are typically morally condemned practices that are illegal too (as is the case regarding those noted in Ch. 1). As a point of clarification, it is not my intention to discuss whether any of these activities *should* be prohibited. It is a fact that they are and, given this fact, my concern is only how one should judge their virtual enactment. In addition, I recognize that POTAs are not homogeneous activities beyond their shared prohibitive status. Some may consider rape and murder to be far worse than, say, discrimination (others may disagree). While accepting their lack of homogeneity, they are nevertheless all worthy of prohibition and so, for this reason, have a status that is at least nominally equivalent. STAs, on the other hand, do not share the same nominal-level prohibitive status; their permissibility within video games is much more lax in cases like virtual assault and murder, which are often considered to be "part of the game", compared to virtual paedophilia, for example, which is banned outright in the UK.[5]

Support for S1 is easily found if one engages in even the most cursory examination of video game content. In numerous single-player video games it is commonplace to maim and kill, even murder (e.g. the *Left 4 Dead* series, or others such as *Killzone* and *Soldier of Fortune*, not to mention the *Grand Theft Auto* series), and, in a growing number, mutilate and even torture (e.g. *Reservoir Dogs*, *24*, *The Punisher* and, arguably, *Brink* and *Red Faction*). As already noted, it is possible to target little girls for extermination (*BioShock*). In some games, acts of violence appear to be an integral part of the gameplay (e.g. *Manhunt 2*, *Postal 2*, *MadWorld*). Switching STAs, now, in a few cases it is possible to witness the cannibalization of victims. The *Resident Evil* series, *Evil Dead* and *F.E.A.R.* (*First Encounter Assault Recon*) all feature cannibalism, although more in the form of a threat to the player than something they engage in themselves. However, in *Stubbs the Zombie in Rebel Without a Pulse*, the player takes on the role of Stubbs the Zombie, who engages in cannibalistic activities. Here, the act of cannibalism seems much more central to the gameplay. Likewise, in the albeit cartoonish video game *Cannibal Warrior*, one can play the role of an "Amazon warrior", who, we are told, must "battle dangerous foes" and capture girls in order to "serve them up for dinner". It is rarely the case, however, that characters engage in acts of rape or incest. An exception to this is *The House of the Dead: Overkill*, where incest is implied by an action, and in *No More Heroes* it is a feature of the game narrative but not interaction. In *Phantasmagoria*, rape is possible, as is the case in the 1982 game *Custer's Revenge* (a game that has received heavy criticism; see Patridge 2011; Sicart 2009). More recently (circa 2006), in the Japanese game *RapeLay*, the entire gameplay is dedicated to hunting down and raping/sexually assaulting a mother and her virgin daughters, although it is also possible to rape other women. *RapeLay* is currently banned in the UK.

Rape is permissible within certain multiplayer gamespaces (e.g. *Sociolotron*), and is not an unheard of practice within others, including *Second Life* (McCabe 2007).[6] In fact, in 2006 it was reported that add-on software (*Rapeplay 1–4*) could be purchased that enabled one avatar to rape another in *Second Life* (Mohney 2006). More recently, a different STA has become (relatively) popular within this space: namely, bestiality (Tan 2007), including a fad involving sex with or possible rape and impregnation by a unicorn (Zjawinski 2007). Such activity led Linden Lab (the creators of *Second Life*) to initiate a tougher "crack-down" on "broadly offensive" behaviour (Tan 2007), which saw the removal of the virtual ageplay space *Wonderland* because of alleged paedophilic activity (Russell 2008; Sky News 2007). ("Ageplay" is the adopting of a virtual child persona by adults.)[7]

It would seem, then, that it is possible, in the UK at least, to engage in a multitude of games involving murder, torture, mutilation and even cannibalism, but not games that involve virtual paedophilia, either against a computer-generated "victim" or, it would seem, in the form of *ageplay* involving (in principle) adults only. Likewise, bestiality in *Second Life* has been subject to a more severe level of moral condemnation and, currently, there are no games that involve virtual necrophilia. Virtual rape, for its part, tends to receive heftier moral sanctioning than other STAs such as murder (see Whitty *et al.* 2011), although virtual rape's legal permissibility is mixed:

available to UK players who enter the online world of *Sociolotron* (for example) but not to those who wish to play the single-player game *RapeLay*.

FRAMING THE QUESTIONS AND GENERAL AIMS

As things stand, within the UK, there is currently a selective prohibition on video game content: that is, a discrepancy in the severity of moral condemnation and even the legal status of certain STAs compared to others that represent POTAs. A key aim of this book is to address the question: *should* it be the case that only some STAs are prohibited (and therefore not others)? If the response is no, is it because one of the following two conditions ought to apply?

(a) Because *all* POTAs are prohibited, *all* STAs should likewise be prohibited.
(b) Irrespective of the prohibited status of POTAs, *no* STAs should be prohibited.

The relationship between POTAs and STAs described by (a), as noted above, is certainly not the current state of play with respect to video game content. As such, what would be required for us to consider that (a) ought to be the case?

In preparing to tackle this question, consider the following, somewhat unremarkable, statement: actual murder (murder$_a$) is not the same as virtual murder (murder$_v$), both in terms of what the activity entails and its consequences. I will not spend time discussing the ways in which murder$_a$ differs from murder$_v$. I simply assert, and therefore take it as a given, that they are not equivalent. Accepting this, consider the following question: given that $x \neq y$, if x is prohibited then should y be prohibited? Perhaps. Perhaps not. There is a case for claiming that whatever conclusion one draws about the prohibitive status of y, this conclusion cannot be based on an appeal to the established prohibited status of x, because x and y are not equivalent. If y is to be prohibited then it must be for some reason other than x's prohibition.

The ambiguity in the relationship between STAs and POTAs is reflected in the comment by David Buckingham when discussing pornographic images of actual children and computer-generated images: "The relationship between fantasy and reality, and the issue of the legality of such activities within online worlds, remains complex and controversial" (2007: 53; quoted in A. Adams 2010: 60). Alongside the legality of STAs is the equally complex and controversial nature of their morality, which is the concern of this book.

Thus, when considering whether it is morally wrong to virtually enact POTAs – be it rape, paedophilia or murder (etc.) – it is important to note that although what the enactment represents is held as morally wrong, this does not necessitate that the enactment itself is morally wrong, either for the same reason as the act itself or for some other reason. But, equally, neither does the fact that it is an enactment negate the possibility that it *is* morally wrong. Saying that $x \neq y$ does not preclude the possibility that a relationship of some kind exists between x and y, even if it is not one of identity, and perhaps it is the nature of this relationship that provides us with an adequate reason for prohibiting y. So even if we cannot use the same reason as that given for the prohibition of x, perhaps we can nevertheless find an equally *compelling* reason to justify why a *representation* of an act that is prohibited should itself be prohibited.

There is, of course, the possibility that a reason for the prohibition of y can be provided even in the absence of any relation between x and y. However, in what is to follow, I shall consider only those accounts that have sought to prohibit STAs based on differing assertions over the relation they hold to POTAs. I shall critically examine each of these putative connections in turn in order to establish which, if any, is sufficient to render STAs morally problematic, which would support a case for their prohibition.[8] In addition, an obvious question that may have struck the reader, and which has not yet been raised, is this: why would anyone want to play games that involve enacting some or all of the STAs described above? Asking why anyone would want to do that implies that there is something wrong with that, whatever *that* may be and, consequently, that there is something wrong with *wanting* to do that. This, of course, is what this book aims to determine. Therefore, as well as focusing on the morality of the virtual act, I shall consider the position of those who would question and even challenge the moral character of gamers who are willing to engage in such activities. What motivates someone to murder, torture, mutilate or even rape within a video game, and should such motivation be subject to moral scrutiny and constraint?

The integration of moral theory centred on character and motivation in a framework that seeks to inform on the issue of selective prohibition reflects the importance I place on *psychological* understanding. Recall from the discussion on play in Chapter 1 that play does not occur in a vacuum; it is a separate space but not too separate. Given this necessary connection, then, in addition to allowing for the possibility of some form of moral purchase, it is my contention that a stronger case can be made for the relevance of psychology – *qua* understanding the psychological processes that connect the subject of play to the same subject outside play – when deliberating over the question of selective prohibition. Ultimately, through evidence and argument, I aim to show that the question of selective video game prohibition is best addressed by a fuller understanding of gamer psychology rather than by seeking to establish whether engaging in a particular STA is morally right or wrong, or whether wanting to virtually enact STAs constitutes evidence of a *morally* flawed character. However, in order to promote psychological

understanding over morality within the context of gamespace, it is first necessary to assess the appropriateness of more traditional moral theories when
applied to STAs, and even those moral arguments that have been specially
devised to address the unique qualities of virtual interaction within single-
and multiplayer gamespace. I consider each of these in turn with the intention of showing them to be, at best, incomplete as a moral framework for
selective prohibition or, at worst, unsuitable when applied to video game
content.

The aims of this book are therefore as follows:

1. Given that $x \neq y$, to critically consider how the relationship between x
   (POTAs) and y (STAs) is construed by different moral theories when
   applied to gamespace, and whether a given moral theory is able to provide a coherent means of assessing the moral status of STAs.
2. In light of (1), to critically evaluate the extent to which the particular
   moral theory is able to justify the *selective* prohibition of video game
   content, or whether it proffers some alternative moral position.
3. Based on (1) and (2), to provide evidence and argument to show that
   no single moral theory provides a complete or cogent moral argument
   for the selective prohibition of video game content.
4. From (3), to argue for the importance of psychological understanding,
   rather than moral judgement, in the question of selective prohibition.

In addressing points (1–4), I draw on video game content that is either
currently available on the UK market or is, in some cases, banned. On occasion, I create hypothetical gameplays in order to assess the appropriateness
of a particular moral approach. I also focus mostly on single-player games,
switching to multiplayer spaces if and when they present additional points
for consideration during the application and/or evaluation of a given moral
theory.

It is also important to stipulate those areas of ethical enquiry that I shall
not be discussing in this book. As already noted, I shall be focusing on gamespace, both single- and multiplayer. However, I shall not be discussing other
potentially playful areas of cyberspace, such as chatrooms or social networking sites, which I accept raise their own moral questions. In addition, I shall
make limited reference to multiplayer spaces such as *Second Life* – often
referred to as sandbox environments – which lack the structure and specific
built-in aims/goals of the games I shall be discussing. Indeed, many who fre-
quent spaces like *Second Life* may feel justified in *not* considering these VEs
to be gamespaces at all. Moreover, I shall not be discussing the moral implications of acquiring virtual assets that require an exchange of non-virtual
funds, as it is possible to do in spaces like *Second Life*, and also within some
spaces with more conventional gaming formats (e.g. *World of Warcraft*, *Eve*

and *Runescape*); nor shall I discuss issues surrounding the theft of such virtual assets if/when they occur outside the rules of the game (see Brenner 2008; Searle 1995; Strikwerda 2012). Finally, at no point in this book do I intend to discuss game theory (for detailed discussion on this topic, see Binmore 1994, 1998).

In the next chapter, I begin my analysis of the morality of gamespace by critically examining Hume's sentimentalism and the later work of neo-sentimentalists such as Jesse Prinz, particularly with regard to the question: does a sense of *disgust* towards STAs constitute a kind of moral wisdom? If the answer is yes, and justifiably so, then perhaps we have found the basis for selective prohibition: namely, that which elicits a sense of disgust (*qua* moral repugnance). However, in order to posit disgust as an arbiter of moral wisdom, both with regard to virtual enactments in general and STAs in particular, the proponent of sentimentalism must overcome the counter-claim that disgust in the context of gamespace, if it is to be acquainted with moral assessment, is nothing more than an expression of moral fallibility rather than wisdom.

THREE

Hume's strength of feeling

The rules of morality... are not conclusions of our reason.
(Hume [1739] 1978: 457)

A few years ago, around the time I first became interested in the issue of taboos within gamespace, I happened to be socializing with a group of university colleagues. One colleague – an avid gamer – began to describe a favourite gaming activity of his: how (*qua* his avatar) he would physically assault virtual characters with a large pink dildo. I remember this causing mild amusement at the time and, if I am honest, a slight sense of puzzlement, but not wariness and certainly not disdain on my part. Later that evening, I reflected on what my colleague had said and began to wonder how I would have reacted if instead he had said that he used the pink dildo to *sexually* assault virtual women, or perhaps even physically assault *just women*, or even that he used it on virtual children. As I introspected on my own feelings, I was interested to gauge whether the thought of any of these acts produced in me a sense of disgust. But perhaps more to the point, irrespective of whether it did or not, should it?

In this chapter, I consider the moral position advanced by David Hume, often referred to as *sentimentalism*. Because this book is concerned with taboos, the sentiment (or emotion) I am interested in is disgust and how this might be used to inform moral judgement within the sentimentalist tradition: as a form of what Hume referred to as disapprobation. In particular, and using the format x (POTAs) $\neq y$ (STAs), I intend to discuss: (a) how disgust has become associated with moral transgressions such as POTAs; (b) how it is, given that x (POTAs) $\neq y$ (STAs), that disgust can be elicited from virtual enactments such as STAs; and (iii) whether the disgust elicited by STAs (at least in some people) should count as a form of moral wisdom or, in light of the *virtual* nature of the enactment, as evidence of moral fallibility. If sentiment (*qua* disgust) is to be considered a form of moral wisdom, then does sentimentalism provide the moral justification required for the selective prohibition of STAs? When responding to this question, in addition to the question of moral wisdom/fallibility, in the final section I evaluate a more recent argument that proffers support for sentimentalism based on a slightly different tack: namely, the alleged potential of violent video games to reduce one's ability to empathize – a faculty of the person that Hume instructs us forms the basis for, and even necessitates, appropriate levels of approbation or disapprobation. Before discussing this further, however, I first present Hume's position in more detail, including an outline of how his theory has been developed in the early part of the twenty-first century by neo-sentimentalists.

MORAL SENTIMENTALISM AND NEO-SENTIMENTALISTS

In an often-quoted passage, Hume introduces his argument for sentimentalism:

> Take any action allow'd to be vicious: Wilful murder, for instance. Examine it in all lights, and see if you can find that matter of fact, or real existence, which you call *vice*. In which-ever way you take it, you find only certain passions, motives, volitions and thoughts. There is no other matter of fact in the case. The vice entirely escapes you, as long as you consider the object. You never can find it, till you turn your reflexion into your own breast, and find a sentiment of disapprobation which arises in you, towards this action. Here is a matter of fact; but 'tis the object of feeling, not of reason. ([1739] 1978: 468–9)

Essentially, what Hume objects to is the pronouncement that there exist moral facts about an action, or that implicit within an act is that thing we call vice or virtue. For Hume, then, the claim that murder is wrong (or any

POTA for that matter) is not something that can be established by perceiving the act directly; nor can one infer it from observing certain tell-tale signs or characteristics within the act itself. In fact, the rightness or wrongness of the act – its vice or virtue – cannot be established by recourse to reason at all. Instead, how we come to judge an action as morally good or bad is determined by what Hume calls a sense of approbation or disapprobation. How we morally judge an action therefore depends on how we feel towards it: that is, the sentiment it elicits from us. The focus of our judgement is based on how *we* feel about the action, not the nature of the act itself. Thus Hume continues:

> [The moral fact] lies in yourself, not in the object. So that when you pronounce any action or character to be vicious, you mean nothing, but that from the constitution of your nature you have a feeling or sentiment of blame from the contemplation of it. Vice and virtue, therefore, may be compar'd to sounds, colours, heat and cold, which, according to modern philosophy, are not qualities in objects, but perceptions in the mind. (*Ibid.*: 469)

To claim that morality stems from a sentiment of approbation or disapprobation that lies within oneself is to reject moral realism: the view that there are absolute moral facts independent of cultural influence. However, as Monique Wonderly (2008) notes, this does not mean that Hume rejects morality or the importance and authority of moral judgements *per se*; for as Hume observes, what could be more important to us and to the regulation of our behaviour than how we feel about a particular act. Moreover, Wonderly holds that Hume advocates a normative theory that recognizes that often moral judgements stem from a shared feeling or common point of view.

Jesse Prinz builds on Hume's idea and, while defending a form of moral relativism, presents what he calls "*constructive sentimentalism*" (2007: 167).[1] This is the view that although moral judgements stem from sentiment – feelings of disapprobation or approbation, as Hume maintains (see Greene *et al.* 2001; Nichols & Mallon 2005) – these sentiments nevertheless form the basis for rules that have their own objective status within the socially constructed space they occupy: "Things that we construct or build come from us, but, once there, they are real entities that we perceive" (Prinz 2007: 168). Prinz's position is compatible with the neo-sentimentalism proffered by Allan Gibbard (1990), who argues that wrongful acts are judged to be so, not simply because one has a negative feeling towards the act, but because such a feeling is appropriate. The addition of this normative element – that the negative feeling of guilt (for example) is not simply something we happen to feel but what we *should* feel – means, for Shaun Nichols, that "even if one has lost any disposition to feel guilt about a certain action, one can still think that feeling guilty is *warranted*" (2008: 258, original emphasis). Nichols goes on to argue that the emotions we feel in relation to a given action have helped shape our cultural norms by determining which are sustained and which are lost. His *affective resonance hypothesis* essentially states: "Norms that prohibit actions to which we are predisposed to be emotionally averse will enjoy enhanced cultural fitness over other norms" (*ibid.*: 269).

For the new generation of sentimentalists such as Prinz and Nichols, whether an action is deemed good or bad, or right or wrong, is in no small part dependent on the emotion we feel towards that action. However, these theorists have built on more traditional Humean sentimentalism by arguing for a degree of objectification within a given space. Thus, if at a given time I experience a sense of disapprobation towards an individual's actions, this does not *as a general rule* – based on how I feel *right now* – make my disapproval grounds for the judgement that what this person is doing is bad; nor does it make my disapproval a good thing, unless the disapproval is warranted.

Having outlined the case for sentimentalism, in the next section I detail how it is that a sense of disapprobation (*qua* disgust) may have come to be associated with what, through our contingent cultural history, we judge to be moral transgressions.

THE ROLE OF DISGUST IN MORAL TRANSGRESSIONS, REAL AND SIMULATED

In a web news article, Bena Roberts (2009) refers to the withdrawn Apple iPhone game *Baby Shaker* as "disgusting". (This game involved shaking a noisy baby in order to stop it crying; one could potentially shake it until it died – an outcome represented by Xs over the baby's eyes.) In a similar tone, and with reference to the airport massacre scene in the game, Tom Chick (2009) asks: "Is *Modern Warfare 2* the most *disgusting* game of the year?" Similarly, Mike Adams (2009) considers the Japanese rape game *Rapelay* to show a *disgusting* lack of morals.

Each author's use of the word "disgusting" is, I suggest, indicative of their negative moral attitude towards the respective game they are reporting. This, it would seem, accords well with Andrew Jones and Julie Fitness's claim that, universally, we "borrow from the lexicon of disgust when describing moral transgressions" (2008: 613). In support of this claim, Judith Danovitch and Paul Bloom note how "children come to find entities like feces and vomit ... disgusting, and ... are able to describe them as such, and ... adults direct the *language* of disgust to what they see as moral violations" (2009: 111, emphasis added).

It may be the case, then, that what we judge to be morally disgusting is largely a product of social conditioning. Such a view is endorsed by Christopher Knapp, who maintains that the objects and events that trigger disgust are not inherently disgusting; rather, associations are "acquired through a socially mediated learning process" (2003: 262). Knapp goes on to concede, however, that such a predominantly social process "does not preclude the contribution of innate structures" (*ibid.*: 263). He talks of potential disgust triggers (PDTs), which we are disposed to be disgusted by, and contrasts these with actual disgust triggers (ADTs), which we *learn* to be disgusted by. The contingent relation between PDTs and ADTs (that is, the means by which a PDT becomes an ADT) is mediated by social conditioning.

By way of a caveat, then, although it may be that the language of disgust is often used as a rhetorical device, one cannot discount the possibility that these learned associations are capable of eliciting the same kinds of visceral response originally used (solely) to dispel our interest in noxious substances – what Edward Royzman *et al.* (2008) refer to as the *moral dyspepsia hypothesis*. In support of this claim, Royzman *et al.* found that descriptions of morally prohibited acts (such as incest) produced oral inhibition, comprising of "nausea, gagging, and diminished appetite" (2008: 100). This has led Leon Kass (2002) to argue that adhering to our sense of repugnance constitutes a kind of *moral wisdom*.[2]

According to Prinz (2007), our moral judgements, particularly where *taboos* are concerned (I contend), are grounded on emotional (disgust-related) responses. As a means of illustrating this point, Prinz asks us to consider why raping a toddler who will never remember the event is wrong. When answering his own question, he considers that to say that it is just wrong is not to fail to have a reason, or to be unable to articulate it. "[W]e are not obviating reason", he declares; rather, "we are explicitly giving one" (*ibid.*: 31). Saying it is wrong *is* the reason; it is *just wrong*.[3] Jonathan Haidt holds a similar position, supported by empirical evidence: "that moral emotions and intuitions drive moral reasoning" (2001: 830), just as Hume proposed. Articulated reasons, then, do not form the basis for disgust (according to Prinz); rather, they are *post hoc* additions that help us justify the moral judgements we make, which are, fundamentally, sentiment-based (however, see Tilo Hartmann's [2011] discussion on rational and experiential processes; see also Ch. 12). In the absence of reason, the sentiment remains, and can even prove reason enough for the moral judgement.

A similar view has been put forward by Dolf Zillmann (2000). In the context of media violence, his *moral sanction theory of delight and repugnance* distinguishes between moral judgements that are formed after deliberation and tend to subscribe to a particular moral theory or ethical code, and the more impulsive moral sanctions that are based on one's readiness to accept a particular moral outcome. Observing someone come to a violent end will more often than not meet with morally sanctioned approval if the recipient is understood to deserve their fate. The extent to which crime matches punishment and the extent to which one might approve of this are seen as a measure of one's "latitude to moral sanction" (*ibid.*: 59): that is, the norma-tive range of retribution one deems morally acceptable (Lachlan & Tam-borini 2008). It should be evident that moral sanction is effectively a form of approbation (delight) or disapprobation (repugnance).

But even if we accept the process by which sentiment has been associated with moral transgressions, how is this association maintained in relation to STAs: acts we know to be virtual and, in the context of gamespace, fictional? Moreover, even if we come to understand the mechanism by which the asso-ciation between the virtual and our sentiment is (possibly) achieved, does this mean the response elicited by the virtual act is a legitimate example of moral wisdom? Before addressing this latter question, let us first consider how sentiment might be elicited by what is known to be fictional.

According to Antonio Damasio's (1994) *somatic marker hypothesis*, somatic markers are sensations – either visceral or non-visceral – that facili-tate efficient decision-making by reducing the number of viable choices available to us. Negative feelings toward a particular option will quickly eliminate that option from the choices available. Conversely, a strong posi-tive feeling may encourage or prioritize the selection of a particular course of action or judgement. Somatic markers are contingently related to exter-nal events and are therefore a product of our education and socialization within a given culture. This process (of education and socialization) typically includes "social conventions and ethical rules" (*ibid.*: 179; recall the neo-sentimentalism of Prinz and Nichols), and amounts to, among other things, the development of associations between particular stimuli and particu-lar somatic states; for at the neuronal level, Damasio informs us, "somatic markers depend on learning within a system that can connect certain cat-egories of entity or event with the enactment of a body state, pleasant or unpleasant" (*ibid.*: 180). The habituation of bodily responses (somatic mark-ers) to external moral and social conventions is such that merely *thinking* about breaking these conventions can trigger a physiological response. As Damasio notes:

> When the choice of option X ... leads to a bad outcome Y, ... [r]e-exposure of the organism to option X, or the *thought* about outcome Y, will now have the power to re-enact the painful body state and thus serve as an automated reminder of bad conse-quences to come. (*Ibid.*: 180, emphasis added)

And again: "Whether the body states are real or *vicarious* ('*as if*'), the cor-responding neural pattern can be made conscious and constitute a feeling" (*ibid.*: 185, emphasis added).

A similar point is made by Daniel Fitzgerald *et al.* (2004) when stating that excitation of the neural pathways underlying our response to disgust-eliciting objects/events can occur even in the absence of external triggers. If the mere thought of taboos is sufficient to elicit disgust then it seems reasonable to conjecture that any *virtual* display of taboos (STAs) will likewise elicit a visceral response. Violating a taboo, it would seem, even if only virtually, has the potential to remain *symbolically* potent. Virtual transgressions are, as the amoralists maintain with some justification (see Ch. 2), innocuous, at least in terms of the virtual act; nevertheless, they have the potential to elicit from us the same types of response that Hume argues signify a breach in the code of values implemented and enforced within a given society. To flaunt these values, even symbolically, risks provoking the severest moral condemnation.

By way of a caveat, however, within the realm of gamespace (or in fact cyberspace in general), there exits the possibility for new interactive spaces, and the construction of new social realities and new forms of embodiment and even morality. Now, if Prinz's constructive sentimentalism, which I contend is compatible with Nichols's affective resonance hypothesis, allows for a socially agreed (and therefore objectified) system of morality to operate relative to, and therefore contingent on, a given space with a given cultural history and evolution, it may be that seemingly universal taboos are in fact a product of constructive sentimentalism, and their *seeming* universality is merely an artefact of certain similarities (universalities) in our biologically and even socially evolved sentiment. If so, then it is important to note that, in the absence of virtual technology, all of these spaces are in fact places where we interact as physically embodied beings. With the advent of VR, however, there exist numerous spaces where this fact does not apply. Therefore, irrespective of whether morality is relative to a given culture with no privileged moral position outside that culture or whether, *contra* Hume, moral absolutes exist, traditionally, either position has been contingent (or supervenes) on the fact that we are physically embodied agents. But what of those spaces in which we are embodied, but not *physically* embodied? In such a space (e.g. gamespace), might deference to sentiment as an arbiter of morality be inappropriate and, in effect, a demonstration of moral fallibility? In such brave new worlds, I am able to engage in virtual acts that in the actual world would be measured along a continuum from saintliness to depravity; but if I am forced to adhere to a form of moral constraint imposed on me by a community's sense of disgust (or disapprobation), then could we not legitimately regard this as a case of what Haidt *et al.* (1993) call *moral dumbfounding* (the entrenched view that a taboo is still morally indefensible even if no subsequent harm to anyone ensues)? One could certainly argue that it *should* be viewed in this way, because any moral objection stands opposed to the more liberal position, which states that one is free to act in any way one wishes so long as it does not cause harm to oneself or others. After all, where is the harm in murdering, torturing and raping pixels, with or without a large pink dildo?

I would argue that a case can be made for moral dumbfounding based on a feeling of disapprobation, at least when this sentiment is directed towards the virtual act itself (the STA); for, within gamespace, no virtual characters are harmed, just as Klimmt *et al.* (2006) noted when articulating the amoralist position (see Ch. 2). Moreover, if Nichols (2008) holds that feelings of guilt or empathy or other sentiment (or lack thereof) should be judged appropriate only if they are warranted, then owing to the contingent nature of gamespace, can we really say that they are warranted in *this* space? If they are, then what are the criteria on which they are based? Yet perhaps a different form of harm is occurring through the enactment of STAs. Perhaps it is the case that, irrespective of whether guilt or empathy (etc.) is warranted – and it is not at all clear that Hume would hold that it is within gamespace – the act of engaging in STAs degrades one's capacity to feel guilt and, importantly, empathy precisely where Hume would maintain it is warranted: towards *actual* people. Whether this is the case or not is effectively an empirical matter (see below). However, if it can be shown that one's capacity for empathy is severely diminished then, based on a criterion of "protecting oneself from harm", we may have *a posteriori* justification for the selective moral prohibition of video game content. Just such a case is made by Wonderly.

DIMINISHED EMPATHY: A CRITERION FOR SELECTIVE PROHIBITION?

Of paramount importance to Hume's moral philosophy is our ability to empathize and, according to Wonderly (2008), this can be diminished through prolonged exposure to extremely violent video games.[4] In support of her argument, Wonderly cites the work of Martin Hoffman (2000), who has carried out extensive research on the integral role played by empathy in orienting individuals towards an ethic of care and justice. She also cites work by Jeanne Funk *et al.* (2004) and Klaus Mathiak and René Weber (2006), which, she claims, shows a negative correlation between video game violence and empathy: the higher the violence, the lower the empathy measured (I shall have more to say on these findings below). Drawing on this work, Wonderly concludes:

> If Hume's conception of empathy is correct, then we now have a strong candidate for the source of moral wrongness in ultra-violent video games. The problem with such games is that they may damage our empathic faculties, and in so doing, they may be directly harming our centers of moral judgment. An impaired capacity for moral judgment may not immediately or invariably translate into aggressive behavior, but such impairment might, at

least initially, only impact one's attitudes toward characters and conduct. One might imagine that a damaged empathic faculty could cause an increased tolerance for moral depravity and a decreased appreciation for virtue. As these attitudes could manifest themselves in any number of ways, their effects might not be readily apparent. The point is that although most violent video gamers aren't out committing vicious crimes, this does not mean that they aren't being affected in other significant, though less obvious ways. (2008: 8)

If it is the case that video games damage our empathic faculties, and empathic faculties are important to our ability to make moral judgements, then indeed we have, as Wonderly reasons, a strong candidate for the source of moral wrongness in these games. I have no qualms regarding the importance of empathy to our ability to make moral judgements and act morally. What I take issue with is Wonderly's *interpretation* of the empirical evidence allegedly supporting the case for reduced empathy within gamers who play extremely (or ultra-)violent video games. Regarding Funk *et al.*'s (2004) study, for example, lower levels of empathy were reported in children, but this was based on measures from a children's empathy questionnaire only. The researchers also talked about measuring increased levels of *fantasy* violence and, importantly, included comments from a qualitative study (Funk 2002; cited in Funk *et al.* 2004), in which it was noted that "children also reported later copying characters' actions in fantasy play, for example saying: 'They try to act like them, like wrestling.' One child qualified his endorsement: 'But not killing. Like if the game has you killing something or whatever'" (Funk *et al.* 2004: 34). What is evident within this last remark is that, even *if* empathy is lower at the time, children are able to differentiate the fantasy violence they imitate from real violence, like killing, which they refrain from emulating (at least, if the one child quoted is to be believed). In addition, Funk *et al.* (2003) found no short-term effects for either lower empathy or increased aggression in children exposed to video violence. They did find long-term effects but cautioned that a direction of cause could not be established from these findings because it could be that more aggressive children and/or those with lower empathy prefer to play violent video games for prolonged periods.

In addition, Marcus Schulzke (2010) questions Wonderly's interpretation of research on the deactivation of brain regions associated with empathic processing (see Mathiak & Weber 2006). He queries how much the fact that the area that controls empathy (the limbic orbitofrontal area of the brain) was inactive during an episode of violent gameplay necessitates (a) that the effect will be long lasting, and (b) that this will produce a significant change in the outlook of the gamer so as to alter his behaviour for the worse when outside gamespace (something even the authors, Mathiak and Weber, are cautious about). In addition, Schulzke points out that Hume emphasized the importance of empathy towards other *people*. Why, then, should we assume that not showing empathy towards an avatar would alter this sentiment towards others? Analogously, should I show empathy towards Ken and Barbie or even a more life-like Bobo doll? In fact, why *should* I show empathy to any virtual object, particularly within the context of *game*space? Is such a normative command based solely on the belief that to not do so would diminish one's capacity for empathy? In other words, it appears that it is not so much that one should show empathy towards virtual characters as it is that not showing empathy, in virtue of one's "violent" actions, will (allegedly) have a detrimental impact on one's psychological make-up. Whether this is the case or not is an empirical matter in need of further testing.

Relevant to this last point is a study by John King *et al.* (2006), who found that when an action was considered appropriate to the context in which it occurred, participants exhibited excitation in the same areas of the brain – the ventromedial frontal cortex and amygdala – irrespective of whether their behaviour was aggressive or compassionate. In other words, irrespective of whether they acted aggressively towards one virtual character (shooting a non-human assailant) or compassionately towards another (an injured human avatar), when this behaviour was considered to be appropriate to the situation (an example of normative action), excitation of the ventromedial frontal cortex and amygdala occurred, compared to no such excitation when participants were asked to engage in contextually inappropriate behaviour (healing the non-human assailant and shooting the injured man). If, within the context of the game, it is appropriate to murder indiscriminately (the normative action), then why should I (*qua* gamer) be expected to show empathy towards the other virtual characters? Even if empathy is diminished in a context-appropriate situation, this does not entail that it will be similarly diminished in a different context: one where it is much more appropriate to show empathy. If we adhere to the advice of Nichols, one must evaluate whether sentiment is warranted within a given context. Within the context of a violent video game, it is not clear that it should be, and certainly Wonderly does not make a convincing case for *why* it should be.

CONCLUSION

Using the framework of Hume's sentimentalism, including the later work of neo-sentimentalists such as Prinz and Nichols, I have considered the role of disgust as an appropriate measure of moral wisdom when applied to gamespace. Owing to the virtual nature of the interactions within gamespace, I have argued that even if STAs elicit a direct visceral response in gamers and/or onlookers that may be expressed as disgust or some other sentiment of disapprobation, this is not sufficient to justify any form of moral condemnation (as sentimentalism would argue). Rather, within the context of gamespace, it is evidence of moral fallibility, for, if acted on, it could prevent individuals from engaging freely on occasions when no harm ensues. Moreover, drawing from Nichols, because of the altered contingencies of gamespace, this would make the reaction (of disgust) unwarranted.

Where a claim to harm is forthcoming (e.g. Wonderly), I have argued that the question of whether engaging in ultra-violent video games degrades one's ability to show empathy is an empirical one and, to date, there is insufficient evidence to support any conclusion either way (see Ch. 5 for discussion on virtual violence and aggression). In short, then, owing to the failure of disapprobation (*qua* disgust) to constitute a form of moral wisdom within gamespace, it follows that sentimentalism cannot be used as a criterion for the selective prohibition of video game content.

In the next chapter, I consider an alternative to sentimentalism: the view that morality is a matter of doing one's duty, and that the rules on how to conduct oneself should be established through the application of reason, not sentiment. Can such a moral system inform judgements on how to conduct oneself within gamespace, and help identify which content to selectively prohibit, if any?

Kant's call of duty

[M]orals is not properly the doctrine of how we are to *make* ourselves happy but of how we are to become *worthy* of happiness.
(Kant [1788] 1997: 108, original emphasis)

In the previous chapter I discussed the role of sentiment within morality,
and the extent to which it can be used to selectively prohibit STAs. In this
chapter, I consider an opposing view presented by Immanuel Kant: that
there is no place for sentiment within moral theorizing, and in fact what one
ought to do, at least in a moral sense, should be driven by duty. Kant, therefore, hoped for a society in which persons not only do the right thing, but
do the right thing for the right reasons, and so treat each other with respect
as autonomous, rational beings (De Marneffe 2001). Having said that, Kant
does not confine his moral theory to an ethic of pure intentionality, in which
one should be indifferent to the accomplishment of what one intended; nevertheless, he does hold that any consideration, on the part of the subject, as
to whether the *outcome* of one's intention is worthy of the moral effort suc-
ceeds only in revealing the subject's immortality (Verweyen 1996).

In this chapter I discuss the work of Kant and those more recent (twenty-first-century) theorists who have sought to apply his moral philosophy to gamespace. In particular, I consider the extent to which the first and second formulations of Kant's categorical imperative can provide the basis for the selective prohibition of video game content.

KANT'S IMPERATIVES

The categorical imperative: first formulation

Talk of morality is essentially talk of what *ought* to be done: one ought to be kind, or one ought to respect others (for example); or, even, one ought not to commit murder. Saying that one ought to do *x* typically indicates that *x* is a good thing to do; whereas saying that *x* is bad is just another way of saying that one should refrain from doing *x*. Kant distinguishes between two types of "ought". One he sees as motivated by personal desire and therefore as having a subjective cause; this he calls the *hypothetical imperative*. The other is driven by recourse to reason, in as much as it stipulates what the rational person ought to do in virtue of being a rational person.[1] This latter "ought" expresses what Kant refers to as the *categorical imperative*. As he explains:

> Now all imperatives command either hypothetically or categorically. The former represent the practical necessity of a possible action as a means for attaining something else that one wants (or possibly may want). The categorical imperative would be one which represented an action as objectively necessary in itself, without reference to another end.   (Kant [1785] 1993: §414)

The hypothetical imperative conveys, conditionally, what one ought to do to achieve some personally desired end. If I want to become an accomplished musician then I ought to practise my craft (practising my craft being the means – or the condition – to that end). To achieve *m* (being an accomplished musician), I ought to do *p* (practise). Saying that one ought not to commit murder, however, is not to say what one ought to do to achieve a desired goal. Kant would not hold that one conditionally ought not to commit murder if one wishes to avoid incarceration (even though, *ceteris paribus*, it is one means to that end); rather, saying that one ought not to commit murder is an end in itself and, moreover, is a conclusion that any rational person would arrive at (I shall consider the link between rationality and morality again in Ch. 10 when discussing social contract theory). The categorical imperative is commanded by reason. To break the categorical imperative is therefore to act not only immorally but also irrationally.

Kant holds that there is but one categorical imperative, although he presents different formulations of it (see Norman 1998 for a discussion). Written here is what is traditionally referred to as the *first formulation*: "Act only according to that maxim whereby you can at the same time will that it should become a universal law" (Kant [1785] 1993: §421). In what is to follow, I discuss this formulation, as well as what is often referred to as the *second formulation* of the categorical imperative, as a means of justifying the selective prohibition of video game content. However, I postpone discussion of either of these until after I have considered how the amoralist, using the hypothetical imperative, might interpret Kant in a way that would favour their view: that STAs should not be of moral concern.

The hypothetical imperative: an argument for the amorality of gamespace

Recent literature that has sought to apply Kantian moral theory to gamespace has focused on the categorical imperative and the extent to which it can be used to sanction violent video game content (see McCormick 2001; Schulzke 2010; Waddington 2007). The amoralist may wish to argue, however, that the first formulation of the categorical imperative provides a formal structure for how to behave towards *other people*, and given that, in the case of single-player games at least, the gamer acts alone, then there are by definition no other people within the gamespace to engage with, morally or otherwise. As such, Kant's first formulation is not applicable to this type of gamespace (I discuss multiplayer space later). Moreover, the amoralist might further insist that, if anything, single-player gamespace is more in keeping with the activities for which the hypothetical imperative was formulated, thereby denouncing any claim to the effect that STAs are a *moral* violation. Thus, the amoralist may assert, given that x (POTAs) ≠ y (STAs), rather than trying to argue for a relationship between x and y that is worthy of moral scrutiny, why not embrace their differences and accept the fact that although the categorical imperative is applicable to POTAs, the hypothetical imperative much more clearly endorses the activity of gamespace. In fact, I consider the player who endorses the hypothetical imperative to be akin to Huizinga's *homo ludens* (introduced in Ch. 1). Recall, that *homo ludens* – the individual who occupies the space of play – engages in an activity with no moral function. As Miguel Sicart states: "*Homo ludens* has no moral duties, no moral dimensions" (2010: 187).

Within the context of single-player games, often it is the case that violent action – be it assault, murder or even torture – is a means to an end. Defeating an opponent enables one to progress, through the acquisition of points or resources (such as equipment or "energy"), or even through information-gathering (a possible context for the use of torture). The manipulation of pixels in order to obtain a desired end seems perfectly compatible with Kant's formulation of the hypothetical imperative and the characterization of *homo ludens* as a seeker of entertainment (*ibid.*). If I desire to win the game, and doing *a, b, c* (etc.) is a means of obtaining that end, then I ought to do *a, b, c* (etc.). The hypothetical "ought" is not decreeing a moral command; rather, in this case, it conveys a simple normative strategy to the gamer – do what ought to be done to win the game. The hypothetical imperative thus encapsulates practical necessity rather than delineating moral obligation; it commands our inclination (do *x* if you want *y*); and, within single-player gamespace, in the absence of other persons, we are free to indulge our inclinations. In Chapter 9, I shall discuss the hypothetical imperative further and, following Sicart's lead, contrast *homo ludens* with the more ethically engaged *homo poieticus* (Floridi & Sanders 2005), particularly in relation to the moral theory of *ethical egoism*.

But what about assaults or murders that occur within certain games, seemingly for the sake of it, in so far as they fail to promote progression within the game and therefore seem gratuitous as a means to that end (e.g. the *Grand Theft Auto* series; see Tavinor 2005)? If one is engaging in such putative gratuity simply because one is seeking to enjoy oneself, rather than, say, because one does not know how to play the game correctly, then the hypothetical imperative would stipulate: if you want to obtain E (enjoyment), and doing *a, b, c* (assault, torture, murder or whatever) is a means of achieving E then one ought to do *a, b, c*. The amoralist could again argue that such indulgence is not a moral matter, and for the moralist to say that it is, through an endorsement of Kant's categorical imperative, requires that she convince us that the categorical imperative can legitimately be applied to gamespace.

The categorical imperative: second formulation

One way in which the proponent of Kantian ethics might try to convince us is through Kant's second formulation of the categorical imperative, which reads: "Act in such a way as to treat humanity, whether in your own person or in the person of another, always at the same time as an end and never simply as a means" (Kant [1785] 1993: §429).

For Kant, people should not be used *solely* as a means to an end. Importantly, however, this does not preclude the possibility of using them as a means to an end on occasion; rather, it proscribes this as an exclusive and exhaustive way to treat other human beings. I can, and often do, treat individuals as a means to an end: when I obtain the services of a car mechanic, for example, or seek to be entertained at the theatre. But I treat them in this way in the full knowledge that they are also autonomous, rational persons who have their own desires: that is, who seek to procure their own ends (Norman 1998). Included within Kant's notion of "persons", of course, is one's own personhood. As he asserts within the second formulation, "whether in your own person or in the person of another"; or, as expressed by Richard Spinello, "that humanity, my own humanity, and those of others, must be respected in every action" (2001: 145). One should, therefore, not treat oneself simply as a means to an end; for as Kant states: "I cannot dispose of man in my own person by mutilating, damaging, or killing him" ([1785] 1993: §429). In terms of gamespace, then, it has been suggested that simulated violence (or, I would argue, any STA) potentially falls foul of Kant's second formulation of the categorical imperative in two interrelated ways: (a) as a demonstrable failing in one's duty to oneself not to engage in practices that are contrary to the categorical imperative; and (b) through *cultivating* practices that are contrary to one's duty to others as expressed within the categorical imperative, thus leading, through this cultivation, to the potential repetition of STAs in the non-virtual world, thereby violating others. In order for the Kantian to defend these claims, however, she must delineate the relationship between POTAs and STAs – given that x (POTA) $\neq y$ (STA) – in such a way as to justify the claim that engaging in STAs (a) violates one's duty to oneself, and (b) will probably result in a failure to do one's duty to others when in the non-virtual realm. The first point can be argued for *a priori*, whereas the second is effectively an empirical matter.

EXTENDING KANT'S ANALOGY: CULTIVATING VIRTUAL CRUELTY

A tack Matt McCormick (2001) and David Waddington (2007) take when postulating a Kantian perspective on normative interactions within gamespace is to extend an analogy Kant himself employs when discussing the treatment of non-human animals (hereafter, "animals"). They point out that Kant does not consider that we have a moral duty towards animals; they are a means to an end rather than an end in themselves. Nevertheless, they both note how Kant argues that we should not be cruel to animals as, by way of analogy from animal to human, this could lead to a failure to do our duty (to apply the categorical imperative) to those around us. As Kant explains:

> Our duties towards animals are merely indirect duties towards humanity. Animal nature has analogies to human nature, and by doing our duties to animals in respect of manifestations which correspond to manifestations of human nature, we directly do our duty towards humanity ... If then any acts of animals are analogous to human acts and spring from the same principles, we have duties towards animals because thus we cultivate the

> corresponding duties towards human beings … If a man shoots his dog because the animal is no longer capable of service, he does not fail in his duty to the dog, for the dog cannot judge, but his act is inhuman and damages in himself that humanity which it is his duty to show towards mankind. If he is not to stifle his human feelings, he must practice kindness towards animals, for he who is cruel to animals becomes hard also in his dealings with men.   ([1930] 1963: 239–40)

For Kant, then, "the right kinds of behaviour and the disposition to do one's duty must be cultivated" (McCormick 2001: 283), because: "Tender feelings towards dumb animals develop humane feelings towards mankind" (Kant [1930] 1963: 240). Waddington further argues that this cultivation could be extended and applied to how we interact within gamespace:

> If animals can be said to be an analogue of humanity, perhaps video-game characters are as well. After all, video-game characters are often representations of humans. If it is wrong to gouge out the eyes of a cat because it inures us to cruelty … then perhaps it is wrong to gouge out the eyes of a video-game character for the same reason.   (2007: 125)

Thus, the argument goes, not only might STAs hinder the cultivation of one's duty by necessarily negating such "dutiful" simulation within gamespace (at least at the time the STA is occurring) but, more than this, they may promote the opposite, and in doing so afford the opportunity to practise being both immoral and subsequently, for Kant, irrational. Therefore, McCormick continues, it is not difficult to imagine Kant saying: "Cultivating cruelty and indifference with regard to virtual suffering and death encourages the same towards real suffering and death" (2001: 283).

For Kant, the idea of cultivating practices that might lead to the negation of one's duty to others is in effect to cultivate an act that is fundamentally irrational. A similar approach has been taken by Neil Levy (although not with explicit reference to Kant). Levy (2003) argues for the importance of rationality to our sense of identity, and says that engaging in certain activities may corrode this. Using the example of bestiality, he argues that such an act is identity-threatening in so far as the more someone engages in it, the more difficult it will be for them "to retain a grip on [their] identity as a full member of our community, and we will find it harder to admit [them] to full membership" (*ibid.*: 454). For Levy, then, not only might the practice of bestiality corrode one's identity as a member of the established community, where such a practice is *not* held as a social (and therefore moral) norm, but the corrosion of this identity would make it harder for such a person to be accepted by others within the community. Perhaps this strikes an intuitive chord with us, even in the case of certain virtual practices: for one is left to wonder how readily those who publicly announce that they engage in virtual rape or paedophilia would be invited to a typical social gathering. Furthermore, to what extent would such a virtual practice corrode one's identity relative to other members of one's non-virtual community or be construed as so altered by them? Perhaps a divergence in identification with one's community would make it harder to satisfy one's moral obligations towards them, and vice versa. Kant alludes to this possibility when discussing certain practices and communal restrictions known to him in his day: "In England butchers and doctors do not sit on a jury because they are accustomed to the sight of death and hardened" ([1930] 1963: 240).

To be clear, I am not comparing the practice of butchers and doctors directly to the act of bestiality (nor would Kant, I expect). Nevertheless, in a much milder and more accustomed form, they illustrate how certain practices – inflicting pain on animals and humans (as butchers and doctors must do on occasion) – or their association with death were held by Kant (and, it would appear, the English judicial system at that time), potentially at least, to harden the individual, thereby making it more difficult for them to act dutifully towards others. In the absence of benefit to society, which Kant would accept being a butcher or doctor has,[2] each respective practice would be morally intolerable.

Cruelty towards humans is morally intolerable because it disrespects people as ends in themselves. But animals are not considered by Kant to be ends in themselves; nevertheless, their treatment is said to elicit the same kind of emotions as would be elicited in the treatment of humans (Brey 1999). However, how is emotion relevant here? After all, Kant's moral theory posits duty above sentiment. Is this not simply sentimentalism in disguise? No. Kant does not consider such feelings to be a measure of morality or the means by which moral decisions should be made, but he does consider that certain emotions are typically congruent with actions that correspond to one's duty to humanity whereas others are not or are less so. These same emotions can be cultivated through the treatment of animals, either through kindness or cruelty, to the betterment or detriment of one's self and, hence, others.

Schulzke (2010), however, is not convinced by the move, through extended analogy, from animal-to-human to avatars-to-human. He does not believe that Kant would endorse the view that, *a priori*, we are failing in our duty to ourselves by engaging in STAs against avatars that are often meant to represent us (humankind), *because* they are meant to represent us. Kant draws the analogy with animals because they share a number of biological and phenomenal similarities to us (e.g. the ability to feel pain).[3] Avatars, on the other hand, share only a superficial similarity to us: certainly not biological, phenomenal or psychological. To further illustrate the problem with such a move, Schulzke continues the analogy (perhaps *ad absurdum*) by asking whether we should extend our indirect moral duties to such things as portraits of humans or even video recordings. One might also wish to include the earlier example (from Ch. 3) of Ken and Barbie, or a more realistic-looking Bobo doll.

Based on an extension of the analogy from animals-to-human to avatar-to-human, a Kantian defence of point (a) – that engaging in STAs demonstrates a failing in one's duty to oneself – appears weak. Moreover, with regard to point (b) (that engaging in STAs cultivates a disposition to violate the categorical imperative to the point where one violates one's duty to other persons), irrespective of the validity of extending the analogy, the outcome is ultimately an empirical matter, as McCormick, Waddington and Schulzke acknowledge. However, the extent to which this virtual violation manifests itself outside the gaming environment in antisocial and otherwise immoral behaviour is a matter of some debate, and certainly empirical findings remain inconclusive. These will be discussed in Chapter 5. In the meantime, let us consider multiplayer spaces and whether Kantian moral theory is applicable, *a priori*, to this type of gamespace.

INTENDING PSYCHOLOGICAL HARM WITHIN MULTIPLAYER SPACES

In the previous section, we saw how the Kantian might argue as follows: "[I]f a person acts cruelly when playing an ultra-violent video game, then this would constitute a violation of that person's duty to his/herself" (Waddington 2007: 124–5). Of course, as Waddington acknowledges, the amoralist may retort that one cannot act cruelly towards pixels; at best one merely simulates cruelty. Within multiplayer gamespaces, however, avatars are often controlled by gamers (although some NPCs may still feature). Consequently, one may be accused of an indirect moral offence against those persons who control the avatar, or even of directly violating one's duty towards them.

The second formulation of the categorical imperative has been applied to what McCormick (2001) refers to as the actions of a *bad sport*. Through the expression of bad sportsmanship – either in victory or defeat – one is said to have disrespected one's opponent. Gloating in victory or wallowing in self-pity after a defeat are each considered to be examples of inappropriate self-focus, at the cost of not paying sufficient respect to one's opponent and fellow gamer. Fairly recently within gamspace (early twenty-first century), an example of what some might call bad sportsmanship has appeared (although it is not exclusive to this space): namely, *tea-bagging* (a.k.a. corpse-humping) in which one's avatar crouches over a defeated ("dead") avatar and moves up and down, raising and lowering its groin over the corpse as an act of (humorous?)

humiliation. There is also the less specific practice of "griefing" (that is, to deliberately cause annoyance to other gamers for one's own amusement).

Thus, while it is not possible to harm another avatar physically, or even humiliate it directly, in multiplayer space indirect and perhaps unintentional harm may be inflicted on a gamer in virtue of the actions carried out on their avatar. There may even be deliberate attempts made to cause harm this way. As Schulzke explains:

> It is not immoral to attack another player-controlled character. Rather, the immorality consists in psychologically harming the person that controls the avatar. Therefore, the exception to the Kantian defence of video games is that actions in the game are immoral when they are *intended* to harm another person psychologically. (2010: 129, emphasis added)

The *intention* to harm, or in other ways be immoral, is of utmost importance within Kant's moral philosophy, irrespective of consequence. There are two ways in which one can *intend* to harm psychologically and for that to come about within multiplayer space: first, through the victim's identification with her avatar; and, second, through violating established status functions. Each of these is not mutually exclusive, of course, for it may be that the single intention to harm violates both.

To understand status functions, one must first understand that the essential characteristic of gamespace is play. As we saw in Chapter 1, according to Whitty and Carr (2006), the fundamental essence of play is the freedom and licence to be creative, and to be set apart from ordinary life. Yet play also depends on rules and other factors contingently related to a given space and time. Consequently, an interesting paradox arises in which freedom within play is created only through constraint. As an example of such constraint, virtual objects/events are assigned a mutually accepted *status function*. This is used to establish coherent play within a cohesive gaming community: formally presented by Philip Brey as "X counts as Y (in context C)" (2003: 278; see also Searle 1995). Thus, two chess players may agree that when playing with *this* chess set (context C), which has a missing king, a wine cork (X) counts as the king (Y). More generally, and more relevant to multiplayer games, it might be established that within the context of a given gamespace (context C), action X (or actions X_1, X_2, X_3, etc.) counts as Y (something it is permissible to do). (See also discussion on social contract theory in Ch. 10.)

In such an environment, through the use of agreed status functions, it may be that one is permitted to engage in virtual rape or murder (rape$_v$ or murder$_v$), or some other STA. In doing so, one can be said to satisfy the first formulation of Kant's categorical imperative, in so far as all those within a given gamespace *will* that murder$_v$ or rape$_v$ (etc.) should become a universal law. In this space, it is permitted to kill$_v$ and be killed$_v$ or rape$_v$ and be raped$_v$. Importantly, such a universal law (or agreed status function) would not (or should not) be considered irrational because, owing to the contingent nature of this environment, with its altered state of embodiment (virtual not physical), one can only be *virtually* raped and/or *virtually* murdered.

However, if the status function of an object/event is not clearly indicated to the satisfaction of all parties (does X_4 also count as Y in this context?), then a conflict born of ambiguity often ensues and the gamespace risks losing its coherence, and the community its cohesion (see Vanacker & Heider 2011 for a recent discussion). The potential for status-function ambiguity is nowhere more apparent than in the types of social interactions possible within multiplayer spaces. Owing to the game-like quality of the events played out in these environments, an element of make-believe inevitably accompanies player interactions.

The extent to which one *intends* to violate established status functions may, in part, be dependent on the extent to which these status functions are explicitly agreed and therefore the extent to which one can be accused of knowingly violating them. However, knowing when a virtual encounter involves simulation compliant with status functions, and when it does not, may not always be easy and, indeed, may not be something that some players want clarifying (Turkle 1995). As Brey notes:

> Interestingly, users of virtual environments sometimes appear as if they want to keep the dividing line between reality and role-playing fuzzy, so as to have the benefits of real-life social interactions while always having the fall-back option of claiming that it is all make-believe. (2003: 281)

One may be genuinely unclear about the permissibility of a given virtual action. But what of those who intentionally violate a status function and, let us say, assault$_v$ or rape$_v$, or murder$_v$ another's avatar when it is not permissible to do so? In such a situation, the gamer would have violated the second formulation of the categorical imperative and used the other gamer's avatar as a means to elicit personal gratification: in effect, as a means to an end.[4] But the avatar is not a person; rather, at best, it *represents* the gamer. Why, then, should one not be able to treat the avatar as a means to an end?

Jessica Wolfendale evidences the occurrence of strong avatar identification through the gamers' use of language. Within the context of *EverQuest*, she notes how gamers may say things like "*I* was ignored" or "*I* never let anyone talk to *me* like that again" (2007: 114, original emphasis). Wolfendale goes on to state: "This identification with the avatar means that harm to avatar is felt as harm to the individual" (*ibid.*). She therefore considers unsolicited aggression or other violations directed towards avatars to be constitutive of real moral harm.[5] Consequently, she rejects the view that the fault is with the gamer who may have too much psychological investment in the avatar. Equally, she rejects as inappropriate the argument that gamers should avoid harm by psychologically distancing themselves from their virtual personas.

Wolfendale compares avatar attachment to the attachment one might feel towards certain possessions, and states that one would not consider it inappropriate for an individual to feel upset or otherwise aggrieved if their car had been stolen or their house burgled. Likewise, it would not be appropriate to advise the victim to distance themselves from such possessions in the future so as to avoid feeling similarly upset if such an incident were to occur again. In such cases where the putatively immoral gamer intentionally targets the avatar of another gamer because they recognize the strength of identification that exists between avatar and gamer (or even the potential for this strength of identification to be in place), then, in light of the gamer's *intention*, the second formulation of Kant's categorical imperative has been violated (for a fuller discussion on the issue of player identification with the avatar, see Young & Whitty 2011a).

In contrast, where the STA (rape$_v$, murder$_v$, etc.) is permitted within a given space, then, on entering that space, one is implicitly willing that the STA becomes a universal law and that others, *qua* an end in themselves, likewise will that this becomes a universal law within *that* gamespace. As an example of such a space, consider *Sociolotron* (mentioned briefly in Ch. 2), which promotes itself as a world with different values and rules, where you are allowed to explore your "darker side" (*Sociolotron 2* was still under construction at time of writing). Virtual sex, both consensual and nonconsensual, is permitted and graphically represented, as is politically incorrect behaviour, including blasphemy and all forms of discrimination (see Young & Whitty 2010 for further discussion). The general philosophy of the game seems to be that if you are given the freedom to express yourself within this space then you should allow others to do the same (if you want to "dish it out" then you should be able to take it, we are told).

In such a space, the agreed status functions may correspond to established offline taboos, only here they are permissible. Importantly, however, it can be the case that some gamers may not always wish to engage in certain permissible behaviours within the virtual space even though they accept and tolerate their occurrence;[6] they may even react with a sense of disgust to the event (i.e. when witnessing the raping of a fellow gamer's avatar, or even their own; see Whitty *et al.* 2011). Such an act would nevertheless be deemed a moral violation (at least within that space) only *if* it contravened a community-agreed status function. But in such a space, and under such circumstances – where one is upset by what is occurring – would it not be a violation of one's duty to oneself to remain in the space enduring further psychological upset? Such an eventuality would appear to contravene one's duty to oneself as stipulated by the second formulation of the categorical imperative.

For those who are content to continue engaging in such activities, however, and do not have an aversive reaction to their occurrence, the Kantian may again consider the empirical question: is such activity not cultivating a practice that is ultimately to the detriment of one's duty to others? So even if one accepts that gamers abide by the agreed status functions of a space, and therefore adhere to the first formulation of the categorical imperative, one may nevertheless wish to challenge the activity's moral worth. Using the animal analogy again, Kant notes how:

> Vivisectionists, who use living animals for their experiments, certainly act cruelly, although their aim is praiseworthy, and they can justify their cruelty, since animals must be regarded as man's instruments; but any such cruelty for sport cannot be justified.
> ([1930] 1963: 240–41)

Perhaps the Kantian can claim that gameplay involving STAs cultivates cruelty in the absence of benefit. In this respect, it is analogous to cruelty for sport, which Kant opposes. However, such a charge still relies on an extended analogy from animal-to-human to avatar-to-human, which is weak. In addition, it is dependent on empirical evidence demonstrating that STAs lead to POTAs: evidence that is, to date, somewhat elusive.

CONCLUSION

The application of Kant's categorical imperative as a means of selectively prohibiting video game content (specifically, STAs) fails regardless of the formulation one adopts. Within single-player games, the first formulation is a non-starter, as there is no other person to consider when willing that action x should become a universal law. In relation to the second formulation, there is likewise no other person towards whom one should act dutifully and treat as an end in themselves. Moreover, the argument from extended analogy is weak and is even vulnerable to a *reductio ad absurdum*, whereby even photographs and such like are considered suitable candidates for moral consideration (Schulzke 2010). Wthin multiplayer gamespace, scholars have applied Kant's second formulation to the issue of bad sportsmanship and the act of disrespecting others. However, this is something that can occur irrespective of the presence of STAs (or any representation in particular, for that matter) and so has no utility when it comes to the question of selective prohibition of *content*. Within this space, the most the Kantian can stipulate is that one should abide by the first formulation when establishing agreed status functions. However, this feasibly permits the universal acceptance (within this space) of virtual rape, murder, or any number of other STAs, thereby discounting the possibility of selective prohibition, unless agreed by the community who occupy that space. Under such circumstances, prohibition is contingent on the fact that a given act is something *they* agree to prohibit. Finally, in the case of those gamers who enter a space that permits an STA they find distressing (even though they accept its permissibility), the Kantian could argue that these people are failing in their duty to protect themselves from psychological harm. However, even if this is the case, and one accepts the Kantian moral judgement on this matter, at best it provides moral guidance on how one should act with regard to oneself, not which content should be selectively prohibited.

The focus on psychological harm is something I shall pursue in more detail at various points throughout the remainder of this book. Among other things, it is certainly an indirect feature of the consequentialist approach to morality, the most famous exponent of which is utilitarianism. Is it that some video game content is associated with a greater degree of negative consequence (increased pain and suffering, for example) than others? If it is, should this "fact" be utilized as a means of justifying the selective prohibition of content?

FIVE

The cost and benefit of virtual violence (and other taboos)

> Nature has placed mankind under the governance of two sovereign masters, *pain* and *pleasure*. It is for them alone to point out what we ought to do, as well as to determine what we shall do.
> (Bentham [1789] 1996: 11, original emphasis)

If doing x brings about y, where y is something unpleasant – meaning x has a negative consequence – then it would seem prudent to avoid doing x. Alternatively, if doing x produces a positive outcome, then common sense would have us do x. However, does engaging in activity x, where x produces a positive outcome, make x the right thing to do, morally? In other words, given its positive consequence, does it necessarily follow that doing x is morally good and so *ought* to be done? Classical utilitarianism – that is, the utilitarianism of Jeremy Bentham and John Stuart Mill – holds that for x to be morally good it must engender (actually, or in principle) a positive outcome in the form of increased happiness. Thus, those acts that produce the most happiness are judged to be the most moral. Conversely, an immoral act is said to be that which produces more pain than happiness.

In this chapter I consider the suitability of classical utilitarianism (here-after, utilitarianism) as a measure of selective prohibition. If engaging in an STA produces an increase in unpleasantness – *qua* antisocial behaviour, for example – then this fact (if indeed it is a fact) would seem to consti-tute reasonable grounds for its prohibition. The association of STAs with negative or positive consequences is, of course, an empirical matter, and much research has been carried out already on the effects of media violence (including video games) on aggression and other forms of antisocial behav-iour. However, before assessing whether it can be empirically shown that doing x (where x = engaging in an STA) brings about y (an unpleasant con-sequence), I shall first outline utilitarianism, contrasting Bentham with Mill where appropriate. After all, if empirical findings are to be evaluated within a utilitarian framework, then it needs to be made clear how happiness is to be measured and whose happiness counts.

THE UTILITARIANISM OF BENTHAM AND MILL

As a measure of consequence, utilitarianism endorses the *principle of utility*, which, according to Bentham:

> approves or disapproves of every action whatsoever, according to the tendency which it appears to have to augment or diminish the happiness of the party whose interest is in question: or what is the same thing in others words, to promote or to oppose that happiness... A thing is said to promote the interest, or be *for* the interest, of an individual, when it tends to add to the sum total of his pleasures: or, what comes to the same thing, to diminish the sum total of his pains.   ([1789] 1996: 12, original emphasis)

For Bentham, then, the principle of utility – also referred to as the *great-est happiness principle* – provides a measure of consequence based on the amount of happiness that consequence provides for the interested party. Importantly, though, in advocating utility as a means by which one can approve or disapprove of an action, Bentham confounds any action that pro-motes happiness (or diminishes unhappiness) with what is judged to be the *right* (or wrong) thing to do; in other words, with what one *ought* to do, morally. As he further explains:

> Of an action that is conformable to the principles of utility one may always say either that it is one that ought to be done, or at least that it is not one that ought not to be done. One may say also, that it is right it should be done; at least that it is not wrong

it should be done: that it is a right action; at least that it is not a
wrong action.   (*Ibid.*: 13)

Mill, like Bentham, endorses the greatest happiness principle as a normative tool: as a measure of what actions ought to be carried out in virtue of
their consequences.

> The creed which accepts as the foundation of morals, Utility, or
> the Greatest Happiness Principle, holds that actions are right
> in proportion as they tend to promote happiness, wrong as
> they tend to produce the reverse of happiness. By happiness is
> intended pleasure, and the absence of pain; by unhappiness, pain
> and the privation of pleasure.   ([1863] 1998: 55)

The two most prominent figures within the utilitarian movement,
Bentham and Mill, share the view that the principle of utility marks out a
good from bad act, in so far as the action that promotes the most happiness
or diminishes the most unhappiness is morally good and, conversely, that
which increases pain or lessens happiness is morally bad. In short, utility is
"the standard of morality" (*ibid.*: 59). However, Mill differs from Bentham
in relation to how one might measure happiness. For Bentham, happiness can be measured quantitatively using a kind of hedonistic calculus
that enables *all* activities to be judged according to the same metric, their
respective utility measure contributing directly to their value. As Bentham
illustrates:

> Prejudice apart, the game of push-pin is of equal value with the
> arts and science of music and poetry. If the game of push-pin
> furnish more pleasure, it is more valuable than either ... If poetry
> and music deserve to be preferred before a game of push-pin, it
> must be because they are calculated to gratify those individuals
> who are most difficult to be pleased.   (1830: 206–7)

In contrast, Mill seeks also to draw a *qualitative* distinction between types of
pleasure – typically distinguishing sensual pleasures from pleasure derived
from more intellectual pursuits; the former – lower pleasures – he regards
as different in kind (not just degree) from the latter, higher pleasures. Thus
Mill argues:

> It is quite compatible with the principle of utility to recognise the
> fact, that some *kinds* of pleasure are more desirable and more
> valuable than others. It would be absurd that while, in estimat-
> ing all other things, quality is considered as well as quantity, the

> estimation of pleasures should be supposed to depend on quantity alone. ([1863] 1998: 56, original emphasis)

As a reaction against Bentham's exclusively quantitative measure of happiness, Mill famously remarks: "It is better to be a human being dissatisfied than a pig satisfied; better to be Socrates dissatisfied than a fool satisfied" (*ibid.*: 57). Unlike Bentham, then, who regards the value of an action as corresponding directly to the happiness derived from it, Mill bestows on some actions (or activities) a more inherent value, which then privileges the type of pleasure they are said to produce, creating, in some cases, what he judged to be a more worthwhile happiness and therefore a more morally commendable action or pursuit.

According to Mill, for an action to be of moral worth it is not enough that it increases happiness *per se*; more than this, it must increase the right sort of happiness or, put another way, happiness produced in pursuit of the right sort of activity. Mill seems to be advocating a pursuit of happiness that is more virtuous: perhaps leading to an increase in one's well-being (see Ch. 8). Thus, better to be Socrates dissatisfied, because what Socrates seeks to make him satisfied and therefore happier is held by Mill to be of greater value than that already achieved by someone content with mere sensual pleasures. In addition, Mill's brand of utilitarianism seeks to commend morally not only the pursuit of intellectual pleasures but the further ideal that one's actions should include, and in fact aim to promote, happiness across wider society, irrespective of how this impacts on one's own happiness (Norman 1998). For Mill, the utilitarian standard:

> is not the agent's own greatest happiness, but the greatest amount of happiness altogether; and if it may possibly be doubted whether a noble character is always the happier for its nobleness, there can be no doubt that it makes other people happier, and that the world in general is immensely a gainer by it. ([1863] 1998: 59)

Mill holds not only that I should *not* engage in an activity that makes me happy *if* at the same time it diminishes the level of general happiness, but also that I should pursue more vigorously those activities from which I am able to derive higher pleasures (characteristic of a more noble pursuit); for, according to Mill, there can be no doubt that these make the world a happier place.

Applying all of this to gamespace: first, it could be argued that within the context of single-player games in which it is permitted to direct STAs towards NPCs, such activity cannot produce negative utility based on an assessment of the consequences for that character because the NPC cannot actually experience pain or any form of displeasure. Therefore, if one assumes that those who play violent video games tend to derive some form of enjoyment from inflicting virtual violence on virtual characters – even allowing for those times when they lose or become frustrated – then, in accordance with Bentham's hedonistic calculus, one must conclude that STAs are morally good things to engage in, at least for those who indulge in them (just like those who played push-pin). This, of course, is a very narrow use of the calculus in so far as it includes only the consequences for the virtual characters (for which there are none) and the *immediate* consequences for the gamer (which, more often than not, are understood to be pleasurable). In addition, we need to include a number of other factors that will probably affect the overall measure of utility arrived at, such as the value placed on the pleasure produced and the scope of the virtual action's consequences.

In accordance with Mill, we might want to consider what *type* of pleasure is being experienced by the gamer. For the sake of argument, let us allow that the pleasure is, by Mill's reckoning, of a more visceral, lower, kind (I will have more to say on this point later). Initially, then, in the absence of any negative utility – because of the impossibility of negative consequences for the NPCs – such *lower* pleasure is sufficient to increase happiness (even if it is just the gamer's). But suppose we were to broaden the evaluative context to include the impact on wider society, even though such "wider society" is not directly involved within the gameplay and therefore the enactment of STAs. By doing this, rather than assessing only the direct and immediate consequences of engaging in STAs (for the gamer), one now has to consider more indirect and remote consequences, and the extent to which these engender negative utility for oneself and others, thereby diminishing more general levels of happiness, perhaps over an extended period of time (all of which goes against Mill's ideal).

Owing to the need for more careful consideration of the remote (potential) consequences of engaging in STAs, such as what the cumulative effects of enjoying virtual violence might be on the gamer (in addition to his exclusive and immediate happiness), it seems pertinent to consider research delineating the possibility of more long-term effects, such as addictive and/or reclusive behaviour. Before that, however, I begin by evaluating what might be viewed as more typical or traditional research looking into the effects of STAs: namely, the association between virtual violence and aggression, and its potential impact on wider society. The purpose of presenting such research findings is to better assess the extent to which incorporating wider and more remote consequences within the hedonistic calculus will culminate in an increase in negative utility.

ON THE ALLEGED NEGATIVE CONSEQUENCES OF VIDEO GAMES: ANTISOCIAL BEHAVIOUR AND ADDICTION

A criticism often voiced against violent video game content (which includes a number of the STAs listed in Ch. 1) is that it increases the likelihood that those who play these games will engage in antisocial behaviour when away from the gaming environment. McCormick (2001), for example, distinguishes between: (a) a *dangerous act*, which is an act that directly increases the risk of harm to self or others (e.g. engaging in a knife-throwing act), (b) a *harmful act*, which is an act that results in direct injury or damage to self or others (e.g. hitting one's assistant with a knife or stabbing oneself in the foot with it), and (c) a *risk-increasing act*, which corresponds to an act that increases the person's chances of committing a dangerous or harmful act (e.g. drinking alcohol before performing a knife-throwing act). For McCormick, video game violence is not a dangerous or harmful act as defined by (a) and (b) because one does not physically harm, nor can one run the risk of physically harming directly, either oneself or another as a result of what is done within the game, much as the amoralist argues (I shall discuss the potential for emotional/psychological harm below). However, for McCormick, engaging in video game violence could be construed as a risk-increasing act, for although no harm is *directly* incurred through engaging in virtual violence, such activity does (allegedly, or at least potentially) increase the risk of engaging in the sorts of dangerous activities that themselves run the risk of directly causing harm to oneself or others.[1]

It may be that any expression of antisocial behaviour, in the form of a dangerous and potentially harmful activity, is directly related to STAs I have previously enacted within the game, in so far as virtual killing/murder may lead to actual murder. Certainly this was the view taken by sensationalist and ill-founded media reports that claimed at the time that violent video games contributed to the US shootings at Columbine High School in 1999, after it was discovered that the perpetrators of this atrocity played violent first-person shooter games and referred to one of them in a video recording made before the murders took place (see Jenkins 1999 for a discussion). Or it may be that the enactment of STAs results in a more generic increase in aggression towards others without necessarily mirroring the specific STA in the form of its corresponding POTA. Such assertions cannot be established *a priori*, of course; there is nothing inherent within the manipulation of pixels or the representational meaning of STAs that would lead one to this conclusion. If such a relationship does hold, however, it is certainly *a posteriori* testable and therefore discoverable (although ethical guidelines on how to carry out research may prohibit certain approaches). In fact, by far the most extensive research on the negative consequences of playing violent video games has involved their alleged association with increased aggression (e.g. leading to more aggressive interactions outside gamespace) or other antisocial behaviour (e.g. being less responsive to someone believed to be in distress) and, related to this, affective and cognitive changes within the gamer (e.g. changes in feelings and attitude towards violence). Research has sought to establish *a posteriori* (or in some cases refute) evidence for a causal connection between virtual enactments of violence and actual violent behaviour and/or thoughts and feelings.

If it can be shown that virtual violence leads to actual violence, then one might seek to extrapolate from this to a more general causal connection between any STA and its corresponding POTA or more general aggressive/ antisocial behaviour (although see below on issues relating to the heterogeneity of STAs). However, even if such a connection can be established, in and of itself this would not be sufficient grounds for a utilitarian claim for the moral prohibition of STAs. In addition, it would need to be established that any (alleged) negative utility outweighed the demonstrably positive contribution video games of this nature make to society (in the form of pleasure gained by the large number who play violent video games, for example, or even from the financial benefits those directly or indirectly involved in a lucrative gaming industry obtain). To begin, then, let us consider evidence for a connection between violent gameplays and an increase in aggression outside the gaming environment.

In a review of previous research, Craig Anderson *et al.* (2003; see also Anderson 2004) reported that many studies found some short-term negative effects of playing video games, including the increased likelihood of aggressive thoughts, emotions and physically and verbally aggressive behaviour. By way of a caveat, however, John Sherry (2001) notes that although violent video games can have an effect on aggression, this effect is smaller than that produced by watching violent television. Moreover, the treatment times in the studies that formed part of his meta-analysis varied somewhat (ranging from 5 to 75 minutes), making it difficult to determine precisely how long the effect actually lasts. In addition, Gabrielle Unsworth and Grant Devilly (2007) reported that levels of aggression were mediated by the player's feelings immediately prior to playing the game, along with their temperament (i.e. their disposition towards aggression). Gary Giumetti and Patrick Markey (2007) likewise found that *only* those with higher levels of anger prior to playing the game were adversely affected, whereas, in a study by Markey and Kelly Scherer (2009), a negative effect occurred only in those with elevated levels of psychoticism (see Markey & Markey 2010 for further discussion of personality factors). Hanneke Polman *et al.* (2008), for their part, found that although actively engaging in a violent video game produced higher levels of aggression than passively watching the same game, this effect occurred only in boys and not girls. Similarly, James Ivory and Sriram Kalyanaraman (2007) found that the more immersed an individual was in a game, the greater their physiological and self-reported levels of arousal and aggression. Related to this, Elly Konijn and Brad Bushman (2007) found that boys who felt more immersed in the game, and identified more with the protagonist, exhibited more aggressive behaviour (see Ch. 12).

There is currently very little literature available on the *long-term* effects of playing violent video games. Ingrid Möller and Barbara Krahé (2009), however, recently conducted a thirty-month longitudinal study in which they found links to aggressive behaviour. Jeroen Lemmens *et al.* (2011) also found longer-term links between pathological (addictive) gaming behaviour in adolescent males and aggression, particularly, although not exclusively, when the virtual content was violent. Again, in contrast to more traditional single-player video games, few studies have focused on *online* (multiplayer) games. Having said that, unlike the findings of Möller and Krahé and Lemmen *et al.*, Dmitri Williams and Marko Skoric's (2005) longitudinal study of massively multiplayer online role-playing game (MMORPG) players found no evidence for the claim that online violent games cause substantial increases in real-world aggression; neither did playing online violent games result in more accepting beliefs about violent behaviours.

More generally, in a comprehensive review of the literature, Christopher Barlett *et al.* (2009) attempted to categorize video game effects as either confirmed, suspected, or speculative (based on weight of evidence). In addition, Anderson *et al.* (2010) recently completed a meta-analytic review of literature on video game violence and its effects. Anderson *et al.* claim to have found that exposure to video games with violent content is a causal risk factor for increased aggressive behaviour, cognition and affect, and decreases empathy and prosocial behaviour. Yet even taking both of these comprehensive reviews into account, there is still disagreement among researchers as to whether playing violent video games leads directly to aggressive behaviour, and so to Anderson *et al.*'s conclusion (see e.g. the responses to Anderson *et al.* 2010: Bushman *et al.* 2010; Ferguson & Kilburn 2010; Huesmann 2010; see also Bensley & Van Eenwyk 2001; Ferguson 2011).

Finally, of interest, because it has implication for future gaming development, Susan Persky and Jim Blascovich (2008) found, while exposing participants to an environment in which they were perceptually surrounded by and therefore immersed in the VE (compared to more traditional desktop games), that their increased sense of presence mediated the relationship between engaging with violent content and aggressive *feelings* but not, importantly, aggressive *behaviour*.[2]

It would seem, then, that in the absence of further evidence, at present, any firm conclusions (either way) must remain speculative. In keeping with this tentative approach, Christopher Ferguson (2007a), in his meta-analytic review on video game violence, warns us (as did Sherry) to treat many of the findings supporting a connection to antisocial behaviour with caution, arguing that the measures of aggression used in most studies lack validity and that often the effect sizes are close to zero. He also suggests that there is a bias in the academic literature in favour of those papers that report statistically significant differences between groups (see also Ferguson 2007b). Because of this, and based on the conflicting evidence reported, any attempt to posit a *direct* causal link between game content and violent offline behaviour should be regarded as overly simplistic, largely uncorroborated and ultimately contentious.

In short, as the empirical evidence remains inconclusive, a direct causal connection between STAs and their corresponding POTAs or more general levels of antisocial behaviour cannot legitimately be said to exist, at least not in terms of the heavily researched topic of virtual violence and actual aggression. However, although the jury is still out (as it were) on the negative effects of video game violence, there is still enough research highlighting *some* connection, with some (increased) risk for some people (Markey & Markey 2010). For Waddington (2007) this potential risk should not be ignored; for, as he acknowledges in a footnote, potential risk – the risk of a risk – is still a risk. A similar cautionary view is voiced by Peter Singer:

> Manufacturers fall back on the simplistic assertion that there is no scientific proof that violent video games lead to violent acts. But sometimes we cannot wait for proof. This seems to be one of those cases: The risks are great and outweigh whatever benefits violent video games may have. The evidence may not be conclusive, but it is too strong to be ignored any longer. (2007: 1)

Thus, if we accept Waddington and Singer's advice, we should include even the *potential* for increased risk within our calculation, regardless of whether empirical proof is presently forthcoming to indicate that this potential is consistently being realized. Before pursuing this point further, however, it is worth acknowledging that, so far, the emphasis has been on the potential risk of changes in the gamer to wider society, in so far as violent video games allegedly elicit violent tendencies (in some) that are transferred from the gaming environment to the actual world, such that the gamer acts aggressively towards those on the outside.[3] But what about negative utility based on how gaming potentially affects the individual in ways that do not result in violent or otherwise antisocial behaviour directed at others?

In the context of more general internet use, Richard Davis (2001: 191) proposed a cognitive-behavioural model of *problematic internet use* (PIU). According to Davis, psychosocial problems (such as depression or loneliness) may make an individual vulnerable to certain maladaptive thoughts about the self – such as "I am only good on the internet" or "I am worthless offline, but online I am someone" or even "I am a failure when I am offline".[4] The resulting need for the kind of "social contact and reinforcement obtained online results in an increased desire to remain in a virtual social life" (*ibid.*: 188). Such maladaptive, internet-biased, thoughts and behaviours are deemed by Davis to be a necessary, proximate cause of PIU.

Scott Caplan *et al.* (2009) note how relatively little attention has been given to gamespace – particularly multiplayer games – in relation to PIU (some exceptions being Gentile *et al.* 2011;[5] Meerkerk *et al.* 2006; Morahan-Martin & Schumacher 2000; and Ng & Wiemer-Hastings 2005). Yet these games are of relevance to the study of PIU not only because they are an increasingly popular form of internet activity but, equally, because they promote inter-personal engagement and potentially complex forms of social interaction, which are an established and even sought-after feature of the gaming experi-ence (see Barnett & Coulson 2010 for a recent detailed review). As a means of measuring this latter point, Ming Liu and Wei Peng devised their own hypothesized construct – called *preference for virtual life* (PVL) – which they define as: "one's cognitions or beliefs that one will perform better, feel better about oneself, and perceive [oneself] to be better treated by others in the online virtual game world than in offline or real life" (2009: 1307).

Liu and Peng found that those scoring high(er) on PVL were more likely to experience psychological dependency on multiplayer games. Caplan *et al.* (2009) likewise found strong predictive associations between PIU and online social behaviour. In addition, however, more specific game-related variables, such as high immersion motivation and use of voice technology (as opposed to text-based communication), were positively associated with PIU. Immer-sion motivation was seen to support the view that individuals were engag-ing in unhealthy escapism (see Billieux *et al.* 2011; Yee 2006a,b), thereby using multiplayer games to avoid more (perceived-to-be) stressful face-to-face encounters, and so further reinforcing their acquired preference for online socializing. The use of voice technology to communicate within these games was seen to facilitate further the player's interpersonal engagement, and so strengthen their sense of online community. In fact, Brian Ng and Peter Wiemer-Hastings (2005) argued that it is the increased social element associated with *online* multiplayer games that attracts the more "hardcore" player, such that players of online games are at a greater risk of developing symptoms characteristic of negative life consequences than offline players.

Problematic internet use in relation to video games does not specifically distinguish violent from non-violent content. However, the same social ele-ments highlighted in the above research on PIU can be found in those mul-tiplayer games that permit more extreme acts of violence compared to those that do not. Yet, even if it can be established that some people or certain groups are more susceptible to the negative effects of video games *per se* – violent or otherwise – either in relation to PIU or by way of increased "real-world" aggression, is this "fact" sufficient to warrant selective prohibition based on utilitarian grounds? For even if the potential for negative utility is included in the utilitarian calculus, ultimately, "[a]ny argument against vio-lent video games on these grounds needs to show that there is a significant possibility that the risks out-weigh the benefits (Waddington 2007: 123). In simple terms, what are the costs and what are the benefits?

Any calculation is far from simple. Not everyone is affected by video games in the same way, much as in the case of other forms of media enter-tainment. Equally, not all members of society, including those gamers who choose not to play violent video games, find their content unpalatable and therefore constitutive of negative utility. Thus the potential risk Waddington and Singer speak of (to wider society) from video game violence, and the documented evidence supporting the claim that there are at least *some* who are more vulnerable to PIU than others, must be weighed against the pleasure (or absence of displeasure) that such games engender. When formulating this calculation, one might also wish to consider the extent to which the happiness derived from playing video games – violent or otherwise – fits within Mill's categorization of lower and higher pleasure. Does the pleasure video games produce constitute a lower or higher kind, and how does one determine this?

In addressing how one might judge the value of two qualitatively different pleasures, Mill has this to say: "Of two pleasures, if there be one to which all or almost all who have experience of both give a decided preference, irrespective of any feeling of moral obligation to prefer it, that is the more desirable pleasure" ([1863] 1998: 56). Thus, according to Mill, the measure of which two pleasures is superior is determined by those who are experienced in both; it is awarded to the one that is consistently preferred by the greater number. Within the context of entertainment, I would not care to hazard a guess as to how many people are sufficiently experienced with ultra-violent video games *and*, say, the opera or the theatre (etc.) to be qualified, under the terms stipulated by Mill, to legitimately select one (preferred) activity over the other, thereby elevating that which is preferred to a qualitatively "higher" level of pleasure. Based on Mill's criterion, I suspect that establishing which pleasure is of a superior quality is somewhat difficult to determine, or could be determined only by a very small number of people. But as Schulzke (2010) acknowledges, some variables are more easily established than others; although he does concede that, in the end, any form of utilitarianism calculus is inherently problematic. For as Schulzke states:

> We have a very good idea of the benefits of video games. Their economic impact is quantifiable as is the number of hours of entertainment they bring to gamers. GTA [*Grand Theft Auto*] alone sold over 66 million games by 2008, evidence that at least this many people derive entertainment from game violence. Other heavily criticized violent games are likewise usually among the top sellers. There are also a number of educational benefits. The improvements in visual perception, hand–eye coordination, and other motor skills from gaming are also well documented. The difficulty only lies in deciding how much these benefits should weigh against any harm that games do, but this is a problem intrinsic to utilitarian theory and should not be counted against violent games. (2010: 131)

Furthermore, in addition to the variables mentioned so far, I recognize that it may be the case that we should not treat STAs as a homogenous group just because they represent a group of behaviours offline that are grouped together solely in virtue of being prohibited (POTAs). It may be that virtual rape or paedophilia or some other STA is different from virtual assault or murder (for example) in terms of the strength of the causal connection between the virtual enactment and the corresponding POTA (or for some other reason yet to be discussed). This lack of homogeneity has, or course, important implications when trying to establish a utilitarian basis for selective prohibition. Might the cost–benefit assessment of one type of STA be different from another? This is far from an impertinent question; rather, it could have important ramifications for any utilitarian outcome geared towards selective prohibition. To date, however, as with more traditional violent gaming content, a causal connection between other less "orthodox" STAs and changes to one's non-gaming behaviour is difficult to validate empirically because there is a distinct paucity of research on the effects of playing video games with content relating to rape and paedophilia (for example).

In addition, although gamers cannot be physically harmed during a game, it may be that certain STAs are responsible for negative psychological effects, not only after the event (in the form of increased desensitization or aggression) but also during the gameplay, such as the unpleasant experience of having one's character raped or witnessing the rape of another within the game. The much-discussed and infamous "Mr Bungle affair", which occurred in 1992 in LambdaMOO, provides just such an example (see Dibbel 1993, and also Turkle 1995 for a more detailed discussion). How one calculates such negative utility is again a difficult question to address at this stage, for there is equally a lack of research on the experiences of gamers who engage in these types of STAs (however, see Whitty et al. 2011 for a recent study). Further research in this area is therefore welcomed.

CONCLUSION

Utilitarianism holds that the morally commendable action is that which brings about the greatest happiness. What this entails is ultimately an empirical question. In the context of video game content (and STAs), this is no different. What I have presented in this chapter is research evidence that, to date, is inconclusive with regard to the consequences both for oneself and for others of engaging in video game violence, thus making the utilitarian cost–benefit analysis difficult to achieve. Moreover, because of the heterogeneity of STAs, even if one could calculate the total increase in happiness that has occurred as a result of, say, virtual murder, and weigh this against the amount of unhappiness produced (even taking into account Mill's higher–lower pleasures distinction), and even if (for the sake of argument) one were to find that more pleasure had been amassed in this case, thus satisfying the greatest happiness principle, should one generalize this consequence across all STAs, or should one weigh up the cost–benefit assessment of each STA on an individual basis? Whether one should or should not is, again, a question better informed by empirical findings that, unfortunately, are currently unavailable.[6] Such (currently unavailable) research findings would also help inform the issue of selective prohibition of video game content within a utilitarian framework.

Having said all that, even if all STAs produce more positive consequences (again, for the sake of argument), one may still object, morally, to the permissibility of STAs, on non-utilitarian grounds. As J. J. C. Smart and Bernard Williams (1973) attest, one may agree with the utilitarian assessment of consequences – that doing A creates more happiness than doing B – but still disagree with the claim that one should do A rather than B. One's preference for B (for being morally committed to this action), despite acknowledging the utility of A, may be for reasons espoused by an opposing moral theory, some of which we have already considered (e.g. Hume and Kant). Moving away from utilitarianism, then, in the next two chapters I present *a priori* arguments for why it is wrong in and of itself to engage in STAs – based on what the interaction represents – irrespective of the utility of the virtual activity.

SIX

Are meanings *virtually* the same?

> It has been said that "games are often *stylized simulations*; developed not just for fidelity to their source domain, but for aesthetic purposes ... [As such, a] game does not as much attempt to implement the real world activity as it attempts to implement a specific stylized *concept* of a real-world activity".
>
> (Juul 2005: 172, original emphasis)

So far, I have considered arguments that have for the most part focused on the morality of the virtual act itself: either through an association with sentiment (Hume and the neo-sentimentalists) or in terms of the consequences for the gamer and her wider society (utilitarianism). Even Kant's deontological argument is in some sense consequentialist when applied to gamespace, or so it has been claimed: in so far as engaging in STAs will cultivate, through an argument from extended analogy, the intention to treat oneself and others immorally (this being the negative "real-world" consequence of STAs). In other words, one (potentially) fails in one's duty to protect oneself from vice and *not* to treat others as a means to an end.

In this chapter I consider an *a priori* argument for the moral appraisal of video game content based on what that content is said to represent – that is, its underlying meaning or *socially significant expression* – irrespective of any cost to oneself or others that may be incurred as a result of playing the game: either through cultivating cruelty or disrespect to others, or other antisocial behaviours, or even in terms of how the representation makes one feel (i.e. disgusted). I assess the extent to which such a position is able to justify the selective prohibition of video game content, and whether any selectivity demanded by this approach matches the current state of STA permissibility within video games. For if it is, as Juul (2005) states (above), that video game representation is stylized, then to what extent is what is represented, in the case of virtual murder or torture or assault or rape (etc.), more about the *idea* of the activity (actual rape, say, in the form of a kind of stylized concept of it) than rape itself, and how might this affect our moral assessment of the STA? In addition, and by way of a refinement to the argument from socially significant expression, I consider the utility of the principle of *sanctioned equivalence* to explaining the current state of play within video game content and its selective prohibition.

SOCIALLY SIGNIFICANT EXPRESSION

Brey (2003) argues that it is precisely because VR typically contains simulations or representations of physical and social reality that it warrants moral policing. As such, the manner in which characters or events within a game are represented, the behaviours they simulate and the interactions permitted them, should all come under moral scrutiny. Thomas Powers, like Brey, recognizes the symbolic significance of VR representation, holding that "what a person intends to do and achieve by acting and uttering, is really part of the world ... [and] is the subject matter for moral judgement, even when his or her agency is mediated by computers" (2003: 193).

What the gamer is communicating, even through the virtual nature of their action, Powers tells us, is *socially significant expression*. It is, therefore, morally wrong to engage in STAs not because they are equivalent to POTAs but because they *represent* them. Or at the very least they should be considered a suitable subject for moral appraisal *because* they represent them. In other words, although x (STA) $\neq y$ (POTA), the relationship between x and y is such that STAs capture what we take POTAs to be: in simple terms, morally bad things. Therefore, when scrutinizing the content of video games, one should evaluate the meaning of the gameplay in terms of the message it conveys. For some, this may have a certain intuitive appeal (see Ch. 3). However, is it really the case that when a player mows down bystanders in the street with an assault rifle (e.g. *Postal 2*) or runs them over in a fast car (*Carmageddon*), one should interpret this as an endorsement of actual murder, either because of what the player is doing or because the game mechanics permit this activity to occur within the gameplay?

If one's response to this question is "No, not necessarily", but this is followed immediately by a caveat that appeals to empirical research on desensitization or increases in antisocial behaviour, then one is effectively resorting to an argument for prohibition based on negative consequences – that is, for some form of utilitarianism that holds that violent games cause more harm than good (see Ch. 5). However, to reiterate, the focus of this chapter is on the morality of the representation itself, or perhaps, more accurately, the meaning inherent within it, irrespective of consequence. Thus we are left to consider whether or to what extent the meaning of the representation should be morally appraised, and whether the outcome of this moral appraisal should form the basis for selective prohibition. Elena Pasquinelli (2010), however, proffers a caveat to what in effect would be censorship when she states that prohibiting violent scenes or other STAs could lead to a blurring of the line between fiction and reality, thereby increasing the confusion over the status of real and imaginary acts: for it suggests that "immoral" actions committed in the virtual world (e.g. gamepace) have the same value as immoral actions (POTAs) committed in the real world, in so far as each must be equally prevented.

Alternatively, if one's answer to the question above is "Yes, it does endorse actual murder and other POTAs" then, presumably, one would seek to morally prohibit such content for that reason alone (although this seems a somewhat extreme view that has little support). It may be, then, that one does not consider that the enactments described above (or similar) are endorsing actual murder *per se*: that is, promoting the idea that we should all leave the gaming world and go out and illegally kill people once we have perfected how to do this virtually. Nevertheless, perhaps one considers that such representations mean for us to enjoy the virtual enactment of actual murder (murder$_a$), and *that* is the meaning implicit within such content. Not "Go out and kill!" but, rather, delight in the *idea* of murder$_a$ or, at least, its stylized enactment as expressed through the gameplay.

This latter view is not unique to video game content, of course. Over the years it has been voiced in relation to a number of other forms of media representation (see Gunter 2008 for a detailed review). Gianluca Di Muzio, for example, when criticizing *slasher* films of the 1970s (like the original *Texas Chainsaw Massacre*) begins by noting:

> [O]ne would want to resist the thesis that it is wrong to read and enjoy Homer's *Iliad* because it contains violence, gore and death. Depictions of violence do not *per se* belong in the category of the morally objectionable only because many instances of real violence do. (2006: 280)

He then goes on to argue that slasher films "not only contain representations of violence and death, but are *devoted primarily or solely* to representing violence and death" (*ibid.*: 281, original emphasis).[1] So much so, he continues, that a slasher film such as *The Texas Chainsaw Massacre* "makes the point of having no moral point" (*ibid.*: 290). What Di Muzio seems to be objecting to here is that (in his view) slasher films present violence/gore as an end in itself: as entertainment. They do not seem to provide (allow, perhaps) the opportunity for the viewer to reflect on the violence graphically represented on the screen, or certainly the depictions of violence do not appear to be instrumental to this reflective end. In fact, at the time of writing, the British Board of Film Classification (BBFC) had just refused to issue a classification for the film *Human Centipede II* because, in their view, the film focuses on: "the sexual arousal of the central character at both the idea and the spectacle of the total degradation, humiliation, mutilation, torture and murder of his naked victims" (see Shoard 2011). The BBFC's objection signifies that they hold that a representation can be wrong in and of itself because of what it represents, and not that it *becomes* wrong only *if* one starts to think and/or feel and/or behave in ways that are morally prohibited in the actual world, when in the actual world (outside the cinema, in this case). It also suggests that the BBFC would endorse the view that engaging in virtual activity x is still morally wrong even if performed by those who do not express equivalent thoughts, feelings and behaviours outside gamespace. In other words, it is wrong in and of itself because of what it *intends to promote*. Having said that, in the case of *Human Centipede II*, the BBFC also felt that the film posed a real, as opposed to a fanciful risk, that harm would be caused to viewers and, as a consequence, that its content would fall foul of the UK obscenity laws. With this latter comment we see how, in the BBFC's considered opinion, *Human Centipede II* not only *commends* the viewer to delight in the morally prohibited but runs the genuine risk of *causing* her to do so.

ON EXPRESSING OBSCENITY

This latter concern is reflected in the UK's Obscene Publications Act 1959, which determines something to be obscene "if its effect or ... the effect of any one of its items is, if taken as a whole, such as to tend to deprave and corrupt persons who are likely, having regard to all the relevant circumstances, to read, see or hear the matter contained or embodied in it" (Section 1[1]). The UK classification of "obscene" is therefore based on whether the material is likely to deprave or corrupt those who have access to it. In other words, what is considered legally obscene is couched in social pathology such that there would be a tendency towards "moral and physical harm caused to vulnerable persons by exposure to obscene writings and images" (Hunter *et al.*

1993: 138). In addition, one's reaction to an obscenity must be more than, say, disgust, even when this involves physical revulsion and/or behavioural aversion (see Ch. 3). One must become (or be in danger of becoming) morally corrupted. Section 1 of the Obscene Publications Act 1959 thus tries to distinguish between what merely offends communal standards of acceptability and what is socially harmful.[2]

What sort of harm are we talking about? Matthew Kieran (2002: 41) defines obscene representations as those that solicit from us cognitive-affective responses towards objects/events that are morally prohibited, to the extent that we are commended "to delight in them". What we are prescribed to delight in, Kieran informs us, are morally prohibited sexual acts; or the infliction of pain or suffering or even death on another, either by one's own hand or vicariously. To commend us to delight in that which is already demarcated as morally prohibited, even taboo, is not only taken to be a measure of the obscene *and* the implied intention of the creator of the material, but also a consequence of it for us, at least if the exposure to obscene material is prolonged.

Thus, it may be argued that obscenity, despite being a legal term, nevertheless confers on an object that which is morally wrong because it morally corrupts; and by "morally corrupts" I mean that it not only *commends* its audience to delight in the morally prohibited but also, and importantly, *causes* them to do so (see Ch. 8 for a discussion on player virtue). For a judgement of "obscenity", then, at least based on the UK definition, there is a consequential component: namely, the real possibility of moral corruption. However, recall how the BBFC's objection to the film *Human Centipede II* was in part based on their view that a representation can be wrong in and of itself, because of what it represents. If STAs are judged to commend us to delight in POTAs then is this alone sufficient justification for selective prohibition of content, irrespective of consequence?

THE PROBLEM OF DISCRIMINATING BETWEEN STAS

A potential problem with socially significant expression as a criterion for selective prohibition is that it may be too broad and thus not sufficiently discriminatory to serve a useful purpose. If the criterion for selective prohibition is based on an opposition to anything that intends us to delight in prohibited behaviour offline, and STAs, in representing POTAs, are taken to be expressing such delight, then how can we distinguish between simulations already permitted within games and those not currently available or for the most part banned? In other words, if it is permissible to engage in STAs that involve assault, mutilation, torture and murder, then should it not be equally permissible to engage in acts of rape, necrophilia, bestiality and child sex (including incest)? Equally, if it is not permissible to engage in STAs of this nature, then how can *any* legally (if not morally) prohibited action be permitted within video games?

Endorsing moral prohibition based on socially significant expression would seem to require us to accept the statement first presenting in Chapter 2: as *all* POTAs are prohibited then *all* STAs should likewise be prohibited. This is because all STAs constitute acts of socially significant expression. This, of course, would require a radical reversal in the way we approach video game content, as clearly the current state of play regarding virtual prohibition does not adhere to this statement and therefore the argument from socially significant expression. A possible way of salvaging the sentiment of the statement above, however, while at the same time allowing for certain violent acts to be permitted, is to clarify what we mean by POTAs, or at least the context in which they occur. This clarification could then be used to better judge the STAs that represent them.

In judging what constitutes a suitable topic for gameplay (or indeed any fiction), or at least in judging what is not totally inappropriate, one might be guided by the principle of *sanctioned equivalence* (Young & Whitty 2011b). Killing, for example, can occur in legitimate or illegitimate ways. A sanctioned equivalent of killing is state-authorized execution, or the death of combatants during a war. Ellen Jordan and Angela Cowan talk of "warrior narratives", whereby we "assume that violence is legitimate and justified when it occurs within a struggle between good and evil" (1995: 728). Torture has been justified in the past by legitimate authorities (Costanzo *et al.* 2007; Soldz 2008), and in some cases still is; or at least its legitimate use is debated (in the ticking-bomb scenario, for example; see Brecher 2007; Opotow 2007). The unofficial "law of the sea" maintains that cannibalism is acceptable, or is at least tolerated, when one's life depends on it and the victim is already dead, or was selected through the mutually agreed drawing of lots. (A similar scenario was famously debated by Lon Fuller in his 1949 paper "The Case of the Speluncean Explorers".) In real life, passengers of Uruguayan Air Force Flight 571 (which crashed in the Andes Mountains on 13 October 1972) survived by resorting to cannibalism. All were Catholic and all received absolution from the Catholic Church. However, it is difficult to think of a sanctioned equivalent in the case of rape or necrophilia, or of cases in which one's life depended on an act of incest or bestiality. Sanctioned equivalence differentiates between equivalent outcomes that are either legitimate or illegitimate. All legitimate outcomes are judged to be essentially *instrumental*: a means to an end. On the other hand, actions that do not have sanctioned equivalence appear *pathological*: an end in themselves.

THE FUN OF BREAKING TABOOS

The principle of sanctioned equivalence offers some insight and a possible explanatory framework for understanding which enactments can be morally justified based on actual moral norms. One can play the role of a soldier defeating the "enemy" or evil mutants/aliens (to whom our normal moral standards "don't apply", for such creatures are beyond the realm of moral obligation). Sanctioned equivalence may even allow the player to question the morality of actions within certain contexts: the use of torture to extract information vital for national security, for example. There are certain similarities in this explanation with that of Zillmann's (2000) *moral sanction theory of delight and repugnance* (see Ch. 3), although the principle of sanctioned equivalence perhaps offers a means of understanding why certain actions are typically morally sanctioned and therefore found to be appealing within a media entertainment context. Sanctioned equivalence is also compatible with the *justice sequence* (Raney & Bryant 2002), which maps the sequence of events in a media portrayal from crime to punishment. If the sequence falls within the normative range of an individual's moral sanctioning, which I would argue typically adheres to the principle of sanctioned equivalence, then the activity (be it film, or in this case video game) will probably meet with approval (although see Haidt & Graham 2007; Haidt & Joseph 2004; Tamborini *et al.* 2012 for studies on cultural variations).

What sanctioned equivalence has difficulty justifying, however, are games like those characteristic of *Manhunt* (1 and 2) or the *Postal* series, which appear to delight in indiscriminate violence (as Di Muzio 2006 accused slasher films of doing; see also Kirkland 2011 for a recent discussion on *survival horror video games*). These games, because they afford the enactment of indiscriminate violence, have courted controversy in the past; and perhaps the principle of sanctioned equivalence should be applied here, resulting in the judgement that these games ought to be morally prohibited. However, perhaps this is precisely the fun of these games: that they allow us to flaunt the principle of sanctioned equivalence and in other ways transgress. In considering the appeal of violent video games and why people are drawn to them, Thomas Nys has this to say:

> My first claim is that an inquiry into this appeal will reveal that their enjoyment *presupposes a moral awareness*, and therefore that morality is included from the start. Knowing that it is wrong is part of the fun and games. The thrill of such virtual actions is precisely that they transgress ethical boundaries.
>
> (2010: 81, original emphasis)

It seems quite probable, then, that enacting STAs holds a certain allure for (some) people; they are gratifying and pleasurable, such that many "identify

71

with bad characters and enjoy committing or observing simulated immoral action" (Schulzke 2011: 63; see also Konijn & Hoorn 2005). Within their "private laboratories" (Jansz 2005: 231), gamers can engage with different emotions and identities in relative safety – relative to the actual world, that is – and invest in their own form of psychological exploration (see also Konijn *et al.* 2011). Similarly, Juul holds that video games "are playgrounds where players can experiment with doing things they would or would not normally do" (2005: 193).[3] In addition, Laurence Ashworth *et al.* (2010) argue that the appeal of certain violent media is not the violence *per se* but the portrayal of dominance that often accompanies it (which they attribute to factors within our evolutionary past). They found that higher levels of dominance by the protagonist in a video game were rated as more appealing, particularly where identification with the virtual character occurred: males identifying with a violent and dominant male avatar, for example (see Ch. 12). Perhaps such perceived dominance contributes to the appeal of such games as *Manhunt* (1 and 2) and the *Postal* series (among others).

One can psychologically explore oneself in single- and multiplayer environments, of course. In single-player spaces, the social significance of one's expression is interpreted and/or evaluated by oneself (see Sicart 2009) as well as those who constitute "wider society" looking on (so to speak), who may take a moral interest in the representations within a given gamespace. Within multiplayer spaces, in contrast, the individual gamer constitutes one of the many within that space who come together to form a particular online (gaming) community. This community is distinct but not mutually excluded from the offline social environment. In fact, when Powers originally talked of socially significant expression, it is fair to say that he had multiplayer environments in mind. However, I do not consider the meaning captured by this term to be restricted to multiplayer spaces and what is represented by the many people therein.

In single-player space, when judging the morality of the representations and enactments, one must be guided by the game mechanics, narrative and degree of constraint imposed on the gamer by the limited plot/gameplay development and choices available. If it is possible to assault$_v$, murder$_v$, torture$_v$ and even rape$_v$ in this space, then this possibility is typically sufficient to decree its *permissibility* (unless such enactments are the result of add-on software or cheats). In multiplayer space, as noted in Chapter 4, it is possible that certain acts are permissible because they have been established by the online community in the form of agreed status functions (see also Ch. 10). One may not wish to engage in a given act, but one accepts that it is permitted within *this* space. In such a context, one's socially significant expression may breach the established conventions of the community-agreed status functions, in which case one may face that community's moral condemnation; but even if one's expression through action does not do this, one may still enact something that contravenes more established offline moral conventions, in which case one may be morally condemned by one's offline (wider) social community. To illustrate, consider the virtual world of *Sociolotron*, where virtual rape is permitted; or the online *World of Gor* (see Bäcke 2011 for a discussion), where it is accepted that men are born free and women are their slaves.

CONCLUSION

When one chooses to shoot a drug dealer in the face, as it is possible to do in *Heavy Rain*, or have sex with and then mug a prostitute in *Grand Theft Auto 4*, one is enabled through the game to become what Jeroen Jansz (2005) calls the *architect of one's own disgust*. If one accepts the appeal of these games – that they are fun to play, partly because they permit moral transgression in an environment where it is "safe" and certainly permitted to do so – then one might be resigned, in light of the inherent play element within video games, to endorse the statement (first presented in Ch. 2) that irrespective of the prohibited status of POTAs, *no* STAs should be prohibited.

Before doing so, however, one might wish to question (a) whether it is indeed *safe* to become the architect of one's own disgust (to borrow Jansz's phrase) within these "private laboratories", and (b) whether, even in play, there are nevertheless certain intrinsic qualities to virtual representation that should be morally prohibited. I have considered the first of these points already in Chapter 4 (Kant) and Chapter 5 (utilitarianism), and return to it again in Chapters 8 and 9. In relation to the second point, I intend to critically examine the view that there is indeed something wrong with games with *certain* ethically contentious content, irrespective of any potential harm that may befall the user. In the next chapter, then, I assess the validity of the argument that asserts that in response to the question "*Should* it be the case that only some STAs are prohibited (and therefore not others)?", the answer is in fact yes; and is yes for a reason established *a priori* – namely, owing to the intrinsic properties of certain virtual representations, which have *incorrigible social meaning.*

SEVEN

There are wrongs and then there are *wrongs*

Some rapes ARE worse than others ... there, I've said it.

(Hitchens 2011: 1)

In the previous chapter I considered the view that STAs should be subject to moral scrutiny because of what they represent: their socially significant expression. The relationship between POTAs and STAs is said to be such that even the virtual enactment of an actual taboo carries potent symbolic meaning; it *means* something in so far as its enactment represents an object and/or event that is of social and/or moral significance outside the gaming realm. For this reason (if for no other), the STA's representative meaning – that is, what it stands for and the message it conveys within the context in which it occurs – warrants moral evaluation. The problem with using socially significant expression as the criterion for selective prohibition, however, is that it is unable to differentiate between those STAs that are presently permitted – as evidenced by the current state of play within video game content – and those that are not (at least within the UK).

In an effort to remedy this predicament, in this chapter I consider an *a priori* attempt to narrow the focus of the socially significant expression said to be present within certain gameplays. Through the use of fictional video games, I evaluate the move to selectively prohibit content with certain alleged intrinsic properties: namely, those that are said to convey *incorrigible social meaning*.

DIFFERENTIATING BETWEEN TABOOS: TWO FICTITIOUS EXAMPLES

Suppose I play a game in which I am able to kill virtual characters at random: ordinary citizens from all walks of life. As noted in Chapter 2, such games already exist; but let us call this fictitious game *S.H.* (short for *Shit Happens*). Suppose I then play a game in which I am able to target, harass and eventually kill individuals categorized in terms of their race/ethnicity, or even their gender, sexual preference, or religious beliefs: a game I shall call *R.A.C.I.S.T.* (which stands for *Rage Against Community: Intercept, Segregate, Terminate*). Let us say that on this occasion I select "Jewish" from the list available on the game menu (I have to select something in order to play the game). With this latter (fictitious) example, we have a game that permits two actions prohibited offline: discrimination and murder.[1] From this, we can pose the question: should video games be allowed to virtually enact (a) discrimination and (b) murder?

Before addressing this question, a related question might first present itself: why would someone want to play a game in which they can murder Jews? Implicit within this question is the assumption that the player must find the game sufficiently enjoyable to continue playing and/or must have anticipated that it would be in order to initiate the play in the first place. Accompanying this question might be an immediate, perhaps even psychologically intuitive, appeal to player motives: something like – surely, such a person must already have a "problem" with Jewish people. (I shall have more to say on player motivation in Ch. 11.) But equally, one could ask: why would someone want to play a game like *S.H.* in which one can murder people at random? (The same assumption regarding enjoyment is made here also.) Surely, such a person must have a "problem" with random citizens.

Must it be the case that playing *S.H.* entails that the player has a negative view of random citizens, such that he would want to kill them, even if only virtually? It does not *necessarily* follow that this is the case. I may consider my victims to be nothing more than targets: nothing more than a simple opportunity to acquire more points within the game (see Hartmann *et al.* 2010; Hartmann & Vorderer 2010; Klimmt *et al.* 2006, 2008 for recent empirical work on this issue). Equally, then, must it be the case that playing *R.A.C.I.S.T. entails* that the player has a negative view of Jewish people, such that he would wish to kill them, even if only virtually? If it does not necessarily follow that the player of *S.H.* has a negative view of random citizens then how could it *necessarily* follow that those who play *R.A.C.I.S.T.* have a negative view of Jewish people? Might the virtual representations of Jewish people within the game be construed simply as targets for the accumulation of points, just as in *S.H.*? Perhaps what is enjoyable about this game is not the targeting of a particular group of people – be they Jewish, Afro-Caribbean, homosexual (etc.) – but the elaborate and ingenious manner in which they can be punished, injured and ultimately put to death: something that is only available within *this* game, let us say.

But even if we accept that playing *R.A.C.I.S.T.* does not entail a negative view of Jewish people (or any other group listed on the game menu), it still seems legitimate to ask: is it nevertheless not *morally wrong* to play a game that involves targeting, harassing and killing Jewish citizens (or any other specific group)? After all, why does such a game have to have elaborate and ingenious means of punishment, injury and death targeted at one group of people in particular? Why can this not be achieved against random citizens? This, of course, rather begs the question: why should the targeting of groups *not* be allowed but the targeting of random citizens permitted? Thus, it seems equally legitimate to ask a follow up question: is it nevertheless not *morally wrong* to play a game that involves the targeting and killing of random citizens? If we permit the latter, as evidenced by the current availability of such games, then should we not permit the former? If not, then why not? What justification could there be for the selective permissibility of virtual murder but not virtual discrimination? Should virtual murder be permissible *only* if it is random, or at least not targeted at a particular (minority) group?

INCORRIGIBLE SOCIAL MEANING

A possible defence of such selective prohibition is provided by Stephanie Patridge (2011), who talks about how certain single-player video games have incorrigible social meaning. By this, she means that some content may represent an association that has deep-rooted (actual) social meaning, even if only localized to a particular society, which may be deemed offensive to certain members of that society and/or even be morally and legally proscribed (see Brenick *et al.* 2007 for discussion on perceived stereotypes in video games). She illustrates this with a fictitious example of a cartoon image of US president Barack Obama eating a watermelon. The association of an African American with a watermelon (and similar imagery), we are told, has "been used as a mechanism to insult and dehumanize African-Americans, and to bind racist Americans together through the practice of telling racially demeaning jokes" (Patridge 2011: 308). She also expands this association to the content of a fictitious video game in which Barack Obama, or in fact any representation of an African American, is navigating his (or her) way through a watermelon field.

The move to generalize from Obama in particular to a more general representation of an African American prevents the charge of "morally offensive" being restricted to cases in which the virtual representation is of a specific (real-life) individual. The virtual character walking through Patridge's watermelon field is not meant to be anyone in particular and so, in that sense, is fictional, but it nevertheless represents a race of people who have been associated in US history with watermelons in a manner that is now held by many (the majority?) in the US to be morally offensive. Patridge recognizes that the association between this image and racism is a contingent fact and localized to US society.[2] Different racist imagery may be found in different societies, each association being similarly contingent. Nevertheless, Patridge's point is that the *epistemic flexibility* we have available to us to create fictions that may be more or less loosely based on real-life contingent associations (objects/events), and therefore the extent to which we are willing, in the pursuit of these fictions, to suspend our disbelief, must be constrained in relation to their potential incorrigible social meaning. Sometimes, she argues, we should reject imaginative and therefore fictional representations if they represent associations that still have morally offensive undertones (recall the discussion on imaginative resistance in Ch. 1).

The representations and virtual enactments targeted by Patridge are those that were once held to be something of a social norm (e.g. institutionalized racism) within the US (for example) but which are no longer viewed in the same way. What she seems less concerned with are actual morally/legally prohibited actions that have never been a social norm. This is alluded to by Patridge when she states: "Consider, for example, the game *Mafia Wars*. The fact that we enjoy playing this game seems to say nothing at all by itself about our attitude towards organized crime" (2011: 307). Organized crime, as far as I am aware, has never been proclaimed as an acceptable social norm in the US. Therefore, what I take Patridge to be saying here is that if we enjoy playing a game that features organized crime, our enjoyment is not necessarily a sign of our approval of organized crime. To be fair, I do not take Patridge to be saying that my enjoyment of playing a game in which an African American navigates his way through a watermelon field is necessarily a sign of my approval of racism. Nor would I take her to say the same about someone who enjoyed murdering virtual Jews in the fictitious game *R.A.C.I.S.T.* What she is saying is as follows:

> [A]s morally challenging representational content begins to
> reflect our actual, shared history of systematic moral violations
> like gender and racial oppression, this serves to limit the meaning

of such imagery, and thereby open the door for associated character evaluations.   (Patridge 2011: 310)

In other words, if the content of a game reflects a one-time moral violation, then this limits the extent to which the content can be said to represent and therefore mean something other than the continued expression of this one-time moral violation. Moreover, although the playing of such a game does not necessitate the moral approval of what the content is said to represent, it does leave the player vulnerable to a charge of *insensitivity*.

Thus, when playing *Mafia Wars*, it would seem that I am not being insensitive because, at least in terms of the history of the US (and the UK), to enact organized crime is not to represent a one-time moral violation (in so far as my enactment does not represent what was once held as a social norm but is *now* accepted as something that should be morally, perhaps even legally, proscribed). For Patridge, then, incorrigible social meaning provides a means of explaining the unease many of us feel towards those who play rape games such as *RapeLay* or *Custer's Revenge*, or even the idea of fictitious games such as *R.A.C.I.S.T.*, or games that hypothetically could feature virtual paedophilia. My aim within this chapter, however, is to consider incorrigible social meaning in a role not originally intended by Patridge: namely, as a criterion for selective prohibition. For if our reason for permitting games that enable the virtual murder of random citizens – such as the fictitious *S.H.* – is that such virtual action does not represent a previous social norm now prohibited, should we not equally permit games that enable the virtual enactment of rape and paedophilia, neither of which represents a one-time norm of society that is now prohibited?

THE PROBLEM WITH INCORRIGIBLE SOCIAL MEANING AS A MEANS OF SELECTIVE PROHIBITION

Patridge considers virtual rape to have incorrigible social meaning because of the "global history and current reality of women's oppression" (2011: 312), but is willing to concede, or at least suggests, that it is perhaps only in a world without gender oppression or other forms of discrimination that such representations will lose their incorrigible social meaning. Perhaps an example supporting this idea can be found in video games that feature gladiatorial combat, such as *Gladius* or *Gladiator: Sword of Vengeance*. During the time of the Roman Empire, such combat would have been the epitome of oppression, at least for those forced to fight owing to their slave status. Yet, now, it would seem that there is little merit to the claim that such video games contain content with incorrigible social meaning. It would seem that, like *Mafia Wars*, I can enjoy playing a gladiatorial-based video game without this action being taken in any way to represent my views on empire-based oppression (there are even children's games that feature gladiators – e.g. Playmobil Gladiator set, complete with arena). But suppose, for a moment, that I live in a world where there is no oppression based on gender. To reiterate, according to Patridge, gender-oppressive images would "likely lose their incorrigible meaning" (*ibid.*). Presumably, in such a world, a game like the Japanese rape game *RapeLay* would no longer be the target for moral scrutiny, at least not based on incorrigible social meaning, just like the gladiator games.

But why wait for such a world to come about? After all, there is no evidence of the US or the UK having a history of oppression against white, middle-class, married heterosexual couples. Suppose, then, in light of this fact, I play a fictitious game entitled *Crazy for Suburbia*. In this game, I take on the role of a predatory man who targets married couples (as described above) and forces them to perform sexual acts on each other, in his presence, and in front of a camcorder, and then kills them. Based strictly on the criterion of incorrigible social meaning, would such a game contain content worthy of moral scrutiny? The answer, it would appear, is no. *Crazy for Suburbia* seems to escape moral censorship on the same grounds as the fictitious game *S.H.* when confining one's scrutiny to incorrigible social meaning. (One might also wish to consider how well a video game featuring male-on-male rape would fare using the same criterion.)

However, at this point, as with the game *R.A.C.I.S.T.*, the reader may be thinking: why would anyone want to play such a game? In response, I will say that, as things stand, this is beside the point, as our focus in this chapter is on the *content* of the video game and not one's motivation for playing. If the question of motivation is introduced then our moral scrutiny will have shifted (see Ch. 11). Having said that, Patridge alludes to player motivation when discussing virtual paedophilia (see also Luck 2009; McCormick 2001), suggesting that those wishing to engage in such activity "expose a flaw in [their] character" (Patridge 2011: 305), but then goes on to concede that we do not know, at present, when and in what way video game interaction is expressive of our character. It is in response to this missing connection that she begins to builds her case for the moral scrutiny of content based on legitimate intrinsic grounds; for anyone who knowingly ignores the incorrigible social meaning of certain video game content – such as the rape in games such as *RapeLay* or *Custer's Revenge* – shows "an obvious vice of character" (*ibid.*: 310). Moreover:

> To insist that one's imagination is one's own private affair, detached from one's own actual commitments and similarly detached from the contextualized moral facts on the ground, amounts minimally, in this case, to a thumbing of one's nose at a requirement of solidarity with the victims of oppression.   (*Ibid.*)

For Patridge, then, to focus our moral scrutiny on video game content with incorrigible social meaning allows us not only to morally assess video games based on the intrinsic features of their content, but also to morally scrutinize the character of those who knowingly ignore this connection. Minimally, she tells us, such a player metaphorically thumbs his nose up at the requirement of solidarity with the victims of oppression; maximally, it would seem, based on the example of virtual paedophilia, it exposes a *flaw* in the person's character (at least in the view of Patridge). But, importantly, as noted above, a case for the moral prohibition of virtual paedophilia does not seem to fit the argument for selective prohibition based on incorrigible social meaning. It does not seem to reflect the contingent nature and history of localized moral violations, as illustrated by the Obama example, or the more general point about rape.

The problem with the case for incorrigible social meaning, when extended beyond Patridge's original role – such that it is now being used as a criterion for selective censorship – is that it allows us only (a) to judge certain STAs and not others for prohibition (e.g. discrimination and rape, and not random killing and paedophilia), and (b) to comment on the character of those who ignore the incorrigible social meaning of video game content *because they ignore it*. Moreover, the extent to which we judge our protagonist to be morally insensitive, or even seek to claim that he has a more severely flawed character, is dependent on the severity of the incorrigible social meaning he chooses to ignore. Compare playing Patridge's game in which the African American traverses the watermelon field to my game *R.A.C.I.S.T.*; is the difference between these and what they potentially represent (in terms of incorrigible social meaning) one of degree or kind? Would playing the latter make the gamer more insensitive than if playing the former? Perhaps the degree of moral insensitivity reflects the degree of moral condemnation typically heaped on the corresponding POTA (i.e. the degree of apparent discrimination represented). Thus, mild racism (however that may be defined) may result in an accusation of mild insensitivity, progressing to gross insensitivity in the case of those who play *R.A.C.I.S.T.* But what of the protagonist who engages in virtual paedophilia: is the worst moral charge we can bestow on him (or her) that of gross insensitivity, or is this enactment different in kind to others such as discrimination or rape (see Luck 2009 for a detailed assessment), such that it falls outside the remit of a moral assessment based on incorrigible social meaning?

CONCLUSION

Based on a continuum of incorrigible social meaning (from mild to severe), it is not clear how one can "progress" from insensitivity to "flawed character" (recall a similar issue surrounding the hypothetical game of chess from Ch. 2). Is there a point at which one's level of (alleged) insensitivity becomes a mark of a flawed character? In addition, as already noted, virtual paedophilia does not fall within the remit of incorrigible social meaning; but even if it did, and if Patridge's position is anything to go by, then I anticipate that a moral champion of video game content would want to accuse the virtual paedophile of more than gross insensitivity. This being the case, it is not clear how one can move from morally insensitive to being morally flawed, other than through what one enacts. But this is not an *explanation* of how they differ morally; if anything, it is a description of the categorization procedure by which we choose to classify such alleged moral character traits (based on virtual behaviours that are said to demonstrate these characteristics). More importantly, though, based solely on the criterion of incorrigible social meaning, one cannot even accuse the paedophile of being insensitive. So how do we establish the charge of "possessing a flawed character"? What other criterion must we use to make this accusation stick (as it were) and how does this support the case for being morally flawed?

One could claim that the fact that paedophilia has never been a one-time social norm of our society that we now hold to be a moral violation is missing the point. Paedophilia is just wrong (recall Prinz's point from Ch. 3, using the example of child rape) so virtual paedophilia is just wrong. Such a claim appeals most strongly to a form of moral appraisal based on either sentimentalism or socially significant expression. But as we saw in Chapters 3 and 6, the problem with using sentimentalism and socially significant expression as respective criteria for selective prohibition is that (a) in the former case, it is vulnerable to a charge of moral dumbfounding, and (b) in the latter, it seems to require, on the face of it, that all STAs be prohibited, which does not match the current state of play with regard to permissible video game content. Even if we include the principle of sanctioned equivalence as a means of distinguishing between, say, virtual rape or paedophilia (on the one hand) and virtual killing in self-defence or during war or even (possibly) certain forms of torture (on the other), this does not provide a means of distinguishing between virtual rape that features within games such as *RapeLay* (banned in the UK) and *random* assault and murder, which are a feature of a number of available video games, and characterized by the fictitious game *S.H.*

In the next chapter, I move away from the representational content of gamespace and turn my attention to the subject of the virtual interaction: the gamer himself. For as Brey notes:

> [W]hether immoral behavior in virtual reality may become acceptable to the offended party may well depend on his or her assessment of the intentions, values and beliefs of the actor.

What may have to be re-established for the offended party is a basic trust that the desire to act immorally in virtual environments does not reflect a fundamental disrespect for the real-life equivalents of the virtual beings or things that are harmed or desecrated in VR. (1999: 9)

While recognizing the worth of Brey's words, when contemplating STAs such as (virtual) paedophilia – even in the knowledge that what is literally occurring amounts to nothing more than the manipulation of pixels – there remains, for many, a strong sense that what is being *enacted* is nevertheless wrong; therefore, there must be something wrong with those who engage in this activity (McCormick 2001). Even if the protagonist expresses the view that their virtual actions do not reflect a similar preference for actual children, and even if we were to believe them, not only does the belief that this is wrong still persist (I contend), but, for many, there remains the compelling, perhaps even entrenched, sense that some form of *contamination* will follow (Coeckelbergh 2007), meaning that there is a real risk that this activity will result in a "spillover" from one realm into the other.

In the next chapter, I discuss issues relating to player character and the extent to which virtue theory is able to inform the selective prohibition of content, based on a consideration of what the virtuous person would and would not do within gamespace.

EIGHT

Virtual virtues, virtual vices

We should not only look at the "message" (violent *content*) but also at what the "medium" does to us, that is, what the game play itself does. Coeckelbergh (2011: 96)

Men acquire a particular quality by constantly acting in a particular way.
(Aristotle, *Nicomachean Ethics*, NE II i, 1103a19–21)

In this chapter I switch focus. Instead of evaluating the morality of a video game's representational content in terms of its socially significant expression or incorrigible social meaning, or the morality of the player's actions based on established rules of morality (e.g. utilitarianism and Kant), my aim is to consider whether STAs are something the virtuous person would engage in. Can the notion of actions that are characteristic of a virtuous person be used as an effective means of assessing the permissibility of video game content? If so, then if *x* is not characteristic of an action P would perform, in virtue of being a virtuous person, does this mean that *x* should be prohibited on moral grounds? The problem with this question, at least within the context of video games, is that it is conditional on x not being something that a virtuous person would do. In the case of POTAs, I take this as a given (in so far as POTAs are things the virtuous person should not engage in); but given that STAs ≠ POTAs, it needs to be made clear what sort of relationship holds, according to virtue theory, between STAs and POTAs (where x = STA) to justify the claim that x is something that P would not engage in. Put simply, it needs to be established whether it is legitimate to claim that a virtuous person would not engage in STAs before considering whether the (virtual) actions of the virtuous can be used as a means of selectively prohibiting video game content.

Before proceeding, however, it is worth noting that those who discuss virtue theory tend to do so with reference to the work of Aristotle as presented in the *Nicomachean Ethics* (NE). Theorists who have engaged with virtue theory in relation to video games are no different. When referring to virtue theory, then, I intend to follow this tradition unless otherwise stated.

In order to evaluate the utility of virtue theory as a suitable criterion for selective prohibition, I begin by presenting selected aspects of Aristotle's virtue ethic, in order to consider the question: would the virtuous person engage in STAs? In addition, I also draw on the work of previous theorists who have incorporated virtue theory within arguments for and against the permissibility of STAs (particularly involving extremely violent gaming content). I intend to show that *a priori* arguments promoting virtue theory are unsustainable in light of the fact that STAs ≠ POTAs, and that *a posteriori* arguments that draw on the alleged negative consequences of simulating vice (what Patridge 2011 refers to as *virtue consequentialism*) are in need of more substantial empirical support before any firm conclusions can be made. I end the chapter by questioning whether virtue theory is able to account for the current state of play, whereby some STAs are permitted and others not.

ARISTOTLE'S VIRTUE ETHIC

In the *Nicomachean Ethics*, Aristotle is concerned with how we should conduct ourselves in order to fare better in life. He argues that faring better equates to achieving happiness – the supreme good – which he considers an end in itself: the ultimate end, in fact. This happiness Aristotle calls *eudaimonia*. The goal of human action is therefore to achieve *eudaimonia*, which one does by acting in accordance with reason. Thus, the route to happiness is reasoned action. As McCormick notes: "[W]e must exercise our reason and govern our behavior with reason in order to achieve happiness" (2001: 285). And again: for "[w]hen reason plays its appropriate role, we exhibit virtue" (*ibid*.). Therefore, to act virtuously is to act in a reasoned way and, in doing so, we achieve happiness (*eudaimonia*).

Eudaimonia is more than a *feeling* of happiness or a simple pleasurable sensation; rather, it consists in *being* happy, and denotes a state of well-being or the act of flourishing. Importantly, Richard Norman (1998) tells us, this form of happiness is not divorced from pleasure, in so far as one will necessarily find pleasure in being happy (in one's well-being and flourishing). The converse is not necessarily true, however: pleasure does not entail happiness *per se*, and certainly not *eudaimonia*. Striving to achieve *eudaimonia*, as we have seen, is considered by Aristotle to be a reasoned pursuit, but this reasoning does not amount to any *intellectual* understanding; one cannot grasp what is required to achieve *eudaimonia* as one might grasp, say, a mathematical theorem. As Aristotle informs us:

> Since the branch of philosophy on which we are at present engaged is not, like the others, theoretical in its aim – because we are studying not to know what goodness is, but how to become good men – we must apply our minds to the problem of how our actions should be performed.   (NE II ii, 1103b27–31)

So how should one become a good person, and how is this related to understanding *how* one ought to act? According to Aristotle, "Moral goodness ... is the result of habit" (NE II i, 1103a12–14). We "become just by performing just acts, temperate by performing temperate ones, brave by performing brave ones" (1103b1–2). So in understanding how to become a good person we are directed to understand the relationship between our actions and our dispositions. Again, Aristotle informs us:

> [L]ike activities produce like dispositions. Hence we must give our activities a certain quality, because it is their characteristic that determines the resulting dispositions. So it is a matter of no little importance what sort of habits we form from the earliest age – it makes a vast difference, or rather all the difference in the world.   (1103b22–6)

Aristotle holds that it is through the repeated performance of just or unjust acts that we likewise become disposed to be just or unjust people: that is, we acquire a disposition towards virtue or vice. But what makes a given action just or unjust (virtue or vice) to begin with? According to Aristotle:

> Acts, to be sure, are called just and temperate when they are such as a just or temperate man would do; but what makes the agent just or temperate is not merely the fact that he does such things,

but the fact that he does them in a way that just and temperate
men do.   (NE II iv, 1105b5–8)

For Aristotle, then, the relationship between *being* and *doing* (Mayo 1958)
is necessarily an intimate one, such that how one identifies an act as possessing the moral properties of "justness" or "temperance" is that it is performed by a just and temperate person. The problem with such a definition
(either of a virtuous act or a virtuous person) is its seeming circularity and
co-dependence. As such, how does one establish, for example, that *I* am a
virtuous person or subsequently that what *I* am doing corresponds to a virtuous act? This is a problem succinctly outlined by N. J. H. Dent:

> [I]f we are to identify who is a just or temperate man we cannot
> tell by looking at what he does. Or, rather and more exactly, we
> cannot go by the fact that he performs just or temperate actions.
> For we cannot identify which are the relevant actions or kind
> of actions until we know what some standard just or temper-
> ate man would do, and compare what we have before us with
> what he does ... [O]nce we have, so to say, got our hands on an
> exemplary just or temperate man we can, by reference to what
> he does, see whether what we do is likewise just and temperate;
> though, of course, we may not have done what was just and tem-
> perate *as* a just or temperate man would have done it. *He* would
> not, for example, be looking to some exemplary person to find
> out what he should be doing; he knows this from his own inner
> resources.   (1975: 323)

Dent's exemplary just or temperate man, because he is a virtuous man,
would not look to others. Instead, he would act from a "fixed and permanent disposition" (NE II iv, 1105a9–b2): a disposition acquired through nurturing – within a particular culture over time. As such, his responses "are
almost second nature" (Walker 1989: 355), because such dispositions have
been "rooted in a civic culture ... in which the right pathways of emotion and
action have been laid down in infancy and fostered by long habits of training and upbringing" (Cottingham 1994: 177) to the point where the virtuous
person "finds it easy to act in accordance with the dispositions and difficult
to act against them" (Walker 1989: 355).

If a *just* man does *x*, then *x* is, in virtue of *him* doing it, a just act; but it
is not enough to say that anyone else found to be doing *x* must likewise be
just in virtue of doing *x*. It is not enough that one should simply do *x*, for one
could accidently do this. Nor is it enough to do *x* on a regular basis, because
one could simply acquiesce to follow the rules that require *x* to be done. As
McCormick notes: "Mere outward conformity with what appears to be good

will not suffice" (2001: 285). Instead, one must do *x* in a manner congruent with the way a just man would approach doing *x*. What way might this be? Aristotle provides instruction:

> [V]irtuous acts are not done in a just or temperate way merely because they have a certain quality, but only if the agent also acts in a certain state, *viz* (1) if he knows what he is doing, (2) if he chooses it, and chooses it for its own sake, and (3) if he does it from a fixed and permanent disposition.   (NE II iv, 1105a31–5)

What Aristotle is telling us here is that the act must be voluntary (one must choose to do it); one must choose it not only by virtue of having a fixed and permanent disposition towards doing *x* (acquired through habit) but, importantly, one must choose to do *x*, and presumably be disposed to choose this option, for its own sake. The "for its own sake" requirement, and also the fact that Aristotle concedes that "they have a certain quality", suggests that one can to some degree assess the quality of virtuous acts independent of the virtuous person's proclivity for engaging in them. This independent assessment Aristotle refers to as the mean, which is the virtuous position located between the vices of excess and deficiency, the paradigm example of this being courage, which sits between rashness (the vice of excess) and coward-ice (the vice of deficiency).

Norman (1998) argues that the mean should be understood relative to a given context. As such, we should exhibit an emotion and/or behaviour appropriate to the context that elicits it. In one context, a certain expression of anger may be too much; on another occasion, within a different context, the same level may be inadequate. This means that, for Aristotle, a given emotion/behaviour should not be judged appropriate in and of itself (in the absence of context), but relative to the context in which it occurs. Thus, we are not blamed for feeling angry, nor for simply being angry *per se*, but "for being angry in a particular way" (NE II v, 1106a1–2) or for "seeking (or shun-ning) the wrong ones [i.e. pleasures or pains], or at the wrong time, or in the wrong way" (NE II iii, 1104b26–7). Conversely, "to have these feelings at the right times on the right grounds towards the right people for the right motive and in the right way is to feel them to an intermediate, that is to say, best degree; and this is the mark of virtue" (NE II vi, 1106b20–23).

To summarize: according to Aristotle, a virtuous act is something that a virtuous person would do; and in carrying out the act one must not simply do *x*, but do it in a manner congruent with the way a virtuous person would do it. However, and importantly, the way a virtuous person would carry out *x* – that is, the level of emotion/behaviour expressed – must be appropriate to the context in which it occurs (to the antecedent and elicit-ing event). With this in mind, then, what would the virtuous person do in the context of video games; that is, what would be an appropriate act within this context?

WOULD THE PRUDENT GAMER SIMULATE VICE?

Aristotle is clear that some acts remain vices irrespective of context in which they occur; nor is the principle of the mean applicable to them.

> But not every action or feeling admits of a mean; because some have names that directly connote depravity, such as malice, shamelessness and envy, and among actions adultery, theft and murder. All these, and more like them, are so called as being evil in themselves; it is not the excess or deficiency of them that is evil. In their case, then, it is impossible to act rightly; one is always wrong. Nor does acting rightly or wrongly in such cases depend upon circumstances – whether a man commits adultery with the right woman or at the right time or in the right way, because to do anything of that kind is simply wrong.
>
> (NE II vi, 1107a9–17)

Aristotle's comments would seem to indicate unequivocally that POTAs are vices and, as such, are not congruent with the actions of the virtuous person. But what of virtual vices such as adultery$_v$, theft$_v$ and murder$_v$ (to use virtual versions of Aristotle's examples above): how would Aristotelian ethics judge these?

We know that Aristotle is concerned more with being good than with what counts as a good act. So the issue for Aristotle is not so much whether murder$_v$ is right or wrong/good or bad but whether engaging in murder$_v$ is what the virtuous person would do: whether, that is, it constitutes a reasoned course of action aimed at achieving *eudaimonia*. Consider, then, the words of Mark Coeckelbergh when discussing video game violence:

> [T]he Aristotelian focus on trajectories of (im)moral develop-ment draws our attention to the time dimension. The moral problem, then, is not so much with committing virtual moral acts as such, but with doing that repeatedly, with training these acts.
>
> (2007: 224)

Likewise, Sicart has this to say:

> Virtue ethics would argue that computer games with unethical content actually reinforce practices and habits that ought not to

be present in the virtuous human being, and that to commit an
act of unethical meaning within a game world is to practice the
wrong habits that will lead to a nonvirtuous life.   (2009: 194)

McCormick (2001) states something similar: that simulated taboo violation
erodes one's virtue because such actions *represent* vice rather than virtue;
and one's intention, even if it is only to *simulate vice*, is damaging to one's
well-being (*eudaimonia*). In fact, for Coeckelbergh (2011), it is not the content of violent video games that need be the focus of concern but the conditions under which we engage this content: notably, in the absence of the
moral gaze of the morally significant other (Vallor 2010). Thus, when commenting on the lack of moral gaze within gamespace, owing to the fact that
others (avatars, especially NPCs) are not construed as morally significant,
Coeckelbergh has this to say:

> [I]f we are unable to imagine that game character as an other,
> we cannot morally evaluate what we do. In this sense, we find
> ourselves in a moral-social desert. The absence of the moral gaze
> allows us and encourages us to *act* as impatient, disembodied,
> insensitive, a-social, and anti-social killers in a pornography of
> slaughter and bloodshed.   (2011: 96, original emphasis)

Putting all of this together: in short, the critical stance of the proponent
of virtue theory is effectively that through engagement with STAs (simulated
vice) one is nurturing a habit that is incongruent with that of the virtuous
person. Knowing *how* to perform acts that are congruent with the virtuous
is referred to by Aristotle as *phronesis*, which translates as a kind of prudence or practical wisdom. *Phronesis* provides the virtuous person with the
know-how to engage in particular instances of virtuous action. Possessing
such prudence, however, "does not make us any more *capable* of doing fine
and just acts" (NE VI xii, 1144a13–14, emphasis added); rather, we are told,
"virtue ensures the correctness of the end at which we aim, and prudence
that of the means towards it" (1144a9–10). The virtuous man uses prudence
(*phronesis*) to arrive at the means of achieving a particular virtuous end. The
argument, articulated separately by Coeckelbergh, Sicart and McCormick,
suggests that engaging in STAs is imprudent because it nurtures in us practices that do not provide a means to a virtuous end and, if anything, take us
away from this goal.

To understand why, let us first ask: why is actual murder (murder$_a$) a vice?
Murder$_a$ does not fit along a continuum from excess to deficiency; either
one murders$_a$ or one does not. Certainly this was understood by Aristotle
(as noted above). Perhaps murder$_a$ is a vice because it is an expression (a
demonstration) of what is unjust. Murder$_a$ is the taking of a life and, as we

saw in Chapter 6 when discussing the principle of sanctioned equivalence, this can be done in legitimate or illegitimate ways: be just or unjust. For the sake of simplicity, then, let us say that murder$_a$ is a vice because it is unjust (one unjustly takes another person's life). The murderer, by carrying out an act of murder$_a$, has engaged in vice in so far as she has done something that is unjust. So what of the person who carries out a virtual murder (murder$_v$): has that person engaged in a vice? If she has, then it cannot be because the act of murder$_v$ is unjust: for although what murder$_v$ *represents* or *simulates* is unjust, the simulation itself is neither just nor unjust (it is just the manipulation of pixels, as the amoralist would say). If it is not unjust, then should the virtuous person be permitted to engage in murder$_v$? On the face of it, it does not seem unreasonable to concede that a virtuous person can play a video game in which she murders a virtual character. After all, the virtuous person has not done something that is unjust (when judged from outside the gaming environment), but only virtually enacted it. But as was noted above, with warnings about the moral danger of such simulation, even the mere enactment of murder, we are told, can potentially corrode one's virtue.

Corrosion suggests a gradual process: the eating away of one's virtue through the repetition of practices that, *if* performed non-virtually, are unjust, which one slowly becomes habituated to. But what does such a virtual performance entail, such that it constitutes the repetitive (virtual) practice of being (virtually) unjust? It would commonly involve the manipulation of buttons on a gaming console, through the use of one's dexterous fingers. Even if one uses a Wii console, the enactment of murder$_v$ is still some distance removed from the actual behaviour required to commit murder$_a$.[1] Perhaps, then, what one is becoming habituated to (or nurtured in) is not the behavioural mechanics of murder$_a$ – analogous, say, to training in hand-to-hand combat – but to a particular way of resolving a particular problem or scenario that, in a particular context (the non-virtual realm), constitutes the vice of murder$_a$, however it may be performed (see also Coeckelbergh 2011).

Is the practice of virtual murder a vice because it (allegedly) corrodes one's disposition to act justly? In terms of *a posteriori* arguments, any such approach would seem to constitute a simple reformulation of arguments from consequentialism discussed in Chapter 5 (as noted earlier, something Patridge [2011] refers to as *virtue consequentialism*). In effect, can it be shown that the simulation of vice (STAs) is associated with an increased disposition towards vice outside the gaming environment, as expressed in immoral behaviour? In other words, does the enactment of STAs actually train one to be more readily disposed to vice, and is this increased disposition manifest through an increase in corresponding behaviour outside the gaming environment? As discussed in Chapter 5, the evidence that this is the case is far from convincing (in fact, see Schulzke's [2010] discussion on the real-world effects of violent video games, including "training killers", for a more detailed rebuttal of this argument). Instead, then, how might one challenge *a priori* the argument from virtue: that it is imprudent to engage in simulated vice?

ON THE POSSIBILITY OF ALTERNATIVE VIRTUES

One might begin by considering Aristotle's view of violence in entertainment and therefore fiction, of which video games can be seen as a simple, although somewhat more technologically advanced, continuation of this tradition. Jon Cogburn and Mark Silcox (2009) discuss Aristotle's use of the Greek word *katharsis*, which scholars tend to interpret as meaning to purge or purify – usually of a particular emotion. (In modern psychology parlance and the psychodynamic tradition, this term is more typically written as *catharsis*, the spelling I shall adopt here.) One may therefore wish to argue as follows: given that STAs ≠ POTAs, if STAs serve a cathartic function for those who engage in them, whereby they (the gamers) can purge themselves of emotions associated with various POTAs in virtue of the STA's representation of a given POTA, then the purging of emotions associated with POTAs, through the enactment of STAs, must be a good thing for oneself and therefore for society. Of course, such *a priori* reasoning depends on certain "truths" that can be established only *a posteriori*: (a) that STAs act in the cathartic way described, and (b) that this has a beneficial effect on the individual and therefore society as a whole. The idea that violent gameplays may have a beneficial effect is certainly not a new one. In Chapter 6, I mentioned Jansz (2005) and his view that video games, even (or especially) violent ones, offer a safe medium for psychological exploration. Whether they do or not, however, is not something that can be established *a priori*.

An alternative approach may be to challenge the Aristotelian view that what is virtuous for one should be virtuous for another, and therefore that one can legitimately have an objective sense of what virtue is. This was certainly the approach adopted by Friedrich Nietzsche, who held that morality, for each of us, is what our own wills create. Thus morality through (Aristotelian) reasoning is replaced, for Nietzsche, "by some gigantic and heroic act of the will" (MacIntyre 1985: 114). Moreover, those who are "stronger of will" (the superman) should not be subject to the same morality as those whose wills are weaker (the herd). As Nietzsche proclaims, "it is *immoral* to say: 'What is good for one is good for another'" ([1888] 2003: §221, original emphasis). Instead: "[W]hat is right for one *cannot* by any means therefore be right for another" (*ibid.*: §228, original emphasis); so much so that "the demand for *one* morality for all is detrimental to precisely the higher men, [for] ... there exists an *order of rank* between man and man, consequently also between morality and morality" (*ibid.*, original emphasis).

Morality, for Nietzsche, is therefore contingent on one's strength of will, as is what should be deemed "moral" or "virtuous", with the consequence that what is a virtue or, conversely, a vice for one may be different for another. What the introduction of Nietzsche's philosophy is designed to highlight is simply that different approaches to virtue theory exist, and arguably none is more opposed to the Aristotelian view than Nietzsche's. If, within our own non-virtual space, one can challenge what constitutes a virtue, or who is virtuous, as Nietzsche does, then how much more might what counts as a virtue be debated within the altered contingencies constitutive of gamespace?

To explain: gamespace is a space where things can be other than they are in our actual world because the contingency relations that exist within this space have been altered (i.e. the rules and costumes of the space that govern how we interact, or even the nature of the environment and our embodiment within it, will all be potentially different). My experience of my virtually embodied self (my avatar) may be as someone with enhanced physical prowess, for example, or special skills, perhaps even with heightened charisma and sex appeal. As a white, heterosexual male, I may present myself within gamespace as a black, homosexual female. Yet who we are within gamespace is but one aspect of this possibility for change. As acknowledged above (with passing reference to altered rules, costumes and governance), the way we represent others and the actions we carry out or permit to occur are also based on altered contingencies. In such a space, what counts as vice and what counts as virtue may not be the same as in our actual world.

It may be that, within a given gamespace, I am virtuous because I take what I want from whom I want: big, strong, small, weak, young or old (perhaps in this world one enacts a kind of Nietzschian view of virtue; see Rauch 2011). Let us allow that, in this space, such behaviour is recognized and accepted as the behaviour of a virtuous man (consider parallels with the *World of Gor*, for example). Granted, my virtuous constitution, so described, would be incompatible with that presented outside this space (or with what should be presented as virtuous if one subscribes to a more typical Aristotelian view of virtue), but in each space I would nevertheless be considered virtuous. Alternatively, while in gamespace, I may relish activities accepted as examples of vice within both the worlds I occupy (real and gaming). Either way, I have an incompatibility of natures (*qua* different ways of behaving) across these divergent spaces. In the first scenario, I am virtuous throughout, although what counts as virtue is quite different within one space than in the other. In the second, I indulge the vices (because *this* gamespace affords me the opportunity to do so).

What this example highlights is that whether my behaviour within gamespace is held to be virtuous or not is irrelevant to its compatibility with what is typically thought of as virtuous in the actual world. Yet, recall how, according to McCormick and other proponents of virtue theory, it is the simulation of *vice* within these virtual worlds that erodes one's virtue. But in the first scenario I am not simulating vice; rather, I am enacting virtue (as conceived of within that space, at least). Ah, but is this not just some philosophical sleight of hand? Surely, whether one conceives of the virtual act as virtuous or non-virtuous is not the point; what is the point, and therefore what is important to virtue theory, is that the virtual enactment is incompatible with what is conceived of as virtuous outside this space. Agreed: this seems to be how virtue theory presents itself; the incompatibility of natures across these two worlds is important. However, conceiving of the virtual act as "virtuous" or "non-virtuous" is not a moot point; for accepting that what one does within gamespace is an example of virtue or vice has important implications for how we come to understand, and therefore decide on the prohibition of, acts that elicit these incompatible natures. If one accepts that, within each world, what I am doing is virtuous, then how can any discrepancy between the virtual and the actual legitimately be called *morally* problematic? In other words, would it not be inappropriate to say that what is held as virtuous within *this* (game) world is morally wrong because it is not considered to be morally virtuous outside this space?

Recall the discussion from Chapter 4 on the status function of multiplayer spaces. Let us allow, then, that the status function of a given space is that X (taking what you want from whom you want) counts as Y (a virtue) in context C (*this* gamespace). If this is agreed by the gaming community, then it represents an alternative moral system. As such, it seems that what we have here are two competing moral practices: one from the actual world and one from within gamespace (in the same way as Aristotle and Nietzsche compete). Therefore, when in gamespace, although I may not be acting in a manner that corresponds to Aristotle's *phronesis* – at least, not based on a morality contingent on our actual world (as Aristotle intended) – I am nevertheless learning how to act morally based on a system of morality contingent on gamespace (or a particular example of that space).

If one accepts this, then perhaps a more informative strategy when deciding on whether to endorse selective prohibition is to consider how the individual is able to cope, psychologically, within spaces with conflicting moral practices, instead of trying to argue that she is only *really* being virtuous in one space compared to the other. The issue of prohibition then becomes a question for psychology not morality. Likewise, if it is a psychological issue when one engages in incompatible virtuous acts then is it not, ultimately, a psychological issue even if one chooses to indulge in simulated vice within a gamespace (i.e. playing a serial killer who is hunted by the authorities)?

Perhaps more than any other moral system, virtue theory is tied to the psychology of the individual, as both virtue theory and psychology are concerned with a person's character. From a psychological perspective, one may enquire: how does a gamer interpret the relationship between incommensurate acts of virtue in these different spaces or, even more straightforwardly, between STAs and the POTAs they represent? The answer to this question may have moral ramifications, and may even be in part determined by what the gamer *perceives* to be a vice or a virtue (see Ch. 12). What it does not require, I contend, is that we try to assign virtual acts either to the category of something a virtuous person would do, or something she would not.

Such a view is compatible with the position adopted by Sicart (2009). According to Sicart, the gamer (or *player-subject*, to use his terminology) is a moral agent because she (*qua* player-subject) is an extension of the person who is a moral agent in non-gamespace (the player-subject is also compatible with Sicart's conception of the gamer as *homo poieticus*; see Ch. 9). However, Sicart accepts that what is deemed morally acceptable within a given space is dependent on a number of interactive factors. First, the game is itself a moral object; its design – including constraints and affordances – can shape the moral choices available and the consequences of those choices (see Hartmann & Vorderer 2010; Pohl 2008; Schrier & Gibson 2010, 2011; Zagal 2009). Second, as just noted, the person playing the game is to a greater or lesser degree a moral agent outside this space, from which is derived the morals of the player-subject created within gamespace. The application of these moral components will also impact on the gamer's experience of the game: whether they will feel morally compromised owing to the moral constraints of the game design or, instead, feel they have the opportunity to explore and reflect on certain moral choices and consequences.

What this means, for Sicart, is that the gaming practice of what may be non-virtuous activities outside gamespace, or radically different practices, does not (in and of itself) lead to the moral corruption of the individual. The gamer's experience of the game should be understood within the context of game design (game as moral object) and person as moral agent. It may be that the game *requires* the gamer to engage in a particular STA (e.g. commit rape in the game), which the person as a moral agent is not prepared to do because it violates their personal moral code; in which case, according to Sicart, the process of *subjectivization* – what the gamer experiences within the game – will cease, because they will disengage from the game. On the other hand, the moral agent – *qua* player-subject – may be prepared to engage in certain activities that would be illegal, immoral or even taboo offline, because they are *a*, or possibly even the *only*, means of playing the game, in which case the subjectivization process would include reflecting on the action in relation to the moral agent's own set of values outside gamespace.[2]

For Sicart, the player-subject may engage in STAs but this takes place within the context of the game and therefore reflects the constraints set by the game as a moral object; what Nicolas Ducheneaut refers to as "the 'laws' of the game embedded in its design" (2010: 137). According to Sicart, in the case of the *mature* moral being there would be no moral corruption, no transfer of values from those evident in the game to the actual world, because the mature moral being is able to understand that the values and unethical content espoused by the gameplay are part of the experience (the subjectivization) of playing the game.

Importantly, though, Sicart concludes that video games "with unethical content should only be marketed to and consumed by virtuous players, those player-subjects who have actually developed their ethical reasoning" (2009: 197). These players know that such provocative content "is only meaningful within the game, because it is related to the game system" (*ibid.*): that, or they will abstain from playing the game altogether. Either way, the moral corruption feared by proponents of virtue theory will be negated.

The contingent relation between the moral system and the space it governs is implicit within Sicart's views. The moral being who understands this contingency relation is free to experience the gamespace (the particular subjectivization) without the threat of this practice leading to a detrimental change in virtuousness. The player-subject derived from the mature moral being is also able to terminate any engagement judged to violate a personal taboo, should they choose to exercise their right to veto. However, if no alternative course of action is available within the game (owing to game mechanic constraints) then the gamer may be forced to withdraw altogether.

CONCLUSION

The view espoused by Sicart certainly seems compatible with the idea that a virtuous person could engage in STAs at least when the STA is related to assault, killing and murder. However, what of the virtuous person who engages in mutilation and torture, or even virtual rape and paedophilia: is it enough to understand such an act as meaningful only within the context of the gamespace? This point raises the question: why would anyone want to do that, irrespective of whether they consider themselves virtuous or not? This question will be addressed in Chapter 11. Moreover, if we hold that the virtuous person may engage in murder$_v$ but not rape$_v$ or paedophilia$_v$, then on what basis are we discriminating these actions? In terms of using virtue theory as a means of selectively prohibiting video game content, and thereby accounting for the current state of play, it seems that either virtue theory bites the bullet and permits any virtual enactment to occur or it must deny all STAs. Moreover, the notion of competing or incompatible virtues across different spaces switches the focus of our appraisal from what the virtuous person would do (because this depends on what is held to be virtuous by a given theory) to what an individual can cope with psychologically when engaged in disparate forms of "virtuous" activity or even "vice".

In the next chapter I present the moral position of ethical egoism as a slightly unorthodox segue into the issue of player motivation (see Ch. 11), and consider the extent to which it matches a potential normative strategy open to gamers to aid their success. In relation to STAs, might such a strategy, by mirroring the principles of ethical egoism, be psychologically damaging to the gamer, especially on leaving the gamespace?

NINE

Doing what it takes to win

For a solitary animal egoism is a virtue that tends to preserve
and improve the species: in any kind of community it becomes a
destructive vice.   (Schrödinger 1992: 101)

In this chapter, I consider the extent to which a strategy available to gamers
to facilitate successful gameplay can be said to endorse (even if inadvertently) the fundamental principles of *ethical egoism* (EE). I then consider
whether adopting this strategy, in light of its similarity to EE, is potentially
damaging to one's psychological well-being when used in conjunction with
STAs and, consequently, whether this potential psychological harm could
justify the prohibition of STAs from video games.

In order to explore these issues, I shall: (i) assess whether EE provides an
internally consistent structure for prescribing how one ought to behave; (ii)
consider the extent to which the aforementioned gaming strategy, while not
necessarily construed by the gamer as a moral principle *per se*, nevertheless
matches the fundamental criterion of self-interest characteristic of EE; (iii)
present an argument for why EE amounts to a psychologically unhealthy

way of behaving; and (iv), given (i–iii), evaluate the extent to which such a strategy, even when adopted against virtual opponents, could prove to be psychologically unhealthy.

One might object to points (i–iii), claiming that they are in many ways redundant, and that point (iv) could be assessed on its own merits in so far as, *a posteriori*, it could be shown that the gaming strategy is psychologically unhealthy (or not, as the case may be), irrespective of any supposed similarity to EE. If such an assessment is achievable, then it could be done without reference to the alleged perniciousness and detrimental psychological effects of EE. Certainly, empirical research has been amassed documenting the effects of playing video games – mostly violent ones and mostly in relation to increased real-world aggression – although, as was discussed in Chapter 5, the findings are far from convincing. However, it is my contention that a richer explanatory account of the effect of video game violence and other STAs can be achieved by engaging with points (i–iii). This will then be used to support my argument that psychology rather than morality should be used to manage the selective prohibition of video game content. For it is my further contention that an analysis of points (i–iii) will reveal support for the argument (developed further in Ch. 12) that the selective prohibition of video game content should be based on a greater understanding of the psychological impact of engaging in these virtual activities, rather than through the imposition of a moral theory established outside gamespace but used to police gamespace through an act of moral transcendence.

In Chapter 12, I discuss ways in which gamers manage decisions within gamespace in light of their own moral systems and/or what the game mechanics affords, and how they (gamers) cope with potentially disparate moral freedoms within these spaces. In the meantime, I would like to explore the possibility of adopting an amoralist strategy when playing games. To clarify, the amoralist strategy I have in mind does not mean that the gamer will not appear to follow a particular moral path or make certain choices with moral consequences within the game, as and when they are required (certain decisions may coincide with a certain moral stance). Instead, it means simply that the gamer does not make decisions as *moral* decisions but, rather, as strategic decisions that he considers will help bring about a successful outcome based on what it means within that game to succeed, or what he holds to be a desired outcome. Such a gamer is, I argue, following Kant's hypothetical imperative, which, in the context of gamespace, is compatible with EE, at least in terms of virtual outcomes and behaviour.

THE HYPOTHETICAL IMPERATIVE REVISITED

Recall from Chapter 4 how I suggested that, in simple terms, from an amoralist perspective, what one ought to do to succeed within gamespace is delineated by Kant's hypothetical imperative. If one desires to win the game, and doing *a*, *b*, *c* (etc.) is a means of achieving that desire (that end), then one ought to do *a*, *b*, *c* (etc.). Even if a game enforces certain moral constraints by restricting the options available, one could simply do what is required – that is, adopt the most probable strategy for success – based on the moral choices available within the game. The decision to act in a certain way (based on the choices available and one's intention within the game), however, does not necessitate nor require that one actually endorse or otherwise embrace a particular moral system, even if one's choice and therefore one's act of doing A rather than B seem to indicate this; rather, it need only mean that one has identified a successful strategy available within the game and, following the hypothetical imperative, chosen to do what one ought to do, pragmatically rather than morally, to succeed.[1] In this respect one is adopting a means of engaging with the gameplay in a manner reminiscent of Huizinga's ([1950] 1992) *homo ludens*.

If, as the amoralist attests, what one does is "just a game", meaning that one's enactments take place in a separate space with its own rules (as discussed in Chs 1 and 4), and if the purpose of the game is to achieve certain goals (which constitute success), and one's motivation for playing in the first place is to achieve these goals, then the hypothetical imperative would seem to be a suitable principle to follow, irrespective of how the morality of one's actions is construed outside the gamespace, or even within it. I say this with the proviso that one's actions must not be detrimental to one's success if (and therefore because) they happen to contravene a system of morality represented within the game. By this, I mean: if one shoots "innocent" people, one must still be able to achieve one's goal of succeeding in the game. If this is not possible, or one is severely hampered by this action, then the hypothetical imperative would not advocate the shooting of innocent people, for strategic rather than moral reasons, unless one's goal was simply to have fun irrespective of success and such action constituted fun for the gamer.[2]

Of course, one may wish to play the game from a particular moral perspective: to switch, as Sicart (2010) argues, from a player characteristic of *homo ludens* to that of *homo poieticus*, whereby one comes to understand that rather than subjugating oneself to the rules of the game, one has the wherewithal to be the steward of one's own ethical system, providing the game design allows for this, of course. For as Sicart points out: "Players can evaluate... behaviour from an ethical perspective, using their moral judgement, but they are still constrained by what is possible and what is not within the game" (*ibid.*: 189). Game design permitting, then, as a player-subject or *homo poieticus*, I may choose to adopt a particular moral perspective, and this will probably affect any decision I make regarding what counts as appropriate or inappropriate action. I may choose to do A rather than B at a particular point in the game, for example, because I consider it my moral duty to do A, or because I believe the character I am playing would consider this to be the case; or it may be that doing A provides the greatest happiness for the greatest number of people (within the game), and I consider that fact to be constitutive of the most moral outcome (etc.). I may even choose to do A in the full knowledge that B would advantage me more, because I consider A to be the morally correct thing to do and do not wish to violate my own moral code, even though what I am doing is "just a game". The point is, as *homo poieticus*, although I may choose to act in accordance with a particular set of moral values (perhaps personal to myself or those of my character within the game), should I *have* to do this? In other words, should I be morally obliged to play the game as a moral being and so endorse a particular moral view and thus be exposed to legitimate moral scrutiny? Or should I be given the freedom, irrespective of morals, to do whatever it takes to succeed or, equally, be permitted to do whatever I find enjoyable (if what I find enjoyable does not coincide with success as decreed by the game mechanics)? Perhaps the nature of gamespace is such that it is legitimate, as Sicart argues, to challenge the morality of game designs that constrain the options available to the player-subject attempting to be *homo poieticus*; perhaps there should be absolute freedom. But is it not equally legitimate to argue that as part of any obligation to provide moral freedom within gamespace there should be the freedom to be immoral or even amoral without incurring moral condemnation for how one chooses to act? As Schulzke notes: "Unreflective play is not immoral; it only misses the benefits of experiencing the game on a moral dimension" (2011: 63).

Those not convinced by arguments for the applicability and therefore suitability of traditional moral theories to the assessment of video game content, or by the strength of the *a priori* arguments for restricted content (see Chs 6 and 7), may be more amenable to the view that the hypothetical imperative provides a simple, practical and amoral guide to conduct within gameplays. The pragmatism inherent within the hypothetical imperative makes it compatible with the amoralist's stance. Interestingly, the motivation to succeed within the game, which has now become the focus of discussion (and for which I am saying one would implement the hypothetical imperative), and the alleged *moral* irrelevance of other characters are both contained within the prescribed principles of the somewhat out of favour moral theory, EE.

Broadly construed, EE is the view that the fundamental moral principle on which to base one's conduct is that of self-interest, regardless of the interests of others (Rachels 1986), a view that may strike those naive to EE as somewhat counter-intuitive for a *moral* theory. As noted, the hypothetical

imperative does not convey a moral ought; it does not constitute a normative position of any notable moral interest. Ethical egoism, on the other hand,
prescribes precisely a means of interaction – a moral ought – that I contend is comparable to a strategy that a gamer could and perhaps should (in a
practical sense) adopt within the game as a means to succeed. To be clear, I
am not saying that during the game the gamer should be *morally* obliged to
look out for his own best interests irrespective of others. Neither am I advocating that if one chooses to conduct oneself in a self-interested way, one is
necessarily endorsing EE. There are two reasons for this worth noting: first,
because one may have chosen to adopt a strategy of self-interest not for reasons of morality but as a normative gaming strategy, and so be following the
hypothetical imperative (rather than intentionally adopting EE) because of
its pragmatic insight; and, second, even if one deliberately or inadvertently
chooses to adhere to the principles of EE within the game, it is not necessarily
the case that one can actually do so. I recognize that there is some legitimacy
to the objection that the self-interest inherent within EE concerns promoting
one's own interest over that of other *people*, not NPCs (as is the case within
single-player gameplays, for example). So, even if one chooses to follow the
principles of EE within the game, at best one may only be engaging in *virtual*
EE or be *symbolically* enacting the role of an egoist; in much the same way as
one would say of the Kantian (within the same context) that he can only virtually or symbolically treat others as an end in themselves. Having accepted
this point, I nevertheless consider an exploration of the relationship between
gaming strategy and EE to be far from redundant or merely academic.

To help understand why, recall the content of single-player video games
as presented in Chapter 2: that in numerous games it is commonplace to
maim, kill and even murder, and, in a growing number, mutilate and torture,
or cannibalize one's victims (*all* of which represent POTAs). Now, if applied
to actual POTAs, would EE claim that one ought to engage in these proscribed activities? Only if it is in one's best interest to do so. However, owing
to the proscriptive nature of POTAs and the severity of the consequences
for those found to have committed such an act, it seems realistic to hold that
it would not be in one's interest to do so. Certainly, any occasion where one
might envisage that it would be to one's advantage may be so contrived as to
be of no value as a practical guide to how one should proceed in life. However, given that STAs ≠ POTAs, even if it is not in one's interest to engage
in POTAs, this does not mean it is not in one's interest to engage in STAs,
especially if doing so increases one's chance of succeeding within the game.
Therefore, if it is shown to be the case that success within video games is
best served by adopting a self-serving strategy equivalent in its approach
to EE but for practical rather than moral reasons,[3] or at least that this is a
legitimate strategy to adopt, then why should one be prohibited from serving
one's best interest (particularly if arguments against the selective prohibition

of STAs in virtue of what they represent are problematic; again, see Chs 6 and 7)? Within the context of gamespace, this could easily involve murdering for self-interest such as personal gain or advancement within the game, or simply pleasure; but, equally, one's best interest might be served by raping a virtual character or possibly even engaging in virtual paedophilia or necrophilia (should the game mechanics make this option available). Why should *these* latter enactments be prohibited if they can be explained with reference to the same gaming strategy underpinning enactments of virtual assault, mutilation, torture or even murder?

As a possible response, if it can be shown that certain gaming strategies inadvertently endorse EE, then perhaps arguments used to challenge the fundamental principle of EE (self-interest irrespective of the interests of others) can be employed to highlight the potential damage playing games that feature the enactment of STAs for self-interest might cause. To be clear, I am not claiming that EE, as a moral theory, advocates murder, mutilation and rape (etc.), because, as already noted, within the context of a non-gaming environment it would typically not be in one's best interest to engage in any of these activities. Equally, it may not be in one's best interest to do this within a game if it hampers one's chances of success. Nevertheless, if it can be shown that EE is a strategy for moral living that is potentially damaging, even when less extreme expressions of self-interest are promoted, then could it not be argued that a gaming strategy that inadvertently endorses EE runs the risk of cultivating a way of interacting with others that is psychologically unhealthy? Moreover, might such risk be even more acute within a gamespace whose gaming mechanics *permit* murder$_v$, torture$_v$, rape$_v$ and all manner of ills (STAs), and therefore where acting in one's self-interest to win the game may require (even encourage) indulging in these STAs? If such concern is shown to be warranted, then one may have a legitimate reason to prohibit STAs; but whether it can explain the current state of play within video games or justify selective prohibition remains to be seen.

In the next section, I shall provide a brief overview of EE and evaluate the extent to which it provides a coherent moral theory, irrespective of whether it is deemed to be an acceptable one.

EXAMINING THE LOGICAL AND MORAL COHERENCE OF ETHICAL EGOISM

As a debated moral theory, EE was at its most prominent during the 1960s and 1970s (see e.g. Baier 1966; Emmons 1969; Facione *et al.* 1978; Machan 1979; Medlin 1970; Rachels 1974; B. Williams 1973). However, within the philosophical literature of the time, Edward Regis Jr informs us, "there [was] no one conception of egoism common to all or most parties in the debate"

(1980: 50). Despite such differences, James Sterba (1979: 92–3) provides a workable definition that I shall adopt here:

(EE): For every person X and every action *y*, X ought to do *y* if and only if *y* is in the overall self-interest of X.

When challenging EE as a moral theory, critics have tended to focus on alleged logical inconsistencies within its structure (e.g. Baumer 1967; Campbell 1972; Medlin 1970), irrespective of how counter-intuitive or unpalatable or even pernicious its principal message may appear to be. Over the years, philosophers have debated the extent to which EE is internally consistent (it has been accused of advocating logical impossibilities), particularly regarding prescribed outcomes (it allegedly instructs *both* A and B to achieve what it is only possible for *either* A or B to achieve). It has also been criticized for being morally incoherent (in so far as it is said to allow that action C is at the same time both morally good and morally bad). A more detailed consideration of each of these challenges is of some value, I contend, not only as a means of establishing the *coherence* of EE as a moral theory (if not its acceptability) but because a closer inspection of EE's essential characteristics, as revealed through a response to these challenges, will help support the case for its compatibility with a strategy for successful gameplay (some might even go so far as to say its utility as a normative gaming strategy).

Ethical egoism promotes the view that each and every one of us ought to act in a way that is in our overall best interest to act. In other words, the pronouncement "*I* should act in a way that suits *my* best interests" should be embraced by one and all as a universal moral truth. However, does the *generalization* (to person X) of such a *singular* prescription (*my* self-interest) reveal a logical inconsistency, thus making the theory internally incoherent? To explain: if EE advocates that I (*qua* person X) should benefit from my actions but also that my neighbour, from his perspective (*qua* person X), should benefit from *his* actions, then if we both seek to benefit from acting on the same object (say, obtaining prize *p*), one of us will benefit less than the other. In the guise of person X, EE would seem to demand that both I and my neighbour benefit the most from each of our respective actions, which, in the case of obtaining prize *p*, cannot be achieved. Thus, it is claimed that EE is logically (and therefore internally) inconsistent (see Österberg 1988 for a detailed discussion).

To resolve this alleged inconsistency, it is important to note that a commonly accepted interpretation of EE holds that it is not that the *outcome* of my action should necessarily benefit me alone but, rather, that I should be *motivated* to act solely in a way that benefits me (Hosper 1961). If my actions happen to benefit others then so be it, but this should not have been a consideration at the time I acted. As Regis points out: although "[EE]

105

must deny that positive action for the good of others is morally obligatory" (1980: 60), this is not the same as saying that it must be proscribed altogether. What this means for EE, then, is that its general proclamation maintains simply that my (or my neighbour's, or whoever conforms to person X's) sole *motivation* for initiating action C is that it will benefit me (or them, in their respective cases); but this does not mean that I (or they) *will* benefit more than others or indeed benefit at all from this action. In other words, although EE holds that one should try to act in a way that is of benefit to oneself above all others, or at least above the benefit one would receive if one acted differently,[4] it does not require, let alone necessitate, that this will actually be achieved. Instead, EE stipulates only that this aim must be realistically achievable. When viewed in this way, EE is not promoting a logical inconsistency. What it does prescribe, which is why it is compatible with the hypothetical imperative, I contend, is that one should be motivated by self-interest alone, irrespective of what the final outcome actually turns out to be, either for oneself or, most definitely, for others.

The difference between the outcome and what one intends can also be used to resolve a further challenge to EE based on moral inconsistency. To illustrate, let us say that as person X it is in my best interest to win prize p; equally, in the form of person X, it is in my neighbour's best interest to do the same. But if I win the prize, then this necessarily entails that I have prevented my neighbour from winning it. As each of us conforms to the generalized person X, I must act in my own self-interest and, *mutatis mutandis*, so must my neighbour. But surely this means that when my neighbour acts in his own best interest he is preventing me from acting in my best interest. Thus, the objection goes, EE is advocating a moral position that is contradictory: for, under such circumstances, it prescribes that person X must both promote self-interest (which is morally good) and prevent it (which is morally bad).[5]

In response, one can reiterate the fact that EE prescribes moral praiseworthiness based on one's motivation to strive for outcomes that are self-serving, not on whether one actually achieves them (Hosper 1961). Moreover, it is not the case, as is perhaps incorrectly alluded to in the scenario above, that EE asserts that one must be motivated to prevent the achievement of self-serving outcomes in another; rather, it is a requirement of EE only that one is motivated to obtain such outcomes for oneself. The motivation (to win prize p) within both myself and my neighbour, and the moral praiseworthiness assigned to this motivation, is therefore perfectly consistent with the teachings of EE. However, it will be the case that if the outcome of my motivation is successful then my neighbour must necessarily be thwarted. But this is not inconsistent with EE, nor does it necessitate that such an outcome could only occur if, and therefore because, I am motivated to *prevent* my neighbour from obtaining that which is in his best interest to obtain. My *intention* to win the prize does not prevent my neighbour from likewise intending this for himself, or indeed achieving it; only my success would prevent this.

But one might object that if I intend P, and P entails that Q cannot be the case, then I must intend that Q cannot be the case. In response I would argue that it is not that I *intend* that Q cannot be the case; rather, under these circumstances, this fact is a logical *outcome* of what I do intend: which is only that P is the case. But the fact that it is a logical or even an empirical outcome of my intention (empirical if my intention is successful) does not alter the fact that what I do intend is consistent with EE because what I intend cannot prevent my neighbour, or any other individual who conforms to person X, from intending the same.[6]

In the next section, I present evidence and argument in support of the claim that certain strategies for successful gameplay endorse EE. Here, I concentrate on examples from single-player games.

MIRRORING ETHICAL EGOISM THROUGH GAMING CHOICES AND STRATEGY

Moral dilemmas are often found within the gameplay of single-player games. In *Fahrenheit* (aka *Indigo Prophecy* in the US), for example, it is contrived that the main character is wanted for murder. He then faces a moral dilemma. He notices a young child is about to slip through the cracked ice and into a freezing lake. Does he save the child but risk exposing himself to nearby police officers, or do nothing and be sure not to put himself at risk? *Heavy Rain*, likewise, contains many such dilemmas, essentially based around how far the gamer (as the main character) would go to save his kidnapped son, who will die at the hands of a serial killer if not found in time (e.g. shooting a drug dealer in the face in order to obtain a clue as to his son's whereabouts). In *The Thing*, potentially any member of one's team (made up of NPCs) can be infected by an alien, which would have detrimental effects on one's chances of success within the game. Even with only the suspicion of infection, one may have to decide between "playing it safe" and killing the suspected team member or letting him live and risking further infection should it transpire that he is, in fact, infected. If he is not, and one does not kill him, then one retains a healthy member of the team. Should one choose the alternative, one commits murder.

Of course, these and any other "moral dilemma" found within gameplays are not actual moral dilemmas; rather, they are simulations of moral dilemmas (although this is not to deny that some gamers may suffer actual anguish when contemplating which decision to make). Within the gamespace, there can and often do occur *enactments* of enforced moral decisions through such simulations. Some games, such as *Heavy Rain* (it could be argued), construct their gameplay around them. Players may even play the game repeatedly and

107

adopt a different moral perspective on each occasion, thereby making different decisions depending on the moral stance they adopt. Moreover, I fully accept that, for some players, simulating moral decisions within these games is a fruitful way for them to explore moral issues and the consequences of their actions (depending, of course, on the consequences afforded/imposed on them by the game mechanics). In the examples above, it may be that what one decides to do stems from, say, utilitarian interests and, therefore, a desire to achieve a greater good, or it may be that one acts out of a sense of duty to the other as a fellow human being (etc.). I do not deny that such moral reasoning may occur. However, here I am interested in an alternative and much more pragmatic approach to gameplay that centres on what the gamer understands to be the decision that will most probably bring about a successful outcome, irrespective of morality. I have argued that this amoral approach is delineated by Kant's hypothetical imperative. Moreover, gamers who adopt such an approach – namely, doing what one has to do to win – may come to think of it as *the* normative strategy for success.

Using *Heavy Rain* as an example, by following the hypothetical imperative, if one wishes to obtain x (a clue as to the whereabouts of one's kidnapped son) and doing y (shooting the drug dealer in the face) is the best (perhaps only) way to obtain x, then one ought to do y. Now it may transpire that doing y brings about negative consequences for oneself that are manifest at a later date within the gameplay. One may not have known this at the time and so will have to address this issue as and when it manifests itself (if one can). Or, one may anticipate negative consequences (within the gameplay) as a result of doing y and so take this fact into account when weighing up whether or not y really is the best option for oneself, and so really is what one ought to do, strategically. We can see, with this latter possibility, a way of thinking about what one ought to do – namely, act in one's best interest, irrespective of others – that has a certain similarity with EE. Of course, it could be said that one is also acting in the interests of the kidnapped son. This is true. But EE does not prohibit an action from benefiting others; it must simply be done with the intention of benefiting oneself first and foremost. Within the game, one's goal (*qua* the character) is to save the son but, more than this, one's goal as a player is to win the game.

As was discussed in Chapter 1, gamespace (*qua* a space of play) is both separate from and connected to the non-gaming environment (or "real" world). One can import personal characteristics into this space (see Bailenson *et al.* 2003; Bailenson & Yee 2005), including one's moral values (recall discussion on Sicart in Ch. 8). Equally, one can be affected by what one experiences here: based on how something is represented within the space and how one interacts with it (see Young & Whitty 2012; also, recall Chs 6 and 7, in which objections to certain sorts of representation were raised based on their perceived socially significant expression and/or incorrigible social meaning). When interacting within a game such as *Heavy Rain*, then – a game that prides itself on the authenticity of its narrative – one is required to make decisions that are meant to emulate real life, albeit in an extreme situation (although sometimes the decisions can appear quite mundane, and realistic for that reason).[7] In fact, it is this juxtaposition between an attempt to simulate real life and the extreme, perhaps even caricatured, nature of the simulation that marks out certain "controversial games" (e.g. the *Grand Theft Auto* series). Decisions made in games with "moral" dilemmas – whether to refrain from rescuing a child that has slipped into icy waters (*Fahrenheit*), or shoot a drug dealer in the face (*Heavy Rain*), or have sex with a prostitute and then mug her (*Grand Theft Auto*) – result in virtual acts that represent a particular moral and even legal violation. The gamer who has chosen to adopt what he holds to be a normative strategy for success, and which I have argued emulates the fundamental principle of EE, is in effect engaging in a narrative, albeit a playful one, that is designed to some degree to represent events that occur in real life. In this space, when one has the opportunity to engage in STAs, *the gamer I am describing* in this chapter bases their decision on reasoning that is compatible with EE's fundamental adherence to the principle of self-interest.

Why should this be a problem? After all, the gamer may declare, it is "just a game". This is true, and perhaps, for some, there is no problem. However, in order to make a more informed decision, I would like to discuss an argument that states that EE is not conducive to one's psychological well-being. In the next section, then, I consider what the danger(s) might be to one's psychological well-being in emulating EE as a normative gaming strategy while engaged in STAs.

IS ETHICAL EGOISM PSYCHOLOGICALLY UNHEALTHY?

Earlier, I presented a case against those who claim that EE lacks both internal and moral consistency. Further objections to EE as a moral theory tend to focus on what it promotes, which is selfishness as a normative course of action, and therefore the likelihood of exploitation. This is formally presented by Laurence Thomas thus:

> For any person *N*, *N* is an egoist if and only if for any person *S* and at any time *T*, *N* is prepared to exploit and take advantage of *S* at *T* if *N* has good reason to believe that he does not thereby adversely affect his long-range interests. (1980: 73)

Thomas is quick to point out, however, that the formulation above does not mean that the egoist:

> must be one who exploits and takes advantage of others at every
> turn. For he must take into account the fact that in doing so he
> risks being discovered which, in general, would not be in his
> interests; and that sometimes the risks are likely to be so great
> that they are simply not worth taking.   (*Ibid.*)

Even with this caveat, EE is still seen by many as an unpalatable moral theory. Thomas's approach, however, is to denounce the legitimacy of EE on psychological rather than moral grounds: in so far as it advocates, he claims, a form of social interaction that is not compatible with psychological well-being, and therefore not sustainable by the non-pathological individual.

Thomas starts from the empirically well-founded premise that people desire to have a positive conception of themselves, the absence of which correlates with psychological problems (Kernis 2003; Pyszczynski *et al.* 2004). Thomas then notes how conceptions of the self are influenced by the way others view us. In order to develop a conception of myself based on the opinion of others, I have to trust the views of at least one other person (I have to believe that their opinion of me is trustworthy). Trust of this kind is typically reciprocated (I trust the individual and reciprocate by acting in a trustworthy fashion towards them). If this does not happen then there can be no mutual trust and typically the relationship quickly breaks down, or certainly changes from one of mutual trust to something else perhaps more controlling and/or destructive (see also Ch. 10 on the social contract). However, as we saw from Thomas's formulation of the ethical egoist's strategy (above), I (*qua* an ethical egoist) am normatively required to take advantage of, even exploit, others when it is to my advantage to do so, including those I trust to inform my self-concept and bolster my self-worth. The ethical egoist, in being normatively required to follow such a strategy, would have to fluctuate between reciprocating trustworthiness and exploitation. Such a requirement, Thomas argues, is not conducive to a stable and therefore psychologically healthy character. Therefore, the type of individual EE disposes us to be cannot be psychologically healthy.

If we start from the position of endorsing Thomas's view, then does it follow that the same underlying problems would transfer to a normative gaming strategy that mirrors EE for practical rather than moral reasons? Owing to the social element intrinsic within online multiplayer games, Thomas's argument has clear application to those who wish to engage socially within this space. It would seem that those desiring successful social interactions, as well as, or even in order, to succeed at the game, would be hampered by EE or the practical equivalent delineated by the hypothetical imperative *if* what one desires is simply to win the game. In multiplayer gamespace, social interactions are real, not virtual; therefore, the same risk of pathology would seem to be a probable outcome of adopting such a strategy if one sought to remain within this space, and especially if one had limited or in other ways impoverished social contact outside gamespace. I shall have more to say on multiplayer space in the next chapter (see also Ch. 12) when considering the role of social contract theory within moral reasoning and its application to gamespace. In the meantime, let us consider the extent to which Thomas's argument is applicable to single-player gamespace.

MIRRORING ETHICAL EGOISM WITHIN SINGLE-PLAYER GAMES

An immediate objection to the idea of the applicability of Thomas's argument to single-player gamespace is that it is not a social space and so does not involve social interaction. In short, there is no other person within this space towards whom one can direct fluctuating levels of trust and exploitation; neither is there anyone present to inform one's self-concept. As such, within single-player gamespace, even if EE is psychologically unhealthy, adopting a strategy that matches its normative behavioural outcomes may lack psychological relevance, at least of the kind postulated by Thomas. However, even if one accepts this criticism, might there be some aspect of engaging in this space that *is* psychologically relevant, and therefore some aspect that can be informed by psychology when considering the permissibility of certain virtual acts? I believe there is. To illustrate, consider the game of chess.

Playing chess involves adopting a strategy, within the rules of the game, that defeats or is intended to defeat one's opponent. In following the hypothetical imperative, in order to be successful at chess one ought to learn the rules and strategies that will enable one to defeat one's opponent. Easier said than done, perhaps, but essentially this is the requirement. In adopting such a strategy, it is not considered immoral for a player to use a much more "powerful" piece – say, the queen – to "take" a pawn. Presumably, one makes such a move to *advantage* oneself (in keeping with the strategy one has devised). It is permitted within the rules and so the move is legitimate; it is not a moral matter. By comparison, in *Heavy Rain*, when one shoots the drug dealer in the face to advantage oneself by gaining valuable information – a legitimate move within this game – should this be a moral matter? Throughout the chapters presented so far, I have considered arguments for and against why this should be the case. What we are considering now, however, is not whether STAs found in games such as *Heavy Rain* are immoral but whether they are psychologically unhealthy, and therefore whether doing what is required to succeed within a game, where doing what is required consists in performing STAs, is psychologically unhealthy (what it means for something to be psychologically unhealthy will be expanded on in Ch. 12). In effect, I am employing the same approach as Thomas by switching from a moral assessment to a psychological one. So, in the absence of the kinds of social interaction held to be problematic by Thomas, what other way might psychology be used to inform selective prohibition?

It may be the case that when one shoots someone in the face as part of an overall strategy for success, one does not construe the object of the virtual assault in the same way as the pawn one has just "taken" in the chess game (Hartmann *et al.* 2010). Perhaps the way *I* construe the virtual human I am (*qua* my avatar) pointing my virtual gun at is not at all analogous to the chess piece, or perhaps it is (again, this is something I shall consider further in Chs 11 and 12). Either way, should my *construal* of the target object – be it pawn or virtual human – make a difference to how my interaction with it is judged, morally? Outside gamespace, if the manner in which I construe an object is radically different from the way my society views it then this should not affect how my action or attitude towards the target object is judged. To explain: suppose that (outside gamespace) I hold that person x is subhuman and/or is simply an object to be used. Because of this construal, I engage in some form of POTA (or wish to). My construal of person x will not justify morally, or legally, my action (or desire) if it is contrary to the moral and legal status granted person x by the society in which I live (based on the legal and moral system it implements, which is why what I do is considered to be a POTA). However, how I cope psychologically, and therefore whether, for me, something *is* psychologically healthy or unhealthy, may very much depend on my construal of that object or event, irrespective of how society views it or the manner of my interaction (be it virtual or actual). Now, one might argue that any individual who construes another human as subhuman or as an object to be used already has psychological problems. This may be so when discussing POTAs. However, what we are really considering here are not POTAs but STAs; and as has been said many times STAs ≠ POTAs. Therefore, irrespective of how society may view STAs, to reiterate, how I construe them in relation to the gamespace in which they occur and the virtual person (or object) I interact with may well impact on how I cope psychologically with what I am doing in this playful space.

CONCLUSION

The debate over the morality of STAs hinges on the relationship between STAs and POTAs. The nature of this relationship is contested, both *a priori* and *a posteriori* (as the preceding chapters have testified). What Thomas's challenge to EE highlights, then, is the important role psychology can play in informing the debate over what constitutes normative action when engaged within a virtual gaming environment. Within single-player gamespace, one may not have to concern oneself with the psychological impact of fluctuations in reciprocity and exploitation of actual others, but one would do well to be informed by how gamers construe these "others" (these NPCs) when engaging in certain strategies involving STAs, and therefore how such construal impacts on the psychological make-up of the gamer, particularly as they transcend spaces with different behavioural norms and categories of permitted action. The extent to which such psychologically pertinent information can be used to selectively prohibit video game content has yet to be established, however, and is ultimately an empirical matter. Evidence and argument in support of psychology as an important means of informing this debate, and therefore as a way of identifying what should count as permissible action, and *why*, will be presented to a lesser degree in Chapter 11 but in more detail in Chapter 12. Before that, however, there is one more moral position I wish to consider, specifically in relation to multiplayer gamespace: namely, social contract theory.

TEN

Agreeing the rules

The problem of the formation of the state, hard as it may sound, is not insoluble, even for a race of devils, granted that they have intelligence. It may be put thus: … [H]ow are we to order their affairs and how establish for them a constitution such that, although their private dispositions may be really antagonistic, they may yet so act as a check upon one another, that, in their public relations, the effect is the same as if they had no such evil sentiments.   (Kant [1795] 1917: 153–4)

In the previous chapter I claimed that there are certain similarities between Kant's hypothetical imperative and EE; arguing that within the context of video games, and in terms of doing what it takes to win, each permits essentially the same underlying strategy. I then drew on Thomas's argument against EE in which he claims that EE necessarily cultivates psychological dysfunction owing to the nature of the social interaction it promotes. I used this to illustrate the importance of psychology as a means of gauging the appropriateness of strategies for success – particularly when engaging in STAs – which manifest the kinds of behavioural consequences permitted by either the hypothetical imperative or EE. As it is the gamer who transcends domains, then perhaps it is important to understand the psychological impact of engaging in STAs within a gaming environment, both on the gamer at the time of the interaction and as she transcends domains and re-enters the non-gaming world: something that can (and should) be done independently of any moral charge.

In the case of single-player games, Thomas's approach lacks application. Nevertheless, his use of an argument based on optimal psychology functioning rather than moral perniciousness (at least in the case of EE) is compatible with my own stance on the importance of psychology when informing decisions on the possible selective prohibition of video game content. I say this in the full knowledge that, when discussing single-player games, the psychological argument I present (see Ch. 12) will need to be different from Thomas's (because his is unsuited to single-player environments). Within multiplayer space, however, Thomas's approach has clearer application; for this type of virtual domain enables the formation of actual social relationships and more often than not requires cooperation in order to implement successful gaming strategies. Yet, as Thomas points out, the pursuit of EE seems to hinder such cooperative strategies and, if sustained, exposes gamers to psychologically unhealthy practices. In contrast, as a form of practical reasoning within a social space, the hypothetical imperative is much more tolerant of strategies that extol the merits of cooperative effort (if working together increases the chance of success and one wishes to succeed, then one ought to work together).

Beyond the practical reasoning of the hypothetical imperative, a *moral* theory that promotes cooperation as a rational means of achieving mutual benefit/success among community members is social contract theory. Therefore, before pursuing the argument for "psychology rather than morality" further in this chapter, I consider social contract theory as a final moral approach to selective prohibition. If, as the approach maintains, moral content and moral authority are established by community assent – as that which facilitates social harmony and cohesion – then could this criterion be used to guide what should be prohibited within video games: namely, that which disrupts social cohesion and harmony? An important factor to consider when applying social contract theory to gamespace, however, is the fact that gamespace is a space of play. Play is, of course, part of social living, but as we saw in Chapter 1 it is also, by design, separate from other social spaces. Issues that will be addressed in this chapter, then, are: (a) whether social contract theory can be used to make moral pronouncements on STAs from a position outside the virtual community; and (b) whether it can provide, for that virtual community, a means of legitimizing their moral authority within the particular space they occupy, and therefore determine what counts as morally appropriate or inappropriate content independently of – and perhaps in (moral) conflict with – the wider social community. Anticipating that it can do both (with qualification), I next consider the impact this will have on the possibility of selective moral proscription. I do this not as an academic exercise, but because I believe that an analysis of social contract theory will add weight to my argument for the role of psychology as a mean of informing guidelines on normative gaming content. Therefore, in keeping with this move, I prepare the ground for my argument for the potential psychological impact of engaging in STAs, particularly as one flits between domains that can have radically different moral content and moral authorities (which will be discussed in detail in Ch. 12). I also discuss the effect this might have on the cohesion and harmony of social living outside gamespace. Before any of that, however, I begin by introducing the rationale for social contract theory, using as my template the work of Thomas Hobbes.

DRAWING UP THE SOCIAL CONTRACT

In *Leviathan*, Hobbes asks us to consider a world with no government, political system or sovereign rule: a world he refers to as the *state of nature*. In the absence of any moral or legal authority, each inhabitant is free to do as they please and, in the case of disputes, act as judge, jury and executioner.[1] As Hobbes states: "[A] free-man *is he that, in those things which by his strength and wit he is able to do, is not hindered to do what he has a will to*" ([1651] 1985: 262, original emphasis).

The state of nature, so envisaged, might be mistaken for the backdrop to some new video game, and would certainly not look out of place among those already available that are set in similarly described fantasy/post-apocalyptic worlds.[2] The similarity continues, in fact, for Hobbes conjectures that without a system of government or recognized authority there would be no industry to speak of and so, in all probability, a scarcity of resources. Any advantage would be gained only as a result of one person's victory over another. Again, in the words of Hobbes: "Competition of Riches, Honour, Command, or other power, inclineth to Contention, Enmity, and War: Because the way of one Competitor, to the attaining of his desire, is to kill, subdue, supplant, or repel the other" (*ibid.*: 161).

For Hobbes, then, such absolute freedom comes at a cost, in so far as the state of nature would be a continual state of war or readiness for war, or, at best, constitute a cold war climate where individuals struggled to gain advantage over others out of a mixture of desire and fear, and where one would have to be constantly vigilant in order to protect what one had gained. Thus Hobbes continues: "[I]n the nature of man, we find three principal causes of quarrel. First, competition; secondly, diffidence; thirdly, glory. The first, maketh men invade for gain; the second, for safety; and the third, for reputation" (*ibid.*: 185). Perhaps such an environment would make for an enticing video game. However, when professed as the natural entailment of ultimate liberty for us, Hobbes anticipates a life that is nasty, brutish and short.

To counter such stark existence, and as a means of prolonging and increasing the quality of one's life, Hobbes argues that duly fearful, but ultimately rational, persons would (and should, because it is the rational thing to do) enter into a contractual agreement whereby they are prepared to sacrifice certain liberties for increased security. As Anthony Holiday notes:

> [H]uman beings reach agreement by a covenant which, being artificial, requires a "common power" to sustain it. Hobbes concludes that the only way to establish such power is for all men "to confer all their power and strength upon one man, or upon one assembly of men, that they may reduce all their wills, by plurality of voices, into one will".
> (2003: 50)

By submitting one's own will to the authority of the sovereign or governing body, one provides the means of legitimizing moral and legal standards within a community of co-signees. Of course, there is no historical contract or record of signatures; nor does one literally sign on the dotted line when entering into this agreement. As Émile Durkheim points out somewhat critically:

> The conception of the social contract is ... very difficult to defend, because it bears no relation to the facts ... [N]ot only are there no societies that have had such an origin, but there are none whose present structure bears the slightest trace of a contractual organization. Thus it is neither a fact derived from history nor a trend that emerges from historical development.
> ([1893] 1984: 151)

Moreover, according to Pekka Sulkunen: "For any will to exist and for any individuals to enter into agreements, society is always already necessary; contracts are the result of society, not its cause" (2007: 326). However, as James Rachels points out, "the story of the 'social contract' need not be intended as a description of historical events. Rather, it is a useful analytical tool, based on the idea that we may understand our moral obligations *as if* they had arisen in this way" (1986: 157, original emphasis).

Rather than as an account of historical fact, reference to a social contract should be understood as having more to do with the *idea* that, given the stark alternative (described by Hobbes), or even the *possibility* of this alternative, rationally minded individuals would consent to the terms of at least some form of social pact (Dunfee & Donaldson 1995), even though "no individual has ever evinced consent" (Holiday 2003: 52). To present the idea of a social contract is therefore to present "a theoretical construct that fits into a theory of social evaluation" (Weirich 2010: 151). In other words, it is a means of encapsulating what is in effect a rational drive towards the mutual recognition and justified standing of others alongside oneself (Scanlon 1998). Understood in this way, the social contract constitutes a macro-social *hypothetical* agreement (Thompson & Hart 2006), whose *tacit consent* (Skyrms 1996) not only enables moral consensus but also justifies moral authority.

The idea of an agreement based on tacit consent is illustrated by Rachels using the analogy of one's involvement within a game:

> Suppose you come upon a group of people playing an elaborate game. It looks like fun and so you join in. After a while, however, you begin to break some of the rules, because that looks like more fun. The others protest; they say that if you are going to play, you must follow the rules. You reply that you never promised to follow the rules. They may rightly respond that this is irrelevant. Perhaps nobody explicitly promised to obey; nevertheless, by joining the game, each person implicitly agrees to abide by the rules that make the game possible.   (1986: 157)

After presenting the analogy, Rachels is quick to highlight a clear discrepancy between it and social living: one *chooses* to join in with a game and, because of this, one can choose to leave, whereas it is much less the case that one is able to choose to be part of the social contract and certainly far harder to opt out.

It is not the concern of this chapter to discuss the extent to which one chooses to opt in or out of the social contract; nor is it my intention to discuss variations of the social contract (Locke [1690] 1980; Rawls 1971; Rousseau [1762] 1973).[3] Instead, I shall consider the extent to which the idea of a social contract provides a suitable means of selectively prohibiting STAs. I shall therefore refer to the *social contract tradition*, which maintains that we have the capacity to live with each other in mutual respect because this is what the rational person would do. The defining feature of the social contract tradition is to bring about social relations on these mutually beneficial terms (De Marneffe 2001). Morality, therefore, provides the framework for social living. Conversely, that which is detrimental to such mutually beneficial social relations is, by definition, morally proscribed.

HYPER- AND LOCAL NORMS WITHIN THE SOCIAL CONTRACT TRADITION

It is not difficult to understand how the permissibility of murder would have a detrimental effect on social living. The same can be said of a number of other actions, including rape, assault and theft. Thomas Donaldson and Thomas Dunfee refer to behaviours characterized within the social contract tradition as *hypernorms* – namely, "principles so fundamental to human existence that ... we would expect them to be reflected in a convergence of religious, philosophical, and cultural beliefs" (1994: 265). Hypernorms are to be contrasted with local norms: expressions of relativistic moral reasoning that reflect more nationally prescribed norms of behaviour (e.g. buying and selling based on an individual system of negotiation – haggling – rather than a fixed price for all). In light of the distinction between hypernorms and local norms, consider the following from Paul Weirich:

> The scope of the social contract varies among theorists. Some take it to govern all aspects of society. I take it to govern just the basic structure of society. People operate within that basic structure to formulate additional social rules and to realize various social arrangements. A social arrangement is constrained by the social contract, but complete details the contract leaves open.
>
> (2010: 150)

Individuals moving from one region to another – perhaps working and in other ways socializing within these different geographical locations – may be influenced in their moral decision-making by local (national) customs, either through willing acceptance or acquiescing to the local norms, which, as noted by Weirich, constitute a more specific, relativistic interpretation within the basic structure that is the universal social contract. However, such acceptance of a local norm is upheld only providing it does not violate what the individual holds to be a hypernorm: that is, an action understood to be fundamental to the social contract (see Spicer *et al.* 2004).

It may be, then, that permitting murder is *a priori* detrimental to social harmony. Likewise, one may consider haggling (rather than providing a fixed price) to be a system of exchange that is not incompatible with the principles of the social contract tradition and therefore not immoral. However, as Rachels (1986) points out, there may be other behaviours construed by some but not by others to be immoral (at the fundamental level of social contract): homosexuality, for example (although this is not the only one). It is my view, which I shall not defend here, that there are no convincing *a priori* reasons to prohibit the practice of homosexuality. Therefore, *if* a persuasive reason is to be provided, articulating why engaging in homosexual acts is detrimental to social cohesion and harmony, it must be established *a posteriori*. (To date, no such evidence is forthcoming.)

Likewise, with STAs, is engaging in virtual violence or other taboo activities detrimental to social cohesion and harmony, and so in breach of the social contract? There are a number of ways to approach this question. First, one might consider STAs as local norms. As such, within the locality of the gaming environment, one may accept that (virtual) assault and murder (for example) is an accepted norm. After all, STAs ≠ POTAs so one is not violating a hypernorm; at worst, one is *symbolizing* its violation. One can move in and out of this space without undermining a norm of behaviour fundamental to the social contract tradition. This being the case, how can we legitimately distinguish STAs such as assault and murder from rape or paedophilia (as is the case in the current state of play)? One would be forced to concede either that all STAs should be prohibited because they symbolize a breach of hypernorms, in so far as they represent those acts vehemently opposed by the social contract tradition, or none should, because they are not *actual* acts that contravene the social contract. (Recall, I discussed a similar point in Ch. 6 in relation to socially significant expression.) Even if we try to differentiate between certain STAs based on their incorrigible social meaning (e.g. rape or racism; as was the case in Ch. 7), which could be argued to have the potential to undermine social harmony and cohesion, one is vulnerable to permitting (on the basis of this criterion alone) paedophilia (again, recall the discussion on this in Ch. 7). Perhaps, then, there are *a posteriori* reasons to prohibit STAs, either *en masse* or selectively, owing to the accumulation of research findings evidencing their detrimental effect on social cohesion and harmony. As we saw in Chapter 5, there is either a paucity of research on the effects of certain types of STAs on those who engage in the activity (e.g. rape$_v$) or, in the case of the negative consequences of more traditional gaming violence (e.g. assault$_v$, killing$_v$, murder$_v$), findings are inconclusive.

The issue of STAs and their relation to the social contract tradition should be understood within the broader context of the social contract's relation to play. Certain behaviours are held to be detrimental to social living (as discussed), but can the behaviour of *play* – that is, any recognized and therefore acknowledged playful act *among adults* – be said to violate the basis for the social contract? Does a behaviour that is playful make it immune to contractually based moral scrutiny? There may be objection raised that play could have negative consequences: someone may be injured, even killed, during play, for example. In response, I would argue that it is clearly not the purpose of play (as typically understood) and therefore one's purpose as a player to intentionally injure or kill people when playing (although hurting an opponent may be accepted within more competitive games/sports). As such, if the social contract establishes that which is moral/immoral – based on social cohesion and harmony – then is play, in light of its ontological status as a separate space, in a position to violate the social contract given that it is *understood* to be separate from non-play behaviour? Why would rational persons be concerned about play?

As already discussed, the rational person may be concerned by certain playful acts (e.g. STAs), not because of what they involve – she may consider the (virtual) *act* to be amoral – but, instead, because of what the act represents (again, see Chs 6 and 7). Alternatively, concern may be expressed out of fear of the detrimental psychological impact STAs may have on the individual, irrespective of whether one labels the virtual acts themselves morally "good" or "bad".[4] Recall from Chapter 1 that although play is a separate space, it is not completely divorced from the non-play realm. There is a necessary degree of connectedness with the world outside play, so an inevitable transcendence across each of these domains. To explore this issue further, I shall consider multiplayer gamespace: first, as constitutive of a separate community with its own social contract; and, second, as housed within the broader non-gaming community.

MULTIPLAYER GAMESPACE

In Chapter 4 I discussed the role of status functions within multiplayer space. Status functions need not be restricted to gamespace but are clearly applicable to it. In that chapter I described how it might be established that within the context of a given space (context C), action X (or actions X_1, X_2, X_3, etc.) counts as Y (something it is permissible to do). On entering the gamespace, one tacitly agrees to abide by the established status functions of that space (this constitutes a much closer analogy to Rachels's games example above).[5] In the case of video games, however, the rules (status functions) may not always be explicitly stated; instead they may be things one discovers as one continues to engage with the gameplay (Tavinor 2008). Alternatively, the gamer may interpret any possible action (i.e. action made possible by the game mechanics) as permitted: "If I can do it, it's allowed". The extent to which possibility equates to permissibility is something the gaming community needs to self-regulate. This is in keeping with the social contract tradition: for moral content/activity and moral authority are each a product of the community's accord. If the community is unable to self-regulate, then this would presumably lead to a lack of social cohesion and harmony, perhaps leading to the ostracizing or even expulsion of the persistent transgressor(s). Where self-regulation does occur, actions that are permitted, even endorsed, may be in marked contrast to those permitted outside the non-gaming space. I illustrated this in Chapter 8 when discussing virtue theory. Fairfield (2008) provides another example with reference to the virtual world of *Eve*: *Eve* is a place where corporate fraud and piracy are part of the fun of the game. Here, acts of deception and the theft of one's virtual assets are permitted under the specifics of this community's social contract. If the status function captured by the idea "fraud is fun" were not in place, and so "were not an implicit norm of the community, the same actions would be treated quite differently" (*ibid.*: 461; see e.g. Strikwerda 2012).

Similarly, and as I discussed in Chapter 4, within the online world of *Sociolotron*, rape is permitted. To reiterate an earlier claim: it is quite plausible that an *a priori* case can be made for why rape and theft/fraud would be detrimental to social cohesion and harmony, and so be viewed as a violation of a hypernorm and therefore outlawed by the social contract tradition. Such POTAs would not be something a community of rational persons would agree to. So why are the equivalent STAs permitted within a gamespace frequented by equally rational persons? Well, given that STAs ≠ POTAs, it does not follow that because POTAs are *a priori* detrimental to social living, STAs would be likewise detrimental to the type of "social living" contingent on gamespace. Accepting the fact that multiplayer gamespace affords the opportunity for actual social interactions, it does not follow from this that all, or in fact *any*, interactions within gamespace are equivalent to social living outside this space.

Given that gamespace is a space of play, it seems perfectly feasible that STAs could be permitted within a community of rational persons, and so form part of an agreed status function in a manner decreed by the social contract tradition. Within this space, moral content would be determined by a community that is itself contingent on the virtual space it occupies and therefore on the virtually embodied nature of its gaming interactions. Moreover, this content would be enforced by the authority bestowed on the community rules (status functions) by the (virtually embodied) community; again, in keeping with social contract tradition. Such local norms – established within the specific social environment of a particular gamespace (be it *Eve* or *Sociolotron*, etc.) – do not contravene actual (offline) hypernorms. Given this, it is my contention that *a priori* claims for selective prohibition based on the social contract tradition are problematic, either because it is not *a priori* apparent that STAs lead to a lack of social cohesion within the virtual community that permits them or that they contravene hypernorms established through the contractarian tradition outside gamespace.

It may be, however, that irrespective of whether STAs are labelled by a particular community as morally good, bad or even amoral, some of its members may nevertheless have difficulty coping psychologically with what they do or see – either within the gamespace itself or, importantly, as they transcend spaces – even when what they do or see is recognized as a form of play (why this might be is discussed in Chs 11 and 12). This being the case, the manner in which this difficulty expresses itself needs to be considered further. Problems in coping may have a detrimental effect on the social cohesion and harmony of the gaming community, in which case either the status function needs to be altered (if agreed) or those members of the community who are having problems with the moral content presumably opt out of engaging in either the STA or the gamespace itself. Now, it may be that a particular member of the community has a problem with a given

STA precisely because they find it morally objectionable, or it may be that they cannot help but find the virtual activity disgusting, and so make moral pronouncements based on sentiment (see Ch. 3). If so, such an objection runs contrary to the moral authority of that space. As such, within the space in which the virtual interaction occurs, the gamer would be unjustified in claiming that the STA is morally wrong, for to do so would be to import a system of morality from outside that space. Alternatively, it may be that they accept its moral permissibility but still find the activity causes them distress or unease (see Whitty *et al.* 2011; see also Richard Bartle's discussion of, and objection to, the act of torture carried out within *World of Warcraft: The Art of Persuasion* on his blog in 2008).

Problems with coping may also impact negatively on the non-gaming community during those occasions when the gamer transcends domains and, owing to her difficulty coping with the disparity between virtual and non-virtual moral freedoms, does something that contravenes the established social contract of non-gamespace, thereby providing grounds for the selective prohibition of STAs. If either of these (or both) proves to be the case then not only is it something that can be established only *a posteriori*, but also it is a matter for psychology to understand and manage, first and foremost, rather than morality. It is therefore the job of psychology to inform what will eventually be decreed as moral judgements concerning selective prohibition and normative gaming content. The point is that moral prohibition, if it is to be established, must occur through an understanding of how individuals cope with STAs, psychologically, rather than by any moral judgement on the rights and wrongs of virtual taboo enactments based on a pre-existing system of morality imported into gamespace from our non-gaming world.

CONCLUSION

Within the social contract tradition, STAs should be understood as a local norm (of gamespace) that does not contravene the hypernorms constitutive of the wider, non-gaming, social contract and, because of this, as also constitutive of a separate social contract drawn up and therefore contingent on the virtually embodied members of the gaming community it serves. The moral authority of this space, established through mutual assent (in the guise of status functions), determines the moral permissibility of STAs within the gaming environment. Any legitimate challenge to the moral authority of this space would, therefore, need to come from within the space – by those members of the community who tacitly agree to abide by its regulations (such that they may decide to alter a particular status function) – or from outside that space *if* it can be shown that the STAs permitted within the space contravene the hypernorms of the wider social contract: a contract which is designed to facilitate more global social cohesion and harmony. If such a challenge (from the wider community) is to be made, then it is my contention that it can only be made based on *a posteriori* evidence – for all *a priori* challenges discussed here have been shown, for various reasons, to be problematic. If such an *a posteriori* challenge is to be established, then it is my view that it must come from psychology.

In Chapter 12 I present the case for psychology as an important arbiter in any attempt to establish normative video games content, and therefore selective prohibition. Before that, however, I present the long overdue response to the question: why would anyone want to do *that*?

ELEVEN

Why would anyone want to do *that*?

The first step towards philosophy is incredulity.
(Denis Diderot, *Last Conversation*)

Recall the fictitious game I introduced in Chapter 7 – *Crazy for Suburbia* – in which white, heterosexual married couples are forced by an intruder (the gamer's character) to perform sexual acts on each other and are then killed. This example could not be said to have incorrigible social meaning for reasons discussed in that chapter, and if it is judged to be worthy of moral prohibition because of its significant social expression (see Ch. 6), then we are left to ponder why the fictitious game *S.H.* (involving random murders) escapes this, or certainly would escape this if currently available games with similar content are anything to go by. A question yet to be considered is why anyone would want to play a game like *Crazy for Suburbia*.

Earlier (in Ch. 6) I noted how Nys (2010) argues that part of the fun of violent games stems from the knowledge that what one is doing is wrong (i.e. such games enable us to enact what would otherwise be prohibited). I assume that the "violating-taboos-equals-fun" factor is therefore part of the *motivation* for playing these games. In addition, I noted how Jansz (2005) argues that violent games provide an arena for psychological exploration; a place where one can engage in STAs free from the moral condemnation (and perhaps even legal constraint) typically associated with POTAs. Here, the gamer can engage in activities designed to elicit certain emotional responses (positive or negative) in a controlled and supposedly safe environment. I also remarked that the question "Why would anyone want to do that?" implies that doing *that* (whatever that may be) is wrong, and therefore that it is wrong to want to do it. When considering the case for selective prohibition, however, one might wish to argue that the onus is on the prosecution (as it were) to establish why it is wrong. An advocate of STAs might argue with some justification that it is not enough to claim that there is nothing morally praiseworthy about engaging in STAs; it must be established that STAs are morally problematic. Following this reasoning, in this chapter, I do not seek to establish what (if anything) is morally praiseworthy about STAs and therefore why *wanting* to engage in *x* is a good thing; rather, I intend only to assess arguments that try to show that *wanting* to engage in *x* is a morally bad thing to do.

BLURRING THE BOUNDARIES BETWEEN FICTION AND REALITY

To begin, I borrow an example from Geert Gooskens (2010), in which a man is watching two actors performing a rape scene. Initially, Gooskens describes a scenario in which the male actor is not *really* sexually aroused by what he is doing; neither is there any intention on his part to humiliate his female acting partner. Through his acting prowess, he makes it appear *as if* he (his character) is a sexually aroused man in the process of raping a woman. For Gooskens, so far so good: there is nothing morally problematic with what is taking place. But then Gooskens alters the scenario slightly. The actor later confides in a friend that when acting out the scene, he discovered that he really felt aroused by what he was doing; the theatrical simulation of rape really turned him on. Gooskens notes that no one was actually harmed in this scene (a point I shall return to) and that the actor has no desire to actually rape someone. Nevertheless, Gooskens maintains, there is something disturbing about his confession; the distinction between the actor and the character he depicts has become too close, blurred even.

For Gooskens, the actor is like the gamer who plays rape games. The unease many of us may feel at the thought of someone playing a rape game is equivalent to the unease felt by the actor's friend: an unease born of the fact that the distinction between actor–character or gamer–avatar has become somewhat nebulous or perhaps collapsed altogether (something Gooskens suggests is the case with those who play rape games, or at least this is what many might intuitively hold to be the case). Importantly, though, Gooskens does not argue that it is ethically wrong *per se* to play rape games; rather, he acknowledges that such activity falls within an ethical grey area. What he does argue is that the actor example explains our intuitive sense of unease at those who play rape games, because of this alleged blurring of boundaries.

Like most analogies, the analogy between the actor and the player-of-rape-games only works to a point. It does what it was intended to do, which is to highlight the intuitive sense we have that the distinction between gamer and avatar has collapsed. However, there is an important difference between the example of the actor being aroused when engaged in his theatrical rape scene and the player of rape games. There *is* a moral issue that has been overlooked in the actor example: an issue that is not relevant to the player of rape games. In simple terms, the job of an actor is to act. Acting involves some form of pretence. But as Howe notes (following the argument of Saltz 1991; see Ch. 1): "[A]ctors do not simply pretend to do actions on stage, but really do actions that *count as* those actions within the conventions of performance" (2008: 571). In acting out Gooskens's rape scene, the actors do not pretend to be involved in a rape as much as they engage in actions designed to convey an act of rape within the context of the play (in this case). Engaging in the type of action that *counts as* rape within a given context requires that whatever behaviour is adopted complies with the agreed conventions of the theatrical performance. Thus Howe continues:

> [T]he responsibility of the actors in such an instance is to carry out the correct performance conventions when prompted by the performance to do so, and this may entail actions that would be highly inappropriate outside the play context. This requires of the actors, not imitation of real actions happening elsewhere, but commitment to really carrying out performance-convention-defined action. (*Ibid.*: 572)

Such are the conventions of acting that, when engaged in the scene, the actor is not meant to feel aroused in the sense described; this ought not to occur. It is certainly something that I am sure his acting partner would find inappropriate. Part of her acting skill is to elicit an emotional response *from the audience*; perhaps sympathy in the case of the rape scene or even sexual arousal if the scene involved actions that *counted as* consensual sex. However, her job is not to elicit this from her acting partner. Conversely, she would not consider it appropriate for her acting partner to use her as a means to that end: namely, eliciting his own sexual arousal during the rape enactment (see also Ch. 4 and Kant's concern about using another as a means to an end). In short, the actor example raises the moral issue of exploitation of the other person; something that is absent in the case of rape games because either (a) the "rape" victim is computer generated or (b), in a multiplayer space such as *Sociolotron*, the "rape" victim acknowledges the permissibility of virtual rape within that space, and presumably the potential for elicited arousal (see Chs 4 and 10).[1]

The normative position within the context of acting (even if it is only tacitly understood to be the case) is that one ought not to use one's fellow actor (*qua* actor) as a means of eliciting sexual arousal. In the example of rape games, there is no tacit agreement that this should not be the case. Nevertheless, the intuitive sense of unease often talked about when discussing these games (as highlighted by Gooskens) is that it should not be the case that one is able to elicit sexual arousal from these gameplays and therefore from what one enacts within them. As Gooskens notes: It is "'better' not to entertain these feelings" (2010: 75); and as this seems to be the purpose of games such as *RapeLay* (the opponent of such games might claim) then, in light of this, one can propose a reason for why such games should no longer continue to exist.

ON THE ISSUE OF VIRTUAL PAEDOPHILIA

The problem the above argument faces is how to move beyond an intuitive sense that one should not elicit sexual arousal from STAs such as rape towards a more rigorous defence of this position. In the case of virtual rape, one could argue, as Patridge does (Ch. 7), that it has incorrigible social meaning and so is morally problematic for that reason. However, the problem with Patridge's argument, as we have seen, is that it charges the player of the rape game with being guilty only of insensitivity. The opponent of rape games seems to seek a reason for prohibition beyond having shown insensitivity to those who were once oppressed. What he may want to claim is that being sexually aroused through the virtual enactment of rape is evidence of a flawed character (see McCormick 2001). Let us consider this claim further. It is not clear why the person has a "flawed" character because they find *virtual* rape sexually arousing; but given that opponents seek to label one's character "flawed", why is having this (alleged) character flaw a problem? After considering various moral positions on the question of STAs in previous chapters, and finding each in its own way problematic, it would seem that if it is a problem it is not unique to virtual rape and, therefore, in the case of rape, it is a problem *only* if it then leads to a desire to engage in *actual* rape, and even more of a problem if it leads to the fulfilment of this desire. Whether this is the case is an empirical question that we are presently unable to answer (see Ch. 5; it is also a point I shall return to briefly below). Thus, however strong our intuition may be, we cannot say that it is a problem *because* it leads to the desire to engage in actual rape. To illustrate why not, when Bryant Paul and Daniel Linz (2008: 35) exposed adults to "barely legal"[2] pornography in order to test assumptions made by the US government in defence of the Child Pornography Protection Act (CPPA) of 1996 – "that virtual child pornography stimulates and whets adults' appetites for sex with children and that such content can result in the sexual abuse or exploitation of minors becoming acceptable to and even preferred by the viewer" – they found that although those who viewed the material were more likely to cognitively associate sexual activity to non-sexual images of minors (based on response latency), there was no evidence that exposure caused participants to be more accepting of child pornography or paedophilia.[3] Extrapolating from what we do know, then, why should we conclude that those who engage in virtual rape or paedophilia or bestiality (etc.) would think/feel/behave in a way congruent with their virtual enactments *when outside the specific gamespace*?[4]

Ignoring the fact that virtual paedophilia is illegal in some countries, including the UK, would the enactment of child sex be any more morally acceptable if the intention of the gameplay was *not* to elicit sexual arousal in the gamer? To explain: consider the video game *BioShock* (mentioned briefly in Chs 1 and 2). In this game it is possible (although not compulsory) to "harvest" – that is kill – creatures called Little Sisters (for the sake of brevity, I shall omit the reason why). These creatures resemble young girls. Presumably, there is no intention on the part of the game designer to elicit arousal, sexual or otherwise, through enacting their murder. There is certainly no evidence of an increase in the desire to "harvest" young girls for real as a result of this game. Suppose, then, that a fictitious game is available whereby, in order to appease the gods, who bestow additional life energy (power) on to one's character, one can engage in paedophilic activities with the captured children of one's enemy. One is not *required* to do this, but it is a way to increase one's energy/power and so increase one's chances of winning the game (see Young in press).[5] Is it *necessarily* the case that, if one chooses to engage in this activity, one is going to be sexually aroused and/or of flawed character? (Recall the discussion in Ch. 9 on the hypothetical imperative.) Perhaps one remains sufficiently detached from what the virtual enactment represents and views it simply as a means of winning the game (see Ch. 12 for the research by Klimmt *et al.* [2006, 2008] on how gamers morally manage their virtual activities), or perhaps one becomes the architect of one's own disgust (as Jansz might say). Possibly. However, consider Morgan Luck's comments:

> A player may enjoy a computer game because, for example, it satisfies her competitive nature, not because it allows her to commit acts of virtual murder *per se*. If this were true, then

virtual murder may not result in the same type of self harm as virtual paedophilia. This in turn may explain why virtual murder is usually considered morally permissible, whilst virtual paedophilia is not.   (2009: 34)

What Luck is acknowledging here is the intuitively compelling position that those who engage in virtual paedophilia must do so because they find the thought of paedophilia enjoyable, rather than for purely competitive reasons. Conversely, players who virtually murder do not necessarily do so because they enjoy the thought of actual murder or wish to engage in such activity for real. However, contrary to this intuitive appeal, if one is *not* sexually aroused or motivated to be sexually aroused by paedophilia or merely the idea of it, then, morally, how is the task afforded the gamer in my fictitious example any different from that afforded the player in *BioShock*? If one type of STA is permitted – the virtual murder of young girls – then should we not permit the other? If, on the other hand, one is sexually aroused as a result of the activity permitted within my fictitious game, then what moral difference does (or should) this make?

In considering this example further, let us compare virtual murder (murder$_v$) with virtual paedophilia (paedophilia$_v$) in more detail. Suppose:

(i)   I engage in murder$_v$ as a means to an end: it helps me progress through the game.
(ii) I engage in murder$_v$ because it is fun, irrespective of whether it helps me progress through the game.
(iii) I engage in paedophilia$_v$ as a means to an end: it helps me progress through the game.
(iv) I engage in paedophilia$_v$ because it is fun, irrespective of whether it helps me progress through the game.

Consider statements (i) and (iii). These provide equivalent reasons for engaging in the virtual activity. If we consider (i) morally acceptable (or not) then we have to consider (iii) likewise morally acceptable (or not). Based on the moral theories presented throughout this book, there is no cogent *a priori* reason to discriminate between them. If a reason is to be provided then it must be established *a posteriori*, perhaps based on the negative consequences of engaging in one compared to the other. To date, and bearing in mind the paucity of research in this area, there is no evidence to justify such discrimination. Does this mean that the same conclusion must be drawn regarding (ii) and (iv)? On the face of it, I would say, yes. However, let us consider the notion of "fun" a bit more to see if we can discriminate between the two statements on the grounds that there may be differences in what this entails in each case.[6]

First, as already noted, for some, these two virtual activities (or similar) are fun things to engage in because they are wrong, in so far as they represent acts that are considered wrong (taboo) in non-gaming space. If one's motivation is simply to enact transgressions virtually in a place where it is safe to do so, then where is the harm? This is a topic we have covered already. The *a priori* argument from extended analogy – from animals-to-humans to avatar-to-humans – discussed in relation to Kant (Ch. 4), to the effect that one fails in one's duty to oneself and so harms oneself, was shown to be weak. Ultimately, then, saying that it is not safe to engage in STAs because one harms oneself and potentially goes on to harm others is an empirical question yet to be addressed with appropriate and sufficient evidence. All that can be said at this stage is that evidence regarding a relationship between virtual violence (e.g. murder$_v$) and increased antisocial behaviour is inconclusive. This being the case, why should there be a relationship between other STAs and their corresponding POTAs? Is there something different about the "fun" elicited in the case of murder$_v$ compared to paedophilia$_v$ (for example) that would make the case for suspecting a relationship between this latter STA and its corresponding POTA?

Suppose that one derives a sense of "fun" from the act of paedophilia$_v$ described in the fictitious game above because one is sexually aroused by it. After all, may come the retort, actual paedophilia (paedophilia$_a$) elicits this type of arousal from the paedophile. Equally, murder$_a$ typically elicits arousal (although not typically sexual), or at least the circumstances leading up to the murder$_a$ do (contract killing aside). Does this mean that those who engage in murder$_v$ experience the same type of arousal (thrill, perhaps) as those who commit murder$_a$? Of course, I imagine that not all murders$_a$ elicit arousal that one (even the perpetrator) might describe as thrilling. That issue aside, however, might there ever be an occasion (based on the technology available to us presently) when the arousal elicited during murder$_v$ is equivalent to murder$_a$?[7] The fact that one knows it is a fiction would suggest not (see Young 2010). However, this is ultimately an empirical question that has not been (and for ethical reasons cannot be) tested.

If one can experience murder$_v$ without experiencing the level of arousal/ emotion typically felt during an actual murder, then why should this not be possible in the case of paedophilia$_v$? Perhaps the level of arousal is not equivalent in either virtual case to its non-virtual counterpart but, nevertheless, arousal is induced because of what the virtual act represents: paedophilia$_a$ or murder$_a$. This arousal may be pleasurable. For the sake of argument, let us say that this is the case: that a degree of pleasurable arousal is elicited by these acts because of what they represent.

It may be, however, that opponents would want to claim that what this scenario highlights is someone who is motivated to play the game – that is, *this* game and not some other – precisely because of what *this* game's interaction represents. If this is the case, then is the gamer wrong to *desire* to play this game *because* of what it represents? Again, we are faced with the same problem of justifying discrimination. If what each game represents is a POTA (as is the case here) then how can we allow one but not the other? Equally, if the gamer is judged to be morally wrong for desiring to play a game involving murder$_v$ or paedophilia$_v$ because of what each respective action represents, then if he is morally wrong in one situation, that person must be morally wrong in the other.

But wait. What does it mean to desire to play the game because of what it represents? What is being represented that the gamer is attracted to? Is the gamer's desire to play the game and the pleasure elicited from the enactment based on the fact that he is engaging in a virtual simulation of a taboo activity (a POTA) because it is a *taboo* activity? In other words, is it not that the fun stems from the fact that what is being enacted is taboo, irrespective of the particulars of the act itself? The appeal of the activity is not, therefore, to enact murder$_a$ or paedophilia$_a$ *per se*, but to enact something taboo, and typically within the context of the gaming narrative.[8] Of course, individual gamers may prefer to enact certain taboos over others (see Ch. 12). Nevertheless, consider the following:

(a) Gamer M desires to engage in murder$_v$ because this activity represents something which is taboo.

(b) Gamer M* desires to engage in murder$_v$ because this activity represents murder$_a$, something she has a desire to do.

(c) Gamer P desires to engage in paedophilia$_v$ because this activity represents something which is taboo.

(d) Gamer P* desires to engage in paedophilia$_v$ because this activity represents paedophilia$_a$, something he has a desire to do.

In the case of (a) and (c), each gamer (M and P) has a desire to engage in a virtual taboo activity because it represents that which is taboo. The object of their desire, and therefore their motivation, is the enactment of something that in the actual world is morally and, in this case, legally prohibited. However, in the case of (b) and (d), each gamer (M* and P*) desires to engage in a particular activity, irrespective of the fact that it is taboo. The typical paedophile does not engage in this activity because it is *taboo*, but because it is what they desire to do. Typically, the same can be said for the murderer.

If one desires to engage in a virtual activity (STA) as a vicarious means of satisfying one's desire to engage in the real thing (POTA), then there seem to be two issues here. First, should STAs be prohibited because they potentially enable those with a desire to engage in POTAs to vicariously satisfy this desire? Second, is it morally problematic to entertain the desire to commit POTAs? The second point is beyond the scope of this book to discuss, as I

am concerned with the virtual enactments of taboos and the selective prohibition of video game content. All I will say is that such a desire would
fall foul of Kant's second formulation of the categorical imperative, as such
an individual would have a desire to treat another as a means to an end
only. As for the first point, someone from, say, a consequentialist perspective may consider that vicariously satisfying one's desire virtually may serve
the greater good: if one could guarantee that the fulfilment of this desire was
restricted to the virtual realm, involving computer-generated characters or
avatars controlled only by adults who accept the status function of the STA's
permissibility. Alternatively, if one sought to prohibit games involving STAs
because they might attract those with a desire to engage in the corresponding POTA, then it would seem that all STAs would have to be prohibited.

Alternatively, if one wished to be selective by arguing that a game involving the virtual enactment of paedophilia (similar to that described above)
would be a magnet to already existing paedophiles or that it might be construed as endorsing its acceptability, by way of a retort, one might ask: are
the games that are available today magnets for already existing murderers,
muggers, torturers, rapists or general thugs? Would only a racist wish to
play the game *R.A.C.I.S.T.*? I have already established that this need not be
the case, and also that those who wish to selectively prohibit certain STAs
(such as racism) must do more than claim that there is nothing good in
playing such a game; they must identify the bad. At best, incorrigible social
meaning only establishes that the gamer motivated to play *R.A.C.I.S.T.* (for
example) shows poor taste and insensitivity, not a flawed character. Perhaps
a similar charge might be put to the player of the hypothetical chess game I
introduced in Chapter 2, in which the act of "taking" one's opponent's piece
is represented in extremely graphic ways. Furthermore, in terms of allegedly
endorsing acceptability, if the answer is yes, then should not all STAs be
morally prohibited, or at least those not adhering to the principles of sanctioned equivalence? If the answer is no then on what moral grounds do we
justify the *selective* moral prohibition of video game content?

As a final point on player motivation, suppose one has a desire only to
enact a taboo (as described above) and decides to play a game in which it
is possible to engage in paedophilia, (again, similar to the game described
above). Suppose one becomes sexually aroused by the enactment within the
game. If this is the case, we still require empirical evidence supporting the
hypothesis that there is a causal connection between this type of arousal
(in someone without previous paedophilic desires) and the sexual arousal
evident in paedophiles to justify any appeal for its moral prohibition. To
say that a paedophile could be vicariously satisfied by virtual paedophilic
activity is not equivalent to saying that someone sexually aroused by this
particular STA would then commit an act of paedophilia. Again, we could
argue that as no such evidence has been found showing an increase in the

desire to kill young children based on the gameplay available in *BioShock*, why then, *mutatis mutandis*, should an unprecedented increase in the corresponding POTA be expected as a result of enacting the virtual paedophilia depicted in my fictitious game? One might wish to appeal to the presence of sexual arousal in the fictitious example, which is (I am assuming) absent in the *BioShock* example: that somehow this is sufficient to elicit the desire to engage in actual paedophilic activities. However, and to reiterate, in the absence of empirical evidence, as intuitively compelling as this may be (to some), it is still mere conjecture.

CONCLUSION

The sense of unease many of us feel towards games involving virtual rape or even fictitious games involving virtual paedophilia, which drives our moral intuition, and which Gooskens (2010) argues involves a blurring of the boundary between the actual world and gamespace, stems from an uncertainty over player motivation, resulting in the question: why would anyone want to do that? There may also be a strong sense of incredulity, such that it is difficult to believe that someone could play a game involving virtual rape or paedophilia without harbouring the desire to engage in the act for real. Consequently, playing such a game is seen by opponents as evidence that these gamers are somehow morally flawed; that there is "something wrong with them".

A closer analysis of player motivation reveals that it is difficult to discriminate, in terms of selective prohibition, murder$_v$ from paedophilia$_v$ (for example) based on what the player desires: so much so that one must either permit both or prohibit both (see Young in press for a detailed discussion). The only way to distinguish between different player motivations (if one is motivated to engage in an STA rather than just play/win the game *per se*) is to consider whether the player wishes to engage in a virtual activity because it represents a *taboo* activity (something prohibited outside gamespace) or whether the player desires to engage in a virtual activity because it represents a pre-existing desire that happens to be taboo. In the latter case, the desire to engage in the actual (taboo) activity exists already. The moral issue, therefore, concerns the desire to enact the STA, because although it symbolizes something that is taboo, it is not enacted simply *because* it is taboo, but because it represents that which is desired (outside gamespace) that happens to be taboo.

In the next chapter, I consider the identity relation that exists between gamers and their avatars, the manner in which they interpret their virtual interactions and other ways they manage their STAs by drawing on empirical evidence detailing the kinds of strategies players adopt to enable successful gaming to occur, where success requires virtually enacting something that is morally prohibited outside gamespace. I do this in order to present a case for the importance of psychology rather than morality when deciding on the criteria for the selective prohibition of video game content. To be clear, it is not my intention to present a particular (established) psychological theory or model that can then be applied to gamespace. Instead, in the next chapter, I present an argument for why psychology is better suited to inform the question of prohibition than morality, and subsequently why decisions about the prohibition of video game content should be based on psychological research rather than moral theories borne outside the virtual space of play. I therefore seek to move away from prohibitive decision-making framed around whether x is morally good or bad towards criteria that take into account whether engaging in x is something that is psychologically manageable. Whether one should selectively prohibit video game content and which, if any, should be prohibited is therefore a question psychology is best suited to answer, not morality.

TWELVE

Coping with virtual taboos

In play, although one *really* plays, in an important sense what one does is also hypothetical: for "what one discovers (if one does) is what it is like to *play at* being X; one does not become X – necessarily". (Howe 2008: 570, original emphasis)

This chapter is concerned not with the morality of STAs but with their psychological impact. How do we cope, psychologically, with the moral freedoms afforded by acts of play, particularly those involving STAs? When we play at X (to borrow Howe's phrase), where X involves some form of STA, how do we manage the reality of this hypothetical? Put another way: how do I cope with the fact that *I* am enacting *this* taboo, be it assault, murder, torture, rape or paedophilia? In addition, how do we manage the *transition* across spaces with potentially different, perhaps incommensurate, moral freedoms; in other words, with the fact that we are able to move in and out of realms in which what is permitted to be done and, importantly, what *I* do can be radically different?[1]

In playing at being X, Howe holds the intuitive view that we do not become X, necessarily; however, there is also a sense in which the possibility of becoming X is not negated by the fact that what one does, initially at least, is merely play at being X. In not negating this possibility, one is left to consider who might be more vulnerable to becoming X, through the act of play, where becoming X involves being the sort of person who would enjoy the activities represented by STAs: namely, POTAs. Or even if one does not become X (in the way described), might the particulars of the play – engaging in STAs – because they are incompatible with the morality of non-gamespace, nevertheless have a potentially negative impact on our psychology and therefore on how we behave, morally (that is, behave within a society that endorses a particular moral system)?

Such questions have a bearing on the view, introduced in Chapter 9 and developed further here, that the selective prohibition of video game content should be based on whether certain activities are psychologically manageable or not. In other words, the permissibility of content should be based on the extent to which we are able to indulge certain moral freedoms (enact STAs) within gamespace in the absence of problems when reverting back to our non-gaming system of morality when engaging in behaviour outside the game. The potential difficulty with the transition from gaming to non-gaming environments, and therefore with reverting back to a previously adhered-to system of morality, is better understood, I contend, through further detailed research on psychological coping. Part of understanding the psychology of the gamer involves recognizing that the gamer, for her part, understands that what she is doing is *symbolically* violating socially accepted taboos and therefore virtually *enacting* some form of immoral, if not illegal, activity: or at least being given the opportunity (required, even) to do this. Accepting this, however, does not necessitate that what the gamer is doing (or being given the opportunity to do) is itself morally wrong. Therefore, prohibition should not stem from moral objections to the virtual content or how one interacts with it (as I hope to have shown) but, rather, from an understanding of psychology. The fact that the gamer recognizes that what they are doing is symbolically violating taboos may impact on how they manage this activity and, therefore, how they interpret and hence morally and psychologically cope with their own virtual actions. This information can then be used to inform questions on selective prohibition.

Even if a player acknowledges that virtual violence and other STAs are "not real", and so recognizes that STAs ≠ POTAs, this fact does not negate the possibility that this same player will nevertheless respond to representations in a moral way (Hartmann *et al.* 2010). Neither does it mean that they will not differentiate between certain types of violence or other STAs (the death of a virtual child, say, compared to a zombie or gangster). However, as we saw in Chapter 3, when considering disgust as a measure of moral wisdom, the fact that an individual may respond in this way or differentiate between different types of prohibited action when played out virtually does not mean that such moral responses are themselves morally justified, or that they count as evidence for the moral inappropriateness of the content in question. This being the case, what it does suggest (when a player feels disgust, irritation or guilt over the virtual act) is "that the killing of video game characters is accompanied by more intense social and moral responses than the 'killing' of chess figures" (Hartmann *et al.* 2010: 341). Thus, it may be that some players perceive the "taking out" of a human character within a game through a lens of social and moral convention that is absent in the case of one chess piece "taking" another (see also Hartmann 2011).

For Hartmann (2011), how gamers experience virtual violence may depend on which type of processing – either rational or experiential (Epstein 1994) – is more prominent during a particular interaction. Rational processing may obviate a sense of guilt or help quell one's disgust at the gory spectacle that occurs when one dispatches an innocent bystander within the game, because it enables the gamer to understand that what she has just done is not real. Those more prone to experiential processing, however, may still react physiologically to the virtual violence in ways analogous (although no doubt in milder form) to how one might anticipate reacting (and so feeling) if the violence were real. For some, the fact that such social and moral conventions are represented and quite probably violated within the gameplay no doubt adds to the enjoyment (Nys 2010); conversely, for others, it may elicit disgust, irritation or guilt in a way that is not expected or required when playing chess.[2] In fact, the cognitive effort needed to keep reminding oneself that what one is doing is "just a game" – and so maintain a sense of detachment – could diminish one's enjoyment altogether (Hartmann *et al.* 2010).

When considering how gamers construe the object of violence, suppose some construe the violation of an avatar in a manner different from, say, the "taking" of a queen by a knight in a game of chess, the former being *viewed* as more morally objectionable than the latter. Just because each act is construed differently – and may even elicit a different reaction from the perpetrator (a sense of guilt, perhaps, in the former case) – does this mean that *we* should bestow on each act a different moral value? And what of those who construe the taking of a chess piece and the violation of an avatar in the same morally inoffensive way: must we conclude that they are morally wrong to do so? Perhaps we should simply acknowledge that although the agent attributes a different moral significance to her actions in virtue of how she reacts to them, this is not sufficient to warrant, let alone establish, a moral ruling.

A lack of psychological detachment in virtue of one's propensity for experiential rather than rational processing has been posited both as a means of facilitating enjoyment (Csikszentmihalyi 1991) and as a contributory factor in explaining why some gamers express the same kinds of social and moral responses to STAs as convention dictates we express in the face of POTAs. Certainly, part of the fun of virtual violence, as already discussed (and I include STAs in this), is that it is "immoral" (*qua* represents that which is immoral); although, as noted above, I accept that not all gamers find all STAs equally appealing. But if one finds it fun to exterminate a group of mutant humanoids in a futuristic world but does not find the thought of massacring hostages in an airport appealing, what does this tell us about the morality of these acts? The way these activities are construed will probably be different for different gamers, but to base moral judgements on what are effectively construals and/or feelings of approbation or disapprobation is to leave oneself vulnerable to a charge of moral dumbfounding (as noted in Ch. 3). As such, although an individual's construal of the particulars of their symbolic enactment may not determine the morality of the activity itself (although see Chs 6 and 7 for a detailed discussion on this point), it may nevertheless affect how they psychologically cope with the disparity between their behaviour within the game and how they interact outside it. This being the case, as a means of judging the *morality* of what one does, despite being psychologically informative, such responses to STAs are nevertheless misleading.

With this in mind, recall from Chapter 8 how Sicart (2009) argues that only those gamers who have developed their ethical reasoning sufficiently will be able to resist the alleged corrupting influence of the "unethical" practices evident in some gameplays, which are feared by virtue theorists to lead to a non-virtuous life. Through their developed ethical reasoning, the morally mature gamer understands that the symbolism is *context*-dependent. However, is an understanding of the contingent relation between a particular moral system and a particular means of interacting and representing enough to avoid the potentially detrimental effects of these altered contingencies on the individual who transcends spaces? Perhaps subserving Sicart's morally mature gamer is a more fundamental psychological process that is affected by the types of interactions afforded by gameplays, not least "unethical" gameplays, and therefore by the potential discrepancy between the moral freedoms afforded within gaming and non-gaming spaces. If so, might this psychological process better explain how we cope (or not) when moving from one space to another? Further, might it explain the potentially positive or negative effects of morally neutral discrepancies between spaces (e.g. being able to fly or change form) as well as those brought about as a result of symbolizing moral extremes in the form of STAs? The possibility of this more fundamental psychological process is something I intend to explore here, in the hope that it will help direct our thinking away from traditional moral theories towards a more effective role for psychology.

Switching from morality to psychology allows that individual STAs can be selectively prohibited on psychological rather than moral grounds. This avoids the problem of how to justify morally the fact that certain STAs are currently permitted and others are not, or are more severely condemned than others, especially given that the activities they represent (POTAs) are uniformly outlawed. If engaging with certain content can be shown to be psychologically damaging (to some, at least), then perhaps we have the basis for selective prohibition that does not require that we adopt a particular moral stance or employ it uniformly across all STAs. The fact that STAs represent activities that are all morally and legally proscribed in our actual world makes the *selective* prohibition of STAs problematic on moral grounds, but the extent to which different STAs have a negative effect on the psychological make-up of individuals is not bound by the same relation that STAs have with POTAs. Irrespective of the uniformly outlawed state of POTAs, the psychological impact of violating these, virtually, need not be uniform and so need not be treated uniformly in the case of judging STAs. Effectively, then, in the absence of a cogent moral argument for selective prohibition, I turn to psychology.

The psychological process I am proposing here (see also Young & Whitty 2012) is morally neutral, but has implications for moral systems such as virtue ethics and the development of the virtuous being (to borrow the phrase from Sicart [2009]) or how we morally manage our virtual actions (see below). The process involves achieving and maintaining *psychological parity*. As part of the continued exploration of the potential psychological impact of engaging in STAs, and therefore the role of psychological parity in this, I consider the issue of moral management: that is, how gamers *interpret* their activities (what meaning the virtual act has for them) and the extent to which they identify with the virtual character carrying out the virtual act.

MORAL MANAGEMENT

> If players are treated only as something affected by games, we miss the way they shape their own gaming experience. Given the medium's interactivity and the myriad interpretations games are open to, such reductionism would lead to an impoverished view of gaming.   (Schulzke 2011: 53)

The way in which gamers cope with violent gameplay is referred to by Klimmt *et al.* (2008) as *moral management*. Moral management, in part, involves cognitively managing the conflict that potentially arises within the gamer between enjoying the gameplay and any aversion they may have towards the violence represented and even virtually engaged in. Moreover, according to Klimmt *et al.* (2006), the same mechanisms of *moral disengagement* (Bandura 2002) found within perpetrators of real-life violence are often found at work within many individuals who play violent video games (e.g. the dehumanization of game characters and the use of euphemistic labelling). As Klimmt *et al.* note:

> [F]indings support the proposition that dealing with moral issues is a cognitive task that players of violent video games have to resolve in order to maintain or enhance their entertainment experience. Therefore, the players' ways to deal with game violence display some similarities to individuals who perform aggressive behavior in real life. (2006: 325)

In support of moral management, Klimmt *et al.* (*ibid.*) interviewed ten players of violent video games, asking them to discuss their thoughts and feelings about playing their favourite games, particularly with a mind to the types of strategies used to cope with the violent behaviour and any moral concerns they may have with this. For some, engaging in moral management was relatively easy because their moral concern was low, matching closely the sentiment of the amoralist declaration "It's just a game" (see below). Of particular interest, however, is their identification of the themes *Game violence as self-defence* (in which gamers justify their actions in terms of "kill or be killed") and *Fighting evil: narrative-normative justification of game violence* (whereby the game narrative positions them as fighting evil). Each of these themes, I would argue, is compatible with the principle of sanctioned equivalence introduced in Chapter 6.

To maintain an identity as "morally virtuous" or as simply "one of the good guys", the gamer may seek to justify their violent acts within the context of the game's pre-determined narrative. The principle of sanctioned equivalence holds that this is much easier to do when violent acts have sanctioned equivalents such as legitimate killing of the enemy or in self-defence, or even if cannibalism is equated with the restoration of health. In the case of torture, again, this may be legitimized as self-defence (of a nation); extracting information by any means necessary will save lives in a "ticking-bomb" scenario, for example. Where there is no sanctioned equivalence (e.g. cases of virtual rape, paedophilia, necrophilia or incest), identifying oneself as virtuous will, no doubt, be much harder to justify (see Hartmann *et al.* 2010; Whitty *et al.* 2011). For some, this may be reason enough not to engage in the activity, either by simply not playing the game or by choosing to avoid that particular possibility within the gameplay (should the game mechanics allow for other options, of course).[3]

For others, however, moral management may simply involve other ways of coping, which, by not adhering to the principle of sanctioned equivalence, allows for more "moral flexibility". Klimmt *et al.* identified further themes that give some insight into what these other coping strategies may be: namely, *Game-reality distinction* (it's just a game and therefore not real) and *Game violence as necessary part of (sports-like) performance* (the nature of the game is such that aggressive action is necessary to win). Gamers who justified their actions within the game with reference to these strategies report thinking of game violence as morally irrelevant or, because it is just a game, as not having any *real* consequences. Within the game, however, such violence was often thought of as a necessary part of winning. Leo Sang-min Whang and Geunyoung Chang (2004: 595) categorized gamers who adopted this type of approach as *off-real world players*. These players are said to "use every possible means to achieve personal success inside the game world", including harming other players, even though they would not do this in the actual world (recall discussion in Ch. 9 on ethical egoism and Kant's hypothetical imperative). Related to this point, Akiko Shibuya *et al.* state: "Players in video games may have few chances to be sympathetic toward victims because players need to win the battle and continue the game" (2008: 536).

Recently, Tilo Hartmann and Peter Vorderer (2010) have argued that violent games often provide moral disengagement cues that enable the gamer to automatically separate their violent actions from their own internalized moral standards.[4] The unrealistic and "fantasy" appearance of the violence, for example, may reinforce the view that it is just a game and therefore not real or clearly unrepresentative of real-life violence (Whitty *et al.* 2011). If these disengagement cues fail, however, Hartmann and Vorderer tell us, it may be that the gamer has to adopt a more reflective strategy of moral management in order to continue enjoying the game: a strategy perhaps in keeping with the principle of sanctioned equivalence noted above.

Sabine Glock and Julia Kneer, when commenting on the findings of a study by Manuel Ladas (2003), note how gamers seemed "to focus on competition, success, thrill, and the virtual simulation of power and control rather than damaging other persons" (2009: 153). Glock and Kneer consider this way of thinking about the game (notably, *not* in saliently aggressive terms) to be suggestive of the existence of *differentiated knowledge structures* in those with prolonged violent game exposure when compared to novice gamers. It may be, they surmise, that novice players associate violent video games with aggression because of media coverage to that effect;[5] however, through "repeated exposure to violent digital games, links to game-specific concepts are strengthened, thereby overrunning [media-related] associations to aggression" (*ibid.*). For Ben DeVane and Kurt Squire, the idea that prolonged engagement with video game violence may actually lead to reduced aggression (see Sherry 2001; also Ch. 5) suggests that experienced players "develop metacognitive understandings of how violence is represented" (2008: 267) within the game: namely, as instrumental to the success of the game, or even as immersed within a narrative that extols the principle of sanctioned equivalence (for example).

Recently, Paul Adachi and Teena Willoughby (2011) found that competition rather than violent content produced greater short-term increases in aggressive behaviour (in a sample of undergraduate students), suggesting that virtual violence may be less influential in elevating aggression than some had previously believed (e.g. Anderson *et al.* 2010). DeVane and Squire go on to note that the meaning players derived from interaction with various media (such as violent video games) must be contextualized. In other words, for researchers to understand the meaning of seemingly or symbolically violent interaction, they must understand what these interactions are taken to mean by those who engaged in them within the context in which they occur. As such, René Weber *et al.* (2009) found marked variation in how gamers respond to violent content in first-person shooter games. When discussing their findings, they make two important points. The first concerns questioning the extent to which a player's aggressive reactions can be traced back to a specific violent episode within the game, or whether the overall context of violence or the "dramaturgy" of game-playing explains their behaviour. Following this, they highlight the importance of studying video games within the context of their interactive gameplays. For as Weber *et al.* conclude: "Due to this unique characteristic, every player creates his or her own specific content that may moderate potentially harmful effects" (*ibid.*: 1033). In support of this idea, Malliet found, when interviewing moderate to heavy video game players, that they "tended to be sceptical towards looking at games as a source of information about reality" (2006: 383), adding that it was not the purpose of games to be realistic.

On the face of it, the meaning of virtual interactions has clear links to types of actual engagement. After all, STAs are meant to *represent* POTAs; they are understood to play this symbolic role within the gameplay and overall narrative. On the other hand, according to Glock and Kneer, and DeVane and Squire, violent acts are not really taken by many gamers to be violent in and of themselves: there occurs what Pasquinelli (2010) identifies as *perceivable discontinuity* between the actual and symbolic act. Gamers may use terms such as "kill" or "assault" when describing certain virtual actions, but the act of virtually killing or assaulting typically seems to be playing a functional role within the game: instrumental to the act of achieving a successful outcome (as was discussed in Ch. 9). Part of that successful outcome may involve maintaining or even enhancing social ties; certainly, it may involve some form of social engagement. In fact, in their survey on gamer characteristics, Jeroen Jansz and Martin Tanis (2007) reported that motivation based on social interaction was the strongest predictor of time spent playing the game. Thus, Juul notes: "The conflict of a game is not antisocial; rather it provides a context for human interaction" (2005: 19). He then continues:

> Controlling a character that hits a character controlled by another player does not mean that one wants to attack that other

person in real life: It means that one enters a complex world of symbolic interactions where attacking someone in a game can be an invitation to friendship, and helping someone in the same game can be a condescending rejection.   (*Ibid.*)

The relationship that holds between gamer and gaming character may also contribute to the psychological investment one makes within the game: towards one's character, others and how one perceives the events unfolding within the gameplay. The way the events unfold will, of course, in part be a response to the choices one makes within the game, which are themselves guided by how one perceives one's character, one's relation to that character and others. Kirstie Farrar *et al.* (2006) reported that gamers who played from a first-person perspective felt less involved in the game than when playing from a third-person perspective in which they could see their avatar. The authors suggest that this is counter-intuitive but surmise that first-person play may be perceived as "no-person" play, owing to the lack of personal avatar presence on the screen. Farrar *et al.* also reported that in a "blood condition" (presence of blood), players found the game to be gorier than the no-blood condition (as one might expect) and also that in the blood condition they behaved more aggressively during the game. This, they speculate, may be because the blood is perceived as a reward for success rather than as a consequence of a violent outcome (see also Przybylski *et al.* 2010). Such a view seems compatible with gamer interpretations reported above, and also with an earlier claim made by Adachi and Willoughby (2011) that it is competition rather than violence that increases aggression (in this case, within the game itself).

PSYCHOLOGICAL PARITY AND PLAYER IDENTIFICATION

Within gamespace, the context in which STAs occur is meant to be playful. Psychological parity amounts to one's sense of continuity of self as one transcends this playful space and the non-gaming world. When playing a game in virtual space, it is undoubtedly *I* who plays, but to what extent do I commit the STA or become the victim of this virtual activity? In other words, do I see myself as playing a game in which STAs occur – in which I am able to manipulate virtual characters to perform these actions – or do *I* engage in STAs? In short, what is the extent of player identification with the virtual protagonist and what is the significance of this, psychologically, particularly in relation to STAs, as one transcends these disparate domains?

With the advent of video game technology, not only has the relationship between audience (or gamer) and media become more (inter)active, but the distinction between gamer and character (protagonist) has been reduced, perhaps even eliminated (see Cohen 2001 for a detailed discussion). As Tom Boellstorf notes within the context of multiplayer spaces such as *Second Life*: avatars "make virtual worlds real, not actual; they are a position from which the self encounters the virtual" (2008: 129). The virtual world is, for Boellstorf, as real as the actual world; it just happens that one's access to this reality is mediated by one's avatar.[6] Klimmt *et al.* likewise have this to say:

> Instead of providing opportunities to follow autonomous characters' actions, playing video games simulates the circumstances of *being* a media character (or holding a social role), for instance, of being a war hero or a police officer. Video games thus seem to facilitate a nondyadic or *monadic* user-character relationship in the sense that players do not perceive the game (main) character as a social entity distinct from themselves, but experience a merging of their own self and the game protagonist. This understanding of a monadic user-character relationship converges with the concept of *identification*.   (2009: 354, original emphasis)

Identification is expressed by Klimmt *et al.* as a set of increased associations between the gamer's self-concept and certain attributes that contingently characterize the online protagonist (e.g. courage, agility, honour, charisma, social status and physical and sexual prowess). In addition, identification is typically defined as a *temporary* state of emotional and cognitive connection with the character (Oatley 1999). As Klimmt *et al.* explain:

> For most people, their image of themselves under the condition of identification with James Bond [for example] would differ substantially from their usual self-image. After game exposure, internal processes (e.g., cognitions about the working day) and external cues (e.g., friends addressing the media user by his/her real name instead of saying "007") will quickly realter the situational self-concept toward the original configuration.
>
> (2009: 356)

Typically one's self-concept (and, as part of that, one's self-image) differs substantially from the protagonist featured in video games, especially violent ones; and, typically, on exiting the game, one's original self-image is restored and is no longer aligned with, say, "007" or perhaps even, Jack, the protagonist from *Madworld* (etc.).[7] Nevertheless, it is my contention that for those gamers whose identity merges strongly with their gameworld character, the restoration of their original self-concept makes salient to them the very discrepancies that mark out the protagonist from themselves. Thus, discrepancies that exist between one's self in the non-gaming world and one's self *qua* gaming character, especially in relation to those characteristics that may be valued – strength, honour, courage, and so on – are made salient as a *loss*: one experiences a loss of strength, a loss of honour, a loss of courage, and so on. If this discrepancy is salient when leaving the gaming environment of single-player games, where often one is the sole gamer, and therefore socially isolated, then how much more, I contend, is there scope for a salient discrepancy between one's gaming and non-gaming self when engaged in social games constitutive of multiplayer space?[8] Liu and Peng offer commentary to that effect:

> [B]y identifying with game characters who can achieve various unusual goals in MMOGs [massively multiplayer online games], gamers may regard themselves as more valuable and successful people in the game world than in the offline real world, and this may lead to unpleasant feelings or withdrawal symptoms when MMOG playing is suddenly unavailable.   (2009: 1307)

Shang Hwa Hsu *et al.* (2009) reported that MMORPG addiction is associated with the player's motivation to develop their character (in order to progress within the game; see also discussion in Ch. 5 on *problematic internet use*). If I identify strongly with my avatar then the avatar's progression and increased status become *my* progression and increased status. Hsu *et al.* also found MMORPG addiction to be associated with emotional attachment to one's avatar, and, on a more communal level, to a strong sense of belonging and obligation to the virtual group.

The gamer, in identifying with the gaming avatar, recognizes or accepts aspects of the avatar's features as representative of their own self-concept, or the self-concept constitutive of a possible self (see Markus & Nurius 1986).[9] This is particularly so when game mechanics allow for the *extensive customization* of one's default avatar. As Boellstorff observes (again, in the context of *Second Life*), very little is left to chance or randomization; instead, one can assume "near-total intentionality with regard to virtual embodiment" (2008: 129). Moreover, such intentional (sometimes time-consuming) customization makes one's virtual self (*qua* avatar) transparent to others.[10] As a participant in his research commented, "I've come to observe that the outward appearance really does communicate a lot about who you are, because it is made up of conscious choices about how you want to present yourself" (*ibid.*: 130). By way of a caveat, however, it may also be the case that the avatar is understood simply as an object one controls within the particular space: instrumental to one's being there, as it were. So, while there may exist valid cases of, for example, online gender swapping, so that players can explore different genders (Ferdinand & Guiller 2011; Hussain & Griffiths 2008), we must also accept that, for some, this may not be the case.[11] As

Searle Huh and Dmitri Williams note: "many male players have quipped that they play a female avatar because it is a pleasing visual object, not a source of identification" (2010: 170).

Recall from Chapter 4 how Wolfendale (2007), within the context of the multiplayer game *EverQuest*, analysed gamers' language and found evidence of gamer–avatar identification (she described how gamers said such things as "*I* was ignored" or "*I* never let anyone talk to *me* like that again"). Kirsten Pohl also notes the blurring of avatar with self in terms of emotional investment when she states:

> We play a game, because we want to win a game ... [But we are also] concerned about the avatar's fate, not only because the avatar is our representative in the fictional world and the instrument we need in order to actually play and win the game, but because we feel for him, we identify with his concerns and want to know how the story turns out for him and for us.
>
> (2008: 100–101)

In addition, Timothy Crick has this to say:

> [W]hen playing in first-person mode ..., the player might notice a shadow that follows the avatar's movements, and they will also see the avatar's reflection when looking through a mirror. Such details ... reinforce the player's sense of being inside the game world and not merely acting on it. (2011: 250)

For some gamers, however, identification may be minimal, its purpose to function purely as a point of agency within the space; what James Newman (2002) refers to as *vehicular embodiment*. Similarly, Mary Fuller and Henry Jenkins describe avatars as offering "traits that are largely capacities for action, fighting skills, modes of transportation, preestablished goals ... [In effect,] little more than a cursor which mediates the player's relationship to the story" (1995: 61; cited in Crick 2011). On the other hand, and as Crick points out, "the stylized designs of iconic avatars, such as Lara Croft in the third-person game Tomb Raider or player-customized designs ... may play an important role in helping the player to identify with the avatar, heightening their affective response to the game" (2011: 250). In fact, Kevin Williams (2011) found that gamers exhibited more aggression when the avatar had been customized to resemble more closely their own physical features compared to a dissimilar-looking avatar engaged in the same violent context.

Bartholomäus Wissmath *et al.* (2009: 117) talk of how the media-user is drawn away from their own physical location into the narrative of the fictional (or virtual) world. *Transportation theory*, as they call it, promotes the

150

idea that the gamer "plunges in the world of a narrative by suspending real-world facts". Moreover, an important antecedent to experiencing transportation is identification with characters immersed within the narrative. For Dorothée Hefner *et al.* (2007), this leads to increased enjoyment. However, for some, it may also lead to heightened aggression within the gameplay (Eastin 2006; Krcmar *et al.* 2011). Ducheneaut, in turn, proffers a view on how the gamer–avatar identity relation may typically manifest itself:

> Virtual worlds and online games are not exotic environments dedicated to the "identity play" of a few, but instead spaces that users move in and out of fluidly, which in turn leads to the construction of a "synthetic" identity that remains fairly stable online and off. (2010: 144)

For the sake of argument, even if Ducheneaut and proponents of this view are correct in what they say about how people typically manifest identity relations across these different spaces, I am nevertheless confident that Ducheneaut would concede that virtual worlds can be, and certainly gamespace has the potential to be, a place for exotic "identity play", particularly if one considers the possibility of using such a space to engage in STAs. In such an environment, would one's identity remain, as Ducheneaut would have us believe, "fairly stable online and off"?

If those components of the self, as represented and experienced through one's avatar, are restricted to gamespace, then a discrepancy will exist between the selves presented and experienced across gaming and non-gaming spaces, a consequence of which, I contend, is the possible disruption of one's psychological parity. Sara Allison *et al.* illustrate the potential starkness of this discrepancy when discussing their patient, Mr A:

> [T]he games allowed Mr. A to express aspects of himself that served a compensatory function psychologically. In other words, he could put on a new identity like a new suit of clothes, becoming someone who walked on water, healed others, and cast lightning bolts, in stark contrast to his daily experience of himself as inadequate. (2006: 384)

Katherine Bessière *et al.* (2007) found that players with lower levels of psychological well-being (e.g. lower self-esteem) tended to rate their avatar more favourably than they did themselves, something that was not found in players with higher rated self-esteem. In addition, identification with one's avatar was found to be more pronounced in those under twenty-seven (Smahel *et al.* 2008).[12] For certain types of player, then, the realization of valued attributes through one's avatar has the potential to create a large discrepancy between one's identity status and social prowess as perceived within the actual world and that attainable within gamespace (see Klimmt *et al.* 2010). Moreover, Amy Gonzales and Jeffrey Hancock (2008) found that repeated *public* presentation of a particular self – say, presenting oneself as extroverted – produced gradual, but long-term shifts in one's self-concept. However, in MMORPGs, the public presentation of one's self is context specific. Typically, the virtual and social environments are vastly different within the gamespace compared to the gamer's "real" world (which may be socially impoverished). As such, it may be extremely difficult to demonstrate one's valued character traits of strength, courage and honour (for example), which are normally demonstrated through one's virtual persona – the dragonslayer, say – in a non-gaming context (see also the discussion by Przybylski *et al.* [2010] on competence, autonomy and relatedness). If one is able to do this, then the characteristics of one's virtual self cease to be context specific and instead transcend domains (Young & Whitty 2011a). If one cannot, then it is my contention that the psychological discrepancy between non-gaming and gaming self (*qua* avatar) is made salient every time one leaves the gamespace.

Sherry Turkle broaches essentially the same issue when, in the context of self and identity, she asks: "How can we be multiple and coherent at the same time?" (1995: 258). In response, and borrowing from Robert Lifton (1993), she considers whether a self that transcends these spaces would be fragmented and lacking moral content, or be a kind of *Protean Self*: coherent and integrated with a moral outlook. Turkle and Lifton seem to accept that there is a clear association between the nature of the self and one's moral tendency. Psychological parity should, therefore, be seen as a development of Turkle's reference to the possible fragmentation or coherence and integration of the self across divergent spaces. However, and importantly, it is my contention that an individual who seeks parity of self (that is, who seeks integration of previously disparate selves born of various exotic identity plays) by favouring a self realized within gamespace would *potentially* have a moral outlook incongruent with our actual world, especially if that self is *defined* by the characteristics and actions of someone who engages in STAs.

In seeking to endorse the view that players are active moral agents (*homo poieticus*), and not mere rule-followers motivated by the entertainment payoff that following the rules provides – which Juul (2005) informs us is the goal of gameplay design (to provide this entertainment) – Sicart has this to say: "as players, we should all be aware that playing is more than just following orders to achieve a goal, that playing is also becoming who we can be in a game, in a world that, more than ever, we have to reclaim as ours" (2010: 194). In reclaiming the gameworld as one's own, one might be expected to invest more, psychologically, in this world. If my psychological investment takes the form of a self (*qua* gamer) who engages in STAs, then how is this going to affect my psychological parity? To have a moral outlook incongruent with the actual world does not mean that actions one engages in within gamespace are necessarily immoral, either as judged within the space or in fact at all. It may be that within gamespace STAs are permitted, or it may be that one supports the amoralist stance and therefore holds that STAs are not a moral matter. Either way, if one seeks to maintain a sense of self that is more in keeping with one's gaming persona, then one runs the risk of preferring to express this self in a manner incompatible with non-gaming morality.

Any discrepancy that exists need not be morally charged, of course, or reflect one's virtuousness (or lack thereof). It may be that in a particular virtual space one has the ability to fly at will, or has an extended social circle. On leaving the space, one can no longer fly at will and, let us say, one's social circle diminishes. How one experiences oneself will therefore change. As noted above, there will not simply be a *lack* of x (be it flying ability or social extension); rather, the lack of x will be made salient as a *loss*: as something that is now missing. In those individuals who identify much less with their avatar (I accept that for some there is no strong avatar identification) or whose avatar and non-gaming self are much more congruent, the discrepancy between the two – in terms of a *psychological disparity* – is smaller, I contend (and certainly this is what the limited available research suggests). As such, it is my further contention that, for these players, there is a much less severe sense of loss (if any) when they return to the "real" world, for while the environment in which they socialize may be different within gamespace, the *extent* to which they socialize may not be so vastly different. As such, their prowess as a social being is not experienced as diminished outside the virtual arena; what Putnam (2000) refers to as *social capital*.

These examples illustrate morally neutral ways in which someone may be affected by differences in their experience and conception of self across spaces. The issue is not whether one is affected by these differences, however, but how one copes with them. How does one integrate this loss within one's continuity of self? Does one compartmentalize different selves such that some form of discontinuity or "double life" is created?[13] After all, one cannot be at the same time one's virtual and non-virtual embodiment. Might there occur, then, a separation of selves that coincides with the dichotomy of corporeal and virtual? Alternatively, perhaps one seeks some form of reconciliation or integration such that one does not lead a "double life" (as it were) but, rather, extends one's self into each respective space by virtue of each respective form of embodiment (corporeal and virtual), thereby maintaining parity of *selfhood*. Either way, what are the psychological implications of each possibility? To date, such an important empirical matter awaits further investigation (although see Williams *et al.* 2011 for a recent study on role-playing within multiplayer space).

CONCLUSION

While accepting the limited experimental evidence available at present on psychological coping, it is nevertheless my contention that striving to maintain psychological parity underlies the virtuousness of which Sicart and even McCormick speak (see Ch. 8). To illustrate, suppose that within a given gamespace I, *qua* player-subject, am a brutal torturer, rapist and murderer. Outside this space, I am none of these things. Yet, knowing that *these* acts of torture, rape and murder are meaningful only within the gameplay, as Sicart would have it, and therefore a product of the game system (something that does not carry the same meaning outside this space) does not eliminate the sense of loss of moral freedom I experience when leaving the gamespace. When transcending spaces, being aware of the context-dependency of the STAs does not negate the sense of loss or the general discrepancy I encounter when moving from gamespace to the actual world. This is something that is present irrespective of the morality of the activity engaged in; it underlies both morally charged and morally neutral activities, although it may be particularly pronounced when engaging in STAs because of the fact that they represent *taboo* activities. Understanding how people manage this discrepancy, irrespective of any alleged immorality of virtual content, should be used to inform any move towards the selective prohibition of video game content, although it has implications for, and application to, cyberspace more generally. To date, however, there is a paucity of such research. More would certainly be welcomed and is indeed required.

THIRTEEN

Conclusion

Throughout this book I have presented a number of traditional moral theories and evaluated their suitability as a means of selectively prohibiting video game content. I have concluded that each, in turn, is unable to explain the current state of play regarding what is permitted and what is not (at least within the UK), either because there is a paucity of evidence from which to draw any firm empirical conclusions or, *a priori*, the theory is unable to justify the selective prohibition of video game content. Moreover, because of the playful element intrinsic to video games, and the altered contingencies characteristic of each gamespace, it is my contention that any moral scrutiny based on a moral system imported from our actual (non-gaming) world is difficult to defend in principle. Consequently, not only is it the case that no single moral approach seems suitable – at least based on evidence accumulated so far – but, more generally, the *idea* of there being any coherent moral system for implementing the selective prohibition of video game content borne outside gamespace seems doomed from the outset.

It is, therefore, my contention that if selective prohibition is to occur then it should be informed by psychology – based on what gamers can cope with, psychologically – rather than stemming from notions of what is morally good or bad about virtual interactions. Now, it may be that as a result of an inability to cope with certain moral freedoms within gamespace, and/or the discrepancy experienced when one moves between morally disparate spaces, the gamer's behaviour is altered in a manner incongruent with what is deemed acceptable outside gamespace (based on a particular moral approach adopted by the gamer's society). If so, then one may wish to challenge the merits of the moral system adopted by that society and the rights and wrongs of morally condemning the gamer's behaviour outside gamespace if/when it is shown to be incongruent with this system of morality. One may wish to do this, but that is not the aim of this book. Instead, what I am arguing is that irrespective of the system of morality adopted by a particular society outside gamespace, accounting for why a gamer's behaviour has changed (if indeed it has), so as to become incongruent with what is morally acceptable to that society, is better explained through an understanding of the psychology of the gamer and how he copes both within gamespace and when transcending that space rather than by attempting to apply a *moral* label – such as "good" or "bad" – to the virtual interactions he chooses to engage in. Thus, psychology can be used to explain behaviour that may be deemed morally inappropriate outside a given gamespace, and so be used in a manner that informs judgements with moral implications and application. All of this can be done, and indeed should be done, I maintain, without resorting to claims that the gamer's *virtual enactments* are morally inappropriate (or even appropriate) in and of themselves.

Having come to this conclusion, as a final point, and in anticipation of a possible objection, suppose someone argues as follows: in my place of work – say, as an internment guard – I am able to engage in activity x (assault and torture, for example) and can psychologically cope with the transition to not doing x when away from my work. I treat each as a distinct space (work/not work) and am psychologically able to manage moving back and forth between them. Should it not be the case, then, that a judgement about whether an action in my workspace should be prohibited or not should also be informed by psychology and not morality? In other words, should it not be the case that, like the argument for gamespace, the prohibition of x, in my clearly demarcated workspace, ought to be based on whether I can psychologically cope with engaging in x and not on whether it is good or bad, right or wrong to do so in this space?

The simple answer is no. Clearly, there is still a moral issue in relation to this example because the object towards which one directs action x is not virtual but actual (recall the unremarkable claim made earlier that murder and virtual murder are not equivalent: $x \neq y$). As such, away from gamespace, a moral system governing what I do should exist independently of whether I can psychologically cope with activity x, or even how I construe it (and, to reiterate, it is not within the remit of this book to evaluate moral practice outside gamespace). In the virtual space of video games, however, one does not enact STAs towards a physically embodied being. What I have argued is that those independent systems of morality that apply to the actual world are an unsatisfactory means of governing the selective prohibition of video game content. Rather, when judging gamespace from the outside, it is more appropriate to use psychology, not morality born of our non-gaming world, to inform judgements about prohibition. I say "from the outside" because it is still appropriate to employ a moral system from within the gamespace itself (i.e. the status functions of multiplayer space). Such a moral system would be born of that space, and would, therefore, be contingent on the unique affordances of the gamespace. As such, it can legitimately be used to judge, morally, how members of a shared gamespace interact with each other, which may have psychological ramifications within that space (e.g. it would be deemed immoral to rape and therefore potentially psychologically traumatize another member of the gamespace unless it is a feature of the agreed status functions).[1]

As it is the individual who transcends the divergent spaces of the gaming and actual worlds, and interacts within both, psychology should override the morality established within a given gamespace (i.e. established status functions) if it is shown that individuals cannot cope with the moral freedoms afforded within that space. As such, judgements about the psychological well-being of the individual should take precedence over a contingent moral system constitutive of gamespace. The extent to which an individual is able to cope, psychologically, is not something that can be established *a priori*. Expressions of how one copes (or does not) psychologically when traversing spaces with independent moral freedoms may include experiencing feelings of shame or guilt when enacting STAs, or fluctuations in self-esteem as one moves between worlds; but such feelings, should they arise, only confirm the importance of psychological understanding to selective prohibition, not the existence of an underlying moral code, expressed through sentiment such as disgust, guilt or shame, which may likewise transcend these spaces.

Notes

1. INTRODUCTION: PLAYING WITH RIGHT AND WRONG

1. Use of the terms "real" or "actual" – as in the real or actual world – is meant simply as a contrast to gamespace.
2. In the multiplayer game *World of Warcraft*, for example, it is not possible for the two rival factions – the Horde and the Alliance – to communicate with each other. This is against the rules and is impossible by design. For Miguel Sicart (2010), such restriction – namely, constraining by design what it is possible for a virtually embodied but social and ethical agent to do – is itself morally dubious. This particular ethical issue is not a concern of this book, however.
3. This formal definition is adapted from Tavinor (2008).
4. In first-person shooter games, the avatar may be implied in virtue of the perspective taken on the screen, and also as that which is in possession of the gun that is visible on the screen.
5. For a detailed discussion on differences between make-believe (*qua* social roles) and make-belief in fiction, see Bäcke (2011).
6. It would perhaps strike us as intuitively the case that if someone played in a Sunday League team *as* David Beckham, declaring to everyone that this was the make-believe case, then his teammates would tell him to stop *playing* around. This would equally be the case if one played football as oneself but made-believe that one was playing for Manchester United (rather than one's Sunday League team). Such cases

are different from someone trying to emulate the skills of Beckham or the success of Manchester United, however.

7. Tamar Szabó Gendler (2000) makes the point I am making here using Rudyard Kipling's poem "The White Man's Burden".

8. This, of course, is not how Coleridge's poem continues; nor are the remaining verses suggestive of this amendment.

9. I borrow this example from Walton & Tanner (1994).

10. In relation to this, according to Martie-Laure Ryan's (1991) *principle of minimal departure*, if aspects of the fictional world are not delineated then we fill in the blanks by extrapolating from what we do know about that world or by importing some understanding from the actual world. This latter process (requirement) is suggestive of an asymmetrical transcendence from actual to fictional world.

11. See also Matravers (2003) for a discussion on the extent to which the narrator of the make-believe is to be trusted.

12. See also Currie (2002) and Matravers (2003) for alternative explanations.

13. In being willing to engage my creative faculty, I should not have to defend this activity by saying "I do not really wish x to occur; it's just make-believe", because imagining (and therefore make-believing that x) does not *entail* that I *wish x* were the case. Wishing x were the case is an act of the imagination, but it is not equivalent to entertaining the possibility of x. See Patridge (2008) for a discussion on morality and imagination in works of fiction and art.

2. TO PROHIBIT OR NOT TO PROHIBIT, THAT IS THE QUESTION

1. See http://uk.gamespot.com/best-of-2010/special-achievement/index.html?page=24 (accessed November 2012).

2. For those unfamiliar with the game, essentially, each player takes it in turn to remove a small item from a two-dimensional cardboard patient using a pair of tweezers. The object of the game is to remove as many items as possible without making a buzzer sound, which, presumably, represents potential damage/harm to the patient.

3. A slightly milder version of what I am suggesting here, involving holographic aliens, can be seen in the film *Star Wars: Episode IV – A New Hope*. More recently, wizard chess (in *Harry Potter and the Philosopher's Stone*) can be seen to convey this idea (again, in a milder form). See also the computer games *Battle Chess* and *Love Chess* (for a more sexual take on the game).

4. Philip Brey (1999) notes how the game *Virtual Surgeon: Open Heart*, which involves the player learning open heart surgery, has been criticized by heart patients and their relatives, who consider it an inappropriate topic to present as a game.

5. In the UK, the 2009 Coroners and Justice Act has made illegal the possession of virtual (or pseudo-)images judged to be paedophilic. Such prohibition has been in place in the Netherlands since 2002, and, at the time of writing, a similar ruling has been proposed in Japan but not yet passed. In 2002 the US Supreme Court ruled that the 1996 Child Pornography Protection Act was unconstitutional. Under this ruling, computer-generated, sexually explicit images of children were permitted. However, in 2003, the PROTECT Act (Section 1466) limited the permissibility of virtual child pornography by prohibiting *obscene* material (obscenity is based on contemporary community standards).

6. Both *Sociolotron* and *Second Life* are sandbox environments and so do not have the kinds of clear gaming objectives characteristic of the video games discussed here. Nevertheless, I include them to give an indication of the sort of enactments (STAs) it is possible to engage in, virtually.

7. One of the concerns with this space was that it was not appropriately policed, and could therefore have been frequented by offline minors who were being asked to engage in virtual sex with adult avatars and potential offline paedophiles.

8. I shall not discuss here what the legal status of STAs ought to be, although on occasion I shall make reference to what it is in the UK.

3. HUME'S STRENGTH OF FEELING

1. See Gerrans & Kennett (2010) for a detailed discussion on sentimentalism (and also what they refer to as *neurosentimentalism*) and moral agency.

2. For a recent discussion on issues of disgust and morality, see Plakias (2012).

3. This is not to say that this is the only reason, or that another reason could not be found articulating why it is wrong.

4. Mark Coeckelbergh (2007) defines empathy as the imaginative process of perspective shifting, which involves: (i) putting oneself in the position of the other person; (ii) imagining oneself in that person's predicament while also retaining the knowledge that one is not that person; and (iii) feeling compassion for that person.

4. KANT'S CALL OF DUTY

1. See Schulte (2012) for a discussion on differences between moral and rational "oughts".

2. Of course, vegetarians may disagree with the benefits of butchery or, at least, with the practice of meat-eating that makes butchery necessary.

3. Elton (2000) speculates that it is perhaps because of the similarity in behaviour that Kant draws the analogy. We do not have a moral duty towards animals or stones, yet kicking a dog would cause "pain" behaviour we recognize, whereas kicking a stone would not. Avatars are likewise able to demonstrate (represent) recognizable pain behaviour.

4. Consider the much-discussed and somewhat infamous example of virtual rape (the "Mr Bungle affair") which occurred in 1992 in LambdaMOO (see Dibbel 1993 and Turkle 1995 for a more detailed discussion).

5. See Vanacker & Heider (2011) for a recent discussion on avatar identification and moral harm in relation to a virtual gallery in *Second Life* showing virtual upskirt images (that is, images taken from beneath an avatar's skirt).

6. Within UK society, one might consider smoking and drinking alcohol to be equivalent non-virtual examples of permissible activities that not all members choose to engage in.

5. THE COST AND BENEFIT OF VIRTUAL VIOLENCE (AND OTHER TABOOS)

1. The effects of video game violence on antisocial behaviour may occur in unexpected or less obvious ways. Tobias Ruthmund *et al.* (2011), for example, found that participants exposed to an aggressive encounter with an NPC, from the perspective of the victim, were less likely to engage cooperatively in a further activity with another participant in a task outside the gaming environment. The authors surmised that this could be the result of mistrust and an enhanced fear of being exploited, both of which stem from an increased form of negative information processing.

2. The word "presence" was originally used by Marvin Minsky (1980). The experience

of presence indicates that one's sense of being somewhere as an embodied agent need not correspond to one's physical location.

3. Emphasizing the risk to wider society is not to deny that becoming more aggressive or otherwise antisocial is itself a negative consequence for the gamer also.

4. Erick Messias *et al.* (2011) reported that adolescents who played video games (including internet use) for five or more hours a day were more likely to report sadness, suicidal ideation or suicidal planning.

5. The authors do not specify whether the video games in this study were multiplayer.

6. One might argue that if it were shown that the consequences for each STA were similar, a form of *rule utilitarianism* could be adopted.

6. ARE MEANINGS *VIRTUALLY* THE SAME?

1. See Woodcock (2012) for a recent discussion on Di Muzio's position in relation to what he (Woodcock) refers to as the argument from reactive attitudes.

2. What is judged to be depraved and corrupting must also be weighed against expert opinion regarding the extent to which the material "is justified as being for the public good on the ground that it is in the interests of science, literature, art or learning, or of other objects of general concern" (Obscene Publications Act 1959, Section 4[1]).

3. Mark Coeckelbergh (2007) questions the notion of gamers as moral explorers and speculates over whether instead they act more like *moral tourists*: consuming alternative morality as perhaps an end in itself, rather than as a means to some form of greater understanding through exploration.

7. THERE ARE WRONGS AND THEN THERE ARE *WRONGS*

1. In 2002, the video game *Grand Theft Auto: Vice City* caused controversy when the main character, Tommy Vercetti, was instructed to "kill Haitians". In 2003, the dialogue was removed from the game (USA Today 2003)

2. In the US in 2003, Los Angeles officials asked manufacturers, suppliers and contractors of computer hardware to refrain from using the terms "master" and "slave" to refer to types of equipment, adding that such terms were unacceptable and offensive (CNN 2003).

8. VIRTUAL VIRTUES, VIRTUAL VICES

1. I accept the elaborate possibility that one could murder someone by activating an automated system through the manipulation of buttons on a console or remote movement.

2. Or it may be that the gamer wishes to explore these immoral acts, which, again, would enable a degree of post-act reflection.

9. DOING WHAT IT TAKES TO WIN

1. Of course, one could utilize the hypothetical imperative to cheat: to do what is required to win the game, even if this means breaking the rules. This is true, if one wishes to win the game by any means, although for those who wish to win by playing within the rules this is not an option. Moreover, if one does not follow the rules then, as Huizinga ([1950] 1992) pointed out, the game and therefore the act of play ends.

2. Juul offers a possible caveat when pointing out that games are typically designed to be entertaining when the player pursues the intended goal of the game (or one of them); as such, "there is no guarantee that pursuing a different goal will provide quality gameplay" (2005: 200).

3. Equivalent in terms of what one does, even if the reason for why one does it is different: practical instead of moral, say.

4. Formulating the prescription in this way precludes the possibility that EE would be forced to prohibit an act that benefited me to the value of, say, £100 but my neighbour to the value of £150. If by acting in any other way I would not have obtained £100 or more, irrespective of what my neighbour obtains through my action, then my action is still morally correct.

5. This example is a variation on the original example used by Baier (1973).

6. One might wish to evoke the principle of double effect here, or at least recognize the similarity in the argument. If, for example, during a war, my country engages in a strategic bombing campaign (intends to do P), and doing so entails *not* Q (Q = there will be no civilian casualties; therefore *not* Q = there will be civilian casualties), then as my country does not intend *not* Q, P is morally justified, or so the argument goes.

7. See Zagal (2011) for a detailed discussion on moral decisions within this game.

10. AGREEING THE RULES

1. Acting as judge, jury and executioner implies an existing legal system. This is not the case so one can make judgements that stems from one's own needs and desires.

2. Plaut (1997: 90) described early online virtual communities as existing in a "relative state of anarchy".

3. For a detailed discussion on this, see Binmore (1994).

4. A contention among social contract theorists and critics is the extent to which the social contract tradition excludes those that one might intuitively feel we have a moral obligation towards, paradigm examples being those with mental disabilities, infants and animals. The concern is that only those who are rational enough to tacitly accept the social contract are bound by it, and we to them. This is not considered to be obviously the case with the examples cited above. Might it be, then, that, like animals and certain humans, avatars are unable to agree to the social contract but we should feel some sense of moral obligation towards them? Such an argument, through comparison with animals (etc.), is a non-starter, I contend. As Kimberly Smith states: "if an animal does not summon up in humans some sense of moral obligation – some sense that it is capable of being wronged – then it isn't a fit candidate for the social contract" (2008: 199). Given this possibility, how much more should we consider an avatar to be incapable of being wronged?

5. It is usually the case that those registering to play an online game will also be required to accept a manufacturer's End User Licence Agreement (EULA) (Fairfield 2008).

11. WHY WOULD ANYONE WANT TO DO *THAT*?

1. By saying that exploitation is absent, I am discounting the infamous example of virtual rape (the "Mr Bungle affair"), which occurred in 1992 in LambdaMOO (see Dibbel 1993; Turkle 1995), or something similar. In this example, there was no agreed status function in place indicating the permissibility of rape, as is the case in multiplayer spaces such as *Sociolotron*. With the LambdaMOO example, I

accept that there is an argument for exploitation. Equally, it may be that a player who acknowledges the permissibility of virtual rape within a given space (e.g. *Sociolotron*) may nevertheless feel exploited. Being exploited and feeling exploited are separate issues, of course.

2. Barely legal pornography uses models who are over eighteen years of age, but who are depicted as being under or just over the legal age of consent.

3. It is worth noting that, as a matter of course, the UK's Child Exploitation and Online Protection Centre sends out notes for editors to the effect that the phrase "child pornography" should be replaced with "child abuse" or "images of child abuse". Use of "child pornography" incorrectly suggests legitimacy and compliance, rather than the actual abuse that has taken place (taken from A. Adams 2010).

4. I accept that one might *fear* the possibility of such an individual escalating his (or her) viewing habits to include images that are of actual abuse, or even to taking part in the abuse itself (see Bourke & Hernandez 2009).

5. Luck (2009) discusses an example in which the goal of the game is to steal the Crown Jewels from the Tower of London. One way of achieving this goal is to sleep with the Beefeater's fifteen-year-old daughter.

6. I accept that engaging in the activity as a means of winning the game may also be fun.

7. One could argue that even with advances in technology equivalent to the science-fiction holodeck simulation, one is still aware that the interaction is virtual. Consequently, the level of arousal may still be arguably different (see Young 2010 for discussion on virtually elicited emotion).

8. This is not to ignore other factors that might motivate play: narrative, graphics, type of competition, etc.

12. COPING WITH VIRTUAL TABOOS

1. The suddenness of the change in environment, embodiment and perhaps even governance that one encounters when moving from our typical social environment to gamespace, made possible by virtual technology, is referred to by Young and Whitty (2012) as *virtual immediacy*.

2. Coeckelbergh (2011) argues that in fact we do not tend to treat gaming characters like mere objects but, to some extent, as a social other, which is why our virtually violent actions are potentially of moral concern. If we did just treat gaming characters as objects then there would be no moral issue to contend with, although it is probably the case (he surmises) that we would not play the game in the first place.

3. In *Call of Duty: Modern Warfare 2*, for example, players are given the option of skipping the "infamous" airport massacre scene.

4. Often violent games present the "enemy" in a caricatured way, which, according to Tobias Greitemeyer and Neil McLatchie (2011), may result in them being perceived by the gamer as less human (even in representation). This may be something that the game design implements to enable moral disengagement or it may be a strategy the gamer employs to morally manage their violent interaction. Either way, according to Greitemeyer and McLatchie, the perception of less humanness – or dehumanization – may be a factor in explaining reports of increased aggression in some gamers outside the game. As a caveat, however, it is worth noting that Greitemeyer and McLatchie's study measured dehumanization (of the outgroup) only indirectly.

5. See also Ivory and Kalyanaraman (2009) for a study looking into different perceptions of abstract (general) and specific violent video games and their perceived effect on aggressive behaviour.

6. One might argue that if the virtual is just as real then the morality of our actual world should apply to gamespace. Even if VR is understood to be real, or to constitute a type of reality, this does not mean that it is based on the same contingency relations as the actual world. Such altered contingencies enable the possibility of altered systems of morality to operate within gamespace.

7. For a more detailed discussion on the relationship between one's self-concept and self-image, see Young & Whitty (2012).

8. Roy Baumeister (1991) argues that individuals (adolescents, in particular) may engage in self-destructive behaviour as a means of escaping from a self that falls short of their own expectations, perhaps gleaned from communal standards. Jung-Hye Kwon *et al.* (2011) apply Baumeister's theory to explain problematic internet use (PIU) among Korean adolescents, concluding that "escape from self" best explains PIU in their sample.

9. According to Hazel Markus and Paula Nurius, possible selves are significant, personalized, yet ultimately social representations of ourselves that we either aspire to be like or fear becoming. They are intimately connected to our current self-concept, and represent our "hopes, fears and fantasies" (1986: 954), derived from what we know of ourselves and the society in which we live.

10. Such customization is often referred to as *skinning*.

11. For further research on gender-related issues, see Greenberg *et al.* (2010); Jenson & de Castell (2010); Williams *et al.* (2009).

12. David Smahel *et al.* (2008) speculate that this is because those twenty-seven and younger have not yet developed a strong sense (or as strong a sense) of identity.

13. See discussion on *psychological doubling* (Lifton 1986) in Burns (2011).

13. CONCLUSION

1. This does not preclude that someone may nevertheless be traumatized by the activity; it just means that what the gamer has done to the other (traumatized) player would not be judged within that space as immoral. If trauma were to become a regular consequence of this permissible virtual activity then the community may take it upon themselves to outlaw the action altogether by amending the agreed status functions. Alternatively, in the absence of collective agreement, individuals who find the STA traumatic may decide to opt out of the community (see Chs 4 and 10).

Bibliography

Adachi, P. J. C. & T. Willoughby 2011. "The Effect of Video Game Competition and Violence on Aggressive Behavior: Which Characteristic Has the Greatest Influence?" *Psychology of Violence* **1**(4): 259–74.

Adams, A. A. 2010. "Virtual Sex with Child Avatars". See Wankel & Malleck (2010), 55–72.

Adams, M. 2009. "Rapelay 'Virtual Raping' Game Shows Disgusting Lack of Morals in Modern Society". *Natural News.com* (14 February). www.naturalnews.com/News_000733_video_games_Rapelay_violence.html (accessed November 2012).

Allison, S. E., L. von Wahlde, T. Shockley & G. O. Gabbard 2006. "The Development of the Self in the Era of the Internet and Role-Playing Fantasy Games". *American Journal of Psychiatry* **163**(3): 381–5.

Anderson, C. A. 2004. "An Update on the Effects of Violent Video Games". *Journal of Adolescence* **27**: 113–22.

Anderson, C. A., L. Berkowitz, E. Donnerstein *et al.* 2003. "The Influence of Media Violence on Youth". *Psychological Science in the Public Interest* **4**(3): 81–110.

Anderson, C. A., A. Shibuya, N. Ihori *et al.* 2010. "Violent Video Game Effects on Aggression, Empathy, and Prosocial Behavior in Eastern and Western Countries: A Meta-Analytic Review". *Psychological Bulletin* **136**(2): 151–73.

Aristotle 1976. *The Nicomachean Ethics*, J. A. K. Thomson (trans.). Harmondsworth: Penguin.

Ashworth, L., M. Pyle & E. Pancer 2010. "The Role of Dominance in the Appeal of Violent Media Depictions". *Journal of Advertising* **39**(4): 121–34.

Bäcke, M. 2011. "Make-believe and Make-belief in Second Life Role Playing Communities". *Convergence: The International Journal of Research into New Media Technologies* **18**(1): 85–92.

Baier, K. 1966. "Moral Obligations". *American Philosophical Quarterly* **3**: 210–26.

Baier, K. 1973. "Ethical Egoism and Interpersonal Compatibility". *Philosophical Studies* **24**: 357–68.

Bailenson, J. N., J. Blascovich, A. C. Beall & J. M. Loomis 2003. "Interpersonal Distance in Immersive Virtual Environments". *Personality and Social Psychology Bulletin* **29**: 819–33.

Bailenson, J. N. & N. Yee 2005. "Digital Chameleons: Automatic Assimilation of Nonverbal Gestures in Immersive Virtual Environments". *Psychological Science* **16**(10): 814–18.

Bandura, A. 2002. "Selective Moral Disengagement in the Exercise of Moral Agency". *Journal of Moral Education* **31**(2): 101–19.

Barlett, C. P., C. A. Anderson & E. L. Swing 2009. "Video Game Effects – Confirmed, Suspected, and Speculative: A Review of the Evidence". *Simulation & Gaming* **40**(3): 377–403.

Barnett, J. & M. Coulson 2010. "Virtually Real: A Psychological Perspective on Massively Multiplayer Online Games". *Review of General Psychology* **14**(2): 167–79.

Bartle, R. 2008. "Torture". *The Everyday Blog of Richard Bartle* (19 November). www.youhaventlived.com/qblog/2008/QBlog191108A.html (accessed November 2012).

Baumeister, R. F. 1991. *Escaping the Self: Alcoholism, Spirituality, Masochism, and Other Flights from the Burden of Selfhood*. New York: HarperCollins.

Baumer, W. H. 1967. "Indefensible Impersonal Egoism". *Philosophical Studies* **17**: 72–5.

Bensley, L. & J. Van Eenwyk 2001. "Video Games and Real-Life Aggression: Review of the Literature". *Journal of Adolescent Health* **29**: 244–57.

Bentham, J. 1830. *Rationale of Reward*. London: Robert Heward. http://books.google.co.uk/books?id=L5Q7AAAAYAAJ&printsec=frontcover&source=gbs_ge_summary_r&cad=0#v=onepage&q&f=false (accessed November 2012).

Bentham, J. [1789] 1996. *An Introduction to the Principles of Morals and Legislation*, J. H. Burns & H. L. A. Hart (eds). Oxford: Clarendon Press.

Bessière, K., A. F. Seay & S. Kiesler 2007. "The Ideal Elf: Identity Exploration in World of Warcraft". *CyberPsychology & Behavior* **10**(4): 530–35.

Billieux, J., J. Chanal, Y. Khazaal, L. Rochat, P. Gay, D. Zullino & M. Van der Linden 2011. "Psychological Predictors of Problematic Involvement in Massively Multiplayer Online Role-Player Games: Illustration in a Sample of Male Cybercafé Players". *Pyschopathology* **44**: 165–71.

Binmore, K. 1994. *Game Theory and the Social Contract, Volume I: Playing Fair*. Cambridge, MA: MIT Press.

Binmore, K. 1998. *Game Theory and the Social Contract, Volume II: Just Playing*. Cambridge, MA: MIT Press.

Biocca, F. 1997. "The Cyborg's Dilemma: Progressive Embodiment in Virtual Environments". *Journal of Computer-Mediated Communication* **3**(2): 1–31.

Boellstorff, T. 2008. *Coming of Age in Second Life: An Anthropologist Explores the Virtually Human*. Princeton, NJ: Princeton University Press.

Booth, W. C. 1988. *The Company We Keep: An Ethics of Fiction*. Berkeley, CA: University of California Press.

Bourke, M. L. & A. E. Hernandez 2009. "The 'Butner Study' Redux: A Report of the Incidence of Hands-on Child Victimization by Child Pornography Offenders". *Journal of Family Violence* **24**: 183–91.

Brecher, B. 2007. *Torture and the Ticking Bomb*. Malden, MA: Blackwell.

Brenick, A., A. Henning, M. Killen, A. O'Connor & M. Collins 2007. "Social Evaluations of Stereotypic Images in Video Games Unfair, Legitimate, or 'Just Entertainment'?" *Youth & Society* **38**(4): 395–419.

Brenner, S. W. 2008. "Fantasy Crime: The Role of Criminal Law in Virtual Worlds". *Vanderbilt Journal of Entertainment and Technology Law* **11**(1): 1–97.

Brey, P. 1999. "The Ethics of Representation and Action in Virtual Reality". *Ethics and Information Technology* **1**: 5–14.

Brey, P. 2003. "The Social Ontology of Virtual Environments". *American Journal of Economics and Sociology* **62**(1): 269–81.

Buckingham, D. (with contributions from N. Whiteman, R. Willett & A. Burn) 2007. "The Impact of the Media on Children and Young People with a Particular Focus on Computer Games and the Internet". Prepared for the Byron Review on Children and New Technology commissioned by the Department for Children, Schools and Families. http://dera.ioe. ac.uk/7363/1/Buckingham%20Impact%20of%20Media%20Literature%20Review%20 for%20the%20Byron%20Review.pdf (accessed January 2013).

Burns, C. P. E. 2011. "Could Digital Gaming be 'Good for the Soul'? Ethics, Theology, & Violent Gaming". See Poels & Malliet (2011), 69–87.

Bushman, B. J., H. R. Rothstein & C. A. Anderson 2010. "Much Ado About Something: Violent Video Game Effects and a School of Red Herring: Reply to Ferguson and Kilburn (2010)". *Psychological Bulletin* **136**(2): 182–7.

Campbell, R. 1972. "A Short Refutation of Ethical Egoism". *Canadian Journal of Philosophy* **2**: 249–54.

Caplan, S., D. Williams & N. Yee 2009. "Problematic Internet Use and Psychosocial Well-being Among MMO Players". *Computers in Human Behavior* **25**: 1312–19.

Cellan-Jones, R. 2008. "Games 'to Outsell' Music, Video". *BBC News* (5 November). http://news.bbc.co.uk/1/hi/7709298.stm (accessed November 2012).

Chick, T. 2009. "Is Modern Warfare 2 the Most Disgusting Game of the Year?" *Fidgit* (10 November). http://fidgit.com/archives/2009/11/is_modern_warfare_2_the_most_d.php (accessed October 2010).

CNN 2003. "'Master' and 'Slave' Computer Labels Unacceptable, Officials Say". *CNN.com* (26 November). http://edition.cnn.com/2003/TECH/ptech/11/26/master.term.reut/ (accessed November 2012).

Coeckelbergh, M. 2007. "Violent Computer Games, Empathy, and Cosmopolitanism". *Ethics and Information Technology* **9**: 219–31.

Coeckelbergh, M. 2011. "Virtue, Empathy, and Vulnerability: Evaluating Violence in Digital Games". See Poels & Malliet (2011), 89–105.

Cogburn, J. & M. Silcox 2009. *Philosophy Through Video Games*. New York: Routledge.

Cohen, J. 2001. "Defining Identification: A Theoretical Look at the Identification of Audiences With Media Characters". *Mass Communication and Society* **4**(3): 245–64.

Costanzo, M., E. Gerrity & M. Brinton Lykes 2007. "Psychologists and the Use of Torture in Interrogations". *Analysis of Social Issues and Public Policy* **7**(1): 7–20.

Cottingham, J. 1994. "Religion, Virtue and Ethical Culture". *Philosophy* **69**(268): 163–80.

Crick, T. 2011. "The Game Body: Toward a Phenomenology of Contemporary Video Gaming". *Games and Culture* **6**(3): 245–58.

Csikszentmihalyi, M. 1991. *Flow: The Psychology of Optimal Experience*. New York: Harper & Row.

Currie, G. 2002. "Desire in Imagination". In *Conceivability and Possibility*, T. Gendler & J. Hawthorne (eds), 200–221. Oxford: Oxford University Press.

Damasio, A. R. 1994. *Descartes' Error: Emotion, Reason, and the Human Brain*. New York: Avon.

Danovitch, J. & P. Bloom 2009. "Children's Extension of Disgust to Physical and Moral Events". *Emotion* **9**(1): 107–12.

Davis, R. A. 2001. "A Cognitive-Behavioral Model of Pathological Internet Use". *Computers in Human Behavior* **17**: 187–95.

De Marneffe, P. 2001. "The Problem of Evil, the Social Contract, and the History of Ethics". *Pacific Philosophical Quarterly* **82**: 11–25.

Dent, N. J. H. 1975. "Virtues and Actions". *Philosophical Quarterly* **25**: 318–35.

DeVane, B. & K. D. Squire 2008. "The Meaning of Race and Violence in Grand Theft Auto: San Andreas". *Games and Culture* **3**(3–4): 264–85.

Dibbel, J. 1993. "A Rape in Cyberspace". *The Village Voice* **38**: 26–42.

Di Muzio, G. 2006. "The Immorality of Horror Films". *International Journal of Applied Philosophy* **20**(2): 277–94.

Donaldson, T. & T. W. Dunfee 1994. "Towards a Unified Conception of Business Ethics: Integrative Social Contracts Theory". *Academy of Management Review* **19**: 252–84.

Ducheneaut, N. 2010. "Massively Multiplayer Online Games as Living Laboratories: Opportunities and Pitfalls". In *Online Worlds: Convergence of the Real and the Virtual*, W. S. Bainbridge (ed.), 135–45. London: Springer.

Dunfee, T. & T. Donaldson 1995. "Contractarian Business Ethics: Current Status and Next Steps". *Business Ethics Quarterly* **5**: 173–86.

Durkheim, E. [1893] 1984. *The Division of Labour in Society*, W. D. Halls (trans.). Basingstoke: Macmillan.

Dutton, D. 2006. "A Naturalist Definition of Art". *Journal of Aesthetics and Art Criticism* **64**(3): 367–77.

Eastin, M. 2006. "Video Game Violence and the Female Game Player: Self- and Opponent-Gender Effects on Presence and Aggressive Thoughts". *Human Communication Research* **32**(3): 351–72.

Elton, M. 2000. "Should Vegetarians Play Video Games?" *Philosophical Papers* **29**(1): 21–42.

Emmons, D. 1969. "Refuting the Egoist". *Personalist* **50**: 309–19.

Entertainment Software Association 2010. Essential Facts about the Computer and Video Game Industry. www.theesa.com/facts/pdfs/ESA_Essential_Facts_2010.PDF (accessed November 2012).

Epstein, S. 1994. "Integration of the Cognitive and Psychodynamic Unconscious". *American Psychologist* **49**: 709–24.

Facione, P. A., D. Scherer & T. Attig 1978. *Values and Society*. Englewood Cliffs, NJ: Prentice-Hall.

Fairfield, J. A. T. 2008. "Anti-social Contracts: The Contractual Governance of Virtual Worlds". *McGill Law Journal* **53**: 427–76.

Farrar, K. M., M. Krcmar & K. L. Nowak 2006. "Contextual Features of Violent Video Games, Mental Models, and Aggression". *Journal of Communication* **56**: 387–405.

Ferdinand, F. & J. Guiller 2011. "'Is That Your Boyfriend?' An Experiential and Theoretical Approach to Understanding Gender-Bending in Virtual Worlds". In *Reinventing Ourselves: Contemporary Concepts of Identity in Virtual Worlds*, A. Peachey & M. Childs (eds), 153–75. London: Springer.

Ferguson, C. J. 2007a. "Evidence for Publication Bias in Video Game Violence Effects Literature: A Meta-analytic Review". *Aggression and Violent Behavior* **12**: 470–82.

Ferguson, C. J. 2007b. "The Good, the Bad and the Ugly: A Meta-analytic Review of Positive and Negative Effects of Violent Video Games". *Psychiatric Quarterly* **78**(4): 309–16.

Ferguson, C. J. 2011. "Video Games and Youth Violence: A Prospective Analysis in Adolescents". *Journal of Youth and Adolescence* **40**: 377–91.

Ferguson, C. J. & J. Kilburn 2010. "Much Ado About Nothing: The Misestimation and Overinterpretation of Violent Video Game Effects in Eastern and Western Nations: Comment on Anderson et al. (2010)". *Psychological Bulletin* **136**(2): 174–8.

Fitzgerald, D. A., S. Posse, G. J. Moore, M. E. Tancer, P. J. Nathan & K. L. Phan 2004. "Neural Correlates of Internally Generated Disgust via Autobiographical Recall: A Functional Magnetic Resonance Imaging Investigation". *Neuroscience Letters* **370**: 91–6.

Floridi, L. & J. W. Sanders 2005. "Internet Ethics: The Constructivist Values of Homo Poieticus". In *The Impact of the Internet on our Moral Lives*, R. J. Cavalier (ed.), 195–215. New York: SUNY Press.

Fuller, L. 1949. "The Case of the Speluncean Explorers". *Harvard Law Review* **62**(4): 616–45.

Fuller, M. & H. Jenkins 1995. "Nintendo and New World Travel Writing: A Dialogue". In *Cybersociety: Computer-mediated Communication and Community*, S. G. Jones (ed.), 57–72. London: Sage.

Funk, J. B. 2002. "What Young Children Experience Playing Violent Video Games". Paper presented at the symposium "Violent Video Games and Aggression" at the meeting of the International Society for Research on Aggression, "The Developmental Origins of Aggressive Behavior", 28–31 July 2002, Montreal, Canada.

Funk, J. B., D. D. Buchman, J. Jenks & H. Bechtoldt 2003. "Playing Violent Video Games, Desensitization, and Moral Evaluation in Children". *Applied Developmental Psychology* **24**: 413–36.

Funk, J. B., H. Bechtoldt-Baldacci, T. Pasold & J. Baumgartner 2004. "Violence Exposure in Real-life, Video Games, Television, Movies, and the Internet: Is there Desensitisation?" *Journal of Adolescence* **27**: 23–39.

Gendler, T. S. 2000. "The Puzzle of Imaginative Resistance". *Journal of Philosophy* **97**(2): 55–81.

Gentile, D. A., H. Choo, A. Liau, T. Sim, D. Li, D. Fung & A. Khoo 2011. "Pathological Video Game Use Among Youths: A Two-Year Longitudinal Study". *Pediatrics* **127**(2): e319–e329.

Gerrans, P. & J. Kennett 2010. "Neurosentimentalism and Moral Agency". *Mind* **119**: 585–614.

Gibbard, A. 1990. *Wise Choices, Apt Feelings: A Theory of Normative Judgment*. Cambridge, MA: Harvard University Press.

Giumetti, G. W. & P. M. Markey 2007. "Violent Video Games and Anger as Predictors of Aggression". *Journal of Research in Personality* **41**(6): 1234–43.

Glock, S. & J. Kneer 2009. "Game Over? The Impact of Knowledge about Violent Digital Games on the Activation of Aggression-Related Concepts". *Journal of Media Psychology* **21**(4): 151–60.

Goffman, E. 1972. *Encounters: Two Studies in the Sociology of Interaction*. New York: Penguin.

Gonzales, A. L. & J. T. Hancock 2008. "Identity Shift in Computer-Mediated Environments". *Media Psychology* **11**: 167–85.

Gooskens, G. 2010. "The Ethical Status of Virtual Actions". *Ethical Perspectives* **17**(1): 59–78.

Greenberg, B. S., J. Sherry, K. Lachlan, K. Lucas & A. Holmstrom 2010. "Orientations to Video Games Among Gender and Age Groups". *Simulation & Gaming* **41**(2): 238–59.

Greene, J. D., R. B. Sommerville, L. E. Nystrom, J. M. Darley & J. Cohen 2001. "An fMRI Investigation of Emotional Engagement in Moral Judgment". *Science* **293**(5537): 2105–8.

Greitemeyer, T. & N. McLatchie 2011. "Denying Humanness to Others: A Newly Discovered Mechanism by which Violent Video Games Increase Aggressive Behavior". *Psychological Science* **22**(5): 659–65.

Gunter, B. 2008. "Media Violence: Is There a Case for Causality?" *American Behavioral Scientist* **51**(8): 1061–122.

Haidt, J. 2001. "The Emotional Dog and Its Rational Tail: A Social Intuitionist Approach to Moral Judgment". *Psychological Review* **108**(4): 814–34.

Haidt, J. & J. Graham 2007. "When Morality Opposes Justice: Conservatives have Moral Intuitions that Liberals may not Recognize". *Social Justice Research* **20**(1): 98–116.

Haidt, J. & C. Joseph 2004. "Intuitive Ethics: How Innately Prepared Intuitions Generate Culturally Variable Virtues". *Daedalus: Special Issue on Human Nature* **133**(4): 55–66.

Haidt, J., S. H. Koller & M. G. Dias 1993. "Affect, Culture, and Morality, or Is It Wrong to Eat Your Dog?" *Journal of Personality and Social Psychology* **65**: 613–28.

Hartmann, T. 2011. "Users' Experiential and Rational Processing of Virtual Violence". See Poels & Malliet (2011), 135–50.

Hartmann, T. & P. Vorderer 2010. "It's Okay to Shoot a Character: Moral Disengagement in Violent Video Games". *Journal of Communication* **60**: 94–119.

Hartmann, T., E. Toz & M. Brandon 2010. "Just a Game? Unjustified Virtual Violence Produces Guilt in Empathetic Players". *Media Psychology* **13**(4): 339–63.

Hefner, D., C. Klimmt & P. Vorderer 2007. "Identification with the Player Character as Determinant of Video Game Enjoyment". In *Proceedings of ICEC 2007, 6th International Conference on Entertainment Computing*, L. Ma, R. Nakatsu & M. Rauterberg (eds), 39–48. Berlin: Springer.

Hitchens, P. 2011. "Some Rapes ARE Worse than Others... There, I've Said It". *Mail Online* (23 May). www.dailymail.co.uk/debate/article-1389647/Ken-Clarke-rape-gaffe-Some-rapes-ARE-worse-others.html (accessed November 2012).

Hobbes, T. [1651] 1985. *Leviathan*, C. D. MacPherson (ed.). Harmondsworth: Penguin.

Hoffman, M. L. 2000. *Empathy and Moral Development: Implications for Caring and Justice*. New York: Cambridge University Press.

Holiday, A. 2003. "Promises Unspoken: A Wittgensteinian Response to the Very Idea of a Social Contract". *Theoria Pietermaritzburg* **102**: 48–64.

Hosper, J. 1961. "Baier and Medlin on Ethical Egoism". *Philosophical Studies* **12**: 10–16.

Howe, L. A. 2008. "Self and Pretence: Playing with Identity". *Journal of Social Philosophy* **39**(4): 564–82.

Hsu, S. H., M. H. Wen & M. C. Wu 2009. "Exploring User Experiences as Predictors of MMORPG Addiction". *Computers and Education* **53**: 990–98.

Huesmann, L. R. 2010. "Nailing the Coffin Shut on Doubts That Violent Video Games Stimulate Aggression: Comment on Anderson et al. (2010)". *Psychological Bulletin* **136**(2): 179–81.

Huh, S. & D. Williams 2010. "Dude Looks Like a Lady: Gender Swapping in an Online Game". In *Online Worlds: Convergence of the Real and the Virtual*, W. S. Bainbridge (ed.), 161–74. London: Springer.

Huizinga, J. [1950] 1992. *Homo Ludens: A Study of the Play-element in Culture*. Boston, MA: Beacon Press.

Hume, D. [1739] 1978. *A Treatise of Human Nature*, L. A. Selby-Bigge (ed.), 2nd edn. Oxford: Oxford University Press.

Hume, D. [1757] 1985. "Of the Standard of Taste". In *Essays: Moral, Political and Literary*, E. F. Miller (ed.), 226–49. Indianapolis, IN: Liberty Fund.

Hunter, I., D. Saunders & D. Williamson 1993. *On Pornography: Literature, Sexuality and Obscenity Law*. London: Macmillan.

Hussain, Z. & M. D. Griffiths 2008. "Gender Swapping and Socializing in Cyberspace: An Exploratory Study". *CyberPsychology & Behavior* **11**: 47–53.

Ivory, J. D. & S. Kalyanaraman 2007. "The Effects of Technological Advancement and Violent Content in Video Games on Players' Feelings of Presence, Involvement, Physiological Arousal, and Aggression". *Journal of Communication* **57**: 532–55.

Ivory, J. D. & S. Kalyanaraman 2009. "Video Games Make People Violent – Well, Maybe Not That Game: Effects of Content and Person Abstraction on Perceptions of Violent Video Games' Effects and Support of Censorship". *Communication Reports* **22**(1): 1–12.

Jansz, J. 2005. "The Emotional Appeal of Violent Video Games for Adolescent Males". *Communication Theory* **15**(3): 219–41.

Jansz, J. & M. Tanis 2007. "Appeal of Playing Online First Person Shooter Games". *CyberPsychology & Behavior* **10**(1): 133–6.

Jenkins, H. 1999. "Congressional Testimony on Media Violence". *MIT Communications Forum*. http://web.mit.edu/comm-forum/papers/jenkins_ct.html (accessed November 2012).

Jenson, J. & S. de Castell 2010. "Gender, Simulation, and Gaming: Research Review and Redirections". *Simulation & Gaming* **41**(1): 51–71.

Jones, A. & J. Fitness 2008. "Moral Hypervigilance: The Influence of Disgust Sensitivity in the Moral Domain". *Emotion* **8**(5): 613–27.

Jordan, E. & A. Cowan 1995. "Warrior Narratives in the Kindergarten Classroom: Renegotiating the Social Contract". *Gender and Society* **9**(6): 727–43.

Juul, J. 2005. *Half-Real: Video Games Between Real Rules and Fictional Games*. Cambridge, MA: MIT Press.

Kant, I. [1795] 1917. *Perpetual Peace: A Philosophical Essay*, M. Campbell-Smith (trans.). London: George Allen & Unwin. http://files.libertyfund.org/files/357/0075_Bk.pdf (accessed November 2012).

Kant, I. [1930] 1963. "Duties Towards Animals and Spirits". In *Lectures on Ethics*, L. Infield (trans.), 239–41. New York: Harper & Row.

Kant, I. [1785] 1993. *Grounding for the Metaphysics of Morals*, J. W. Ellington (trans.). Indianapolis, IN: Hackett.

Kant, I. [1788] 1997. *Critique of Practical Reason*, M. Gregor (trans.). Cambridge: Cambridge University Press.

Kass, L. R. 2002. *Life, Liberty, and the Defense of Dignity: The Challenge for Bioethics*. San Francisco, CA: Encounter Books.

Kernis, M. H. 2003. "Toward a Conceptualization of Optimal Self-Esteem". *Psychological Inquiry* **14**(1): 1–26.

Kieran, M. 2002. "On Obscenity: The Thrill and Repulsion of the Morally Prohibited". *Philosophy and Phenomenological Research* **64**(1): 31–55.

King, J. A., R. J. R. Blair, D. G. V. Mitchell, R. J. Dolan & N. Burgess 2006. "Doing the Right Thing: A Common Neural Circuit for Appropriate Violent or Compassionate Behaviour". *NeuroImage* **30**(3): 1069–76.

Kirkland, E. 2011. "Morality in Survival Horror Games". See Poels & Malliet (2011), 287–301.

Klimmt, C., H. Schmid, A. Nosper, T. Hartmann & P. Vorderer 2006. "How Players Manage Moral Concerns to Make Video Game Violence Enjoyable". *Communications* **31**: 309–28.

Klimmt, C., H. Schmid, A. Nosper, T. Hartmann & P. Vorderer 2008. "'Moral Management': Dealing with Moral Concerns to Maintain Enjoyment of Violent Video Games". In *Computer Games as a Sociocultural Phenomenon: Games Without Frontiers – Wars Without Tears*, A. Sudmann-Jahn & R. Stockmann (eds), 108–18. Hampshire: Palgrave Macmillan.

Klimmt, C., D. Hefner & P. Vorderer 2009. "The Video Game Experience as 'True' Identification: A Theory of Enjoyable Alterations of Players' Self-Perception". *Communication Theory* **19**: 351–73.

Klimmt, C., D. Hefner, P. Vorderer, C. Roth & C. Blake 2010. "Identification With Video Game Characters as Automatic Shift of Self-Perceptions". *Media Psychology* **13**(4): 323–38.

Knapp, C. 2003. "De-Moralizing Disgustingness". *Philosophy and Phenomenological Research* **66**(2): 253–78.

Konijn, E. A. & B. J. Bushman 2007. "I Wish I Were a Warrior: The Role of Wishful Identification on the Effects of Violent Video Games on Aggression in Adolescent Boys". *Developmental Psychology* **43**(4): 1038–44.

Konijn, E. A. & J. F. Hoorn 2005. "Some Like it Bad: Testing a Model for Perceiving and Experiencing Fictional Characters". *Media Psychology* **7**(2): 107–44.

Konijn, E. A., J. H. Walma van der Molen & J. F. Hoorn 2011. "Babies versus Bogeys: In-Game Manipulation of Empathy in Violent Video Games". See Poels & Malliet (2011), 151–76.

Krcmar, M., K. Farrar & R. McGloin 2011. "The Effects of Video Game Realism on Attention, Retention and Aggressive Outcomes". *Computers in Human Behavior* **27**(1): 432–9.

Kwon, J.-H., C.-S. Chung & J. Lee 2011. "The Effects of Escape from Self and Interpersonal Relationship on the Pathological Use of Internet Games". *Community Mental Health Journal* **47**(1): 113–21.

Lachlan, K. & R. Tamborini 2008. "The Effect of Perpetrator Motive and Dispositional Attributes on Enjoyment of Television Violence and Attitudes Toward Victims". *Journal of Broadcasting & Electronic Media* **52**(1): 136–52.

Lack, J. 2008. "Censoring Provocative Art is the Worst Advert for 2012". *Guardian* (26

August). www.guardian.co.uk/artanddesign/2008/aug/26/art.olympics2012 (accessed November 2012).

Ladas, M. 2003. "Eine Befragung von 2141 Computerspielern zu Wirkung und Nutzung von Gewalt" [A survey of 2,141 computer game players on effect and use of violence]. In *Virtuelle Welten – reale Gewalt* [Virtual worlds – real violence], F. Rötzer (ed.), 26–35. Hannover: Hans Heise Verlag.

Lemmens, J. S., P. M. Valkenburg & J. Peter 2011. "Psychosocial Causes and Consequences of Pathological Gaming". *Computers in Human Behavior* **27**(1): 144–52.

Levy, N. 2003. "What (if Anything) Is Wrong with Bestiality?" *Journal of Social Philosophy* **34**(3): 444–56.

Lifton, R. J. 1986. *The Nazi Doctors: Medical Killing and the Psychology of Genocide.* New York: Basic Books.

Lifton, R. J. 1993. *The Protean Self: Human Resilience in an Age of Fragmentation.* New York: Basic Books.

Liu, M. & W. Peng 2009. "Cognitive and Psychological Predictors of the Negative Outcomes Associated with Playing MMOGs (Massively Multiplayer Online Games)". *Computers in Human Behavior* **25**: 1306–11.

Locke, J. [1690] 1980. *The Second Treatise of Civil Government*, C. B. MacPherson (ed.). Indianapolis, IN: Hackett.

Luck, M. 2009. "The Gamer's Dilemma: An Analysis of the Arguments for the Moral Distinction Between Virtual Murder and Virtual Paedophilia". *Ethics and Information Technology* **11**: 31–6.

Machan, T. R. 1979. "Recent Work in Ethical Egoism". *American Philosophical Quarterly* **16**(1): 1–15.

MacIntyre, A. 1985. *After Virtue.* London: Duckworth.

Malliet, S. 2006. "An Exploration of Adolescents' Perceptions of Videogame Realism". *Learning, Media and Technology* **31**(4): 377–94.

Markey, P. M. & C. N. Markey 2010. "Vulnerability to Violent Video Games: A Review and Integration of Personality Research". *Review of General Psychology* **14**(2): 82–91.

Markey, P. M. & K. Scherer 2009. "An Examination of Psychoticism and Motion Capture Controls as Moderators of the Effects of Violent Video Games". *Computers in Human Behavior* **25**(2): 407–11.

Markus, H. & P. Nurius 1986. "Possible Selves". *American Psychologist* **41**: 954–69.

Mathiak, K. & R. Weber 2006. "Towards Brain Correlates of Natural Behavior: fMRI during Violent Video Games". *Human Brain Mapping* **27**: 948–56.

Matravers, D. 2003. "Fictional Assent and the (So-Called) 'Puzzle of Imaginative Resistance'". In *Imagination, Philosophy and the Arts*, M. Kieran & D. I. Lopes (eds), 91–106. London: Routledge.

Mayo, B. 1958. *Virtue and the Moral Life.* New York: Macmillan.

McCabe, J. 2007. "Rape in Second Life". *The F Word: Contemporary UK Feminism* (30 April). www.thefword.org.uk/blog/2007/04/rape_in_second (accessed November 2012).

McCormick, M. 2001. "Is it Wrong to Play Violent Video Games?" *Ethics and Information Technology* **3**(4): 277–87.

Medlin, B. 1970. "Ultimate Principles and Ethical Egoism". In *Morality and Rational Self-Interest*, D. P. Gauthier (ed.), 56–63. Englewood Cliffs, NJ: Prentice-Hall.

Meerkerk, G. J., R. J. Van Den Eijnden & H. F. Garretsen 2006. "Predicting Compulsive Internet Use: It's all about Sex!" *CyberPsychology & Behavior* **9**: 95–103.

Messias, E., J. Castro, A. Saini, M. Usman & D. Peeples 2011. "Sadness, Suicide, and Their Association with Video Game and Internet Overuse among Teens: Results from the Youth Risk Behavior Survey 2007 and 2009". *Suicide and Life-Threatening Behavior* **41**(3): 307–15.

Mey, K. 2007. *Art & Obscenity.* New York: Palgrave Macmillan.

Mill, J. S. [1863] 1998. *Utilitarianism*, C. Crisp (ed.). Oxford: Oxford University Press.

Minsky, M. 1980. "Telepresence". *OMNI* **2**: 45–51.

Modell, A. H. 1990. *Other Times, Other Realities: Toward a Theory of Psychoanalytic Treatment*. Cambridge, MA: Harvard University Press.

Mohney, C. 2006. "Second Life: Rape for Sale". *Valleywag* (15 December). http://gawker.com/news/second-life/second-life-rape-for-sale-222099.php (accessed November 2012).

Möller, I. & B. Krahé 2009. "Exposure to Violent Video Games and Aggression in German Adolescents: A Longitudinal Analysis". *Aggressive Behavior* **35**(1): 75–89.

Morahan-Martin, J. & P. Schumacher 2000. "Incidence and Correlates of Pathological Internet use Among College Students". *Computers in Human Behavior* **16**: 13–29.

Moran, R. 1994. "The Expression of Feeling in Imagination". *Philosophical Review* **103**(1): 75–106.

Newman, J. 2002. "The Myth of the Ergodic Videogame: Some Thoughts on Player–Character Relationships in Videogames". *Game Studies* [online] **2**: 1–8. www.gamestudies.org/0102/newman/ (accessed January 2013).

Ng, B. D. & P. Wiemer-Hastings 2005. "Addiction to the Internet and Online Gaming". *CyberPsychology & Behavior* **8**: 110–13.

Nichols, S. 2008. "Sentimentalism Naturalized". In *Moral Psychology: The Evolution of Morality, Volume 2*, W. Sinnott-Armstrong (ed.), 255–74. Cambridge, MA: MIT Press.

Nichols, S. & R. Mallon 2005. "Moral Dilemmas and Moral Rules". *Cognition* **100**(3): 530–42.

Nietzsche, F. [1888] 2003. *Beyond Good and Evil*, R. J. Hollingdale (trans.). London: Penguin.

Norman, R. 1998. *The Moral Philosophers: An Introduction to Ethics*, 2nd edn. Oxford: Oxford University Press.

Nussbaum, M. C. 1992. *Love's Knowledge: Essays on Philosophy and Literature*. Oxford: Oxford University Press.

Nys, T. 2010. "Virtual Ethics". *Ethical Perspectives* **17**(1): 79–93.

Oatley, K. 1999. "Meeting of Minds: Dialogue, Sympathy, and Identification in Reading Fiction". *Poetics* **26**: 439–54.

Opotow, S. 2007. "Moral Exclusion and Torture: The Ticking Bomb Scenario and the Slippery Ethical Slope". *Peace and Conflict: Journal of Peace Psychology* **13**(4): 457–61.

Österberg, J. 1988. *Self and Others: A Study of Ethical Egoism*. London: Kluwer Academic.

Parés, N. & R. Parés 2006. "Towards a Model for a Virtual Reality Experience: The Virtual Subjectiveness". *Presence* **15**(5): 524–38.

Pasquinelli, E. 2010. "The Illusion of Reality: Cognitive Aspects and Ethical Drawbacks". See Wankel & Malleck (2010), 197–215.

Patridge, S. 2008. "Monstrous Thoughts and the Moral Identity Thesis". *Journal of Value Inquiry* **42**: 187–210.

Patridge, S. 2011. "The Incorrigible Social Meaning of Video Game Imagery". *Ethics and Information Technology* **13**(4): 303–12.

Paul, B. & D. G. Linz 2008. "The Effects of Exposure to Virtual Child Pornography on Viewer Cognition and Attitudes Toward Deviant Sexual Behavior". *Communication Research* **35**(1): 3–38.

Persky, S. & J. Blascovich 2008. "Immersive Virtual Video Game Play and Presence: Influences on Aggressive Feelings and Behavior". *Presence* **17**(1): 57–72.

Plakias, A. 2012. "The Good and the Gross". *Ethical Theory and Moral Practice*. http://rd.springer.com/article/10.1007/s10677-012-9334-y (accessed November 2012).

Plaut, S. E. 1997. "Online Ethics: Social Contracts in the Virtual Community". *Journal of Sex Education and Therapy* **22**(1): 84–91.

Poels, K. & S. Malliet (eds) 2011. *Vice City Virtue: Moral Issues in Digital Game Play*. Leuven: Acco Academic.

Pohl, K. 2008. "Ethical Reflection and Involvement in Computer Games". In *Conference*

Proceedings of the Philosophy of Computer Games, S. Günzel, M. Liebe & D. Mersch (eds), 92–107. Potsdam: Potsdam University Press.

Polman, H., B. Orobio de Castro & M. A. G. van Aken 2008. "Experimental Study of the Differential Effects of Playing Versus Watching Violent Video Games on Children's Aggressive Behaviour". *Aggressive Behavior* **34**(3): 256–64.

Powers, T. M. 2003. "Real Wrongs in Virtual Communities". *Ethics in Information Technology* **5**: 191–8.

Prigg, M. 2009. "Violent Video Game Breaks Records with 4.7m Sales in a Day". *London Evening Standard* (13 November). www.thisislondon.co.uk/standard/article-23769128-violent-video-game-breaks-records-with-47m-sales-in-a-day.do (accessed November 2012).

Prinz, J. J. 2007. *The Emotional Construction of Morals*. Oxford: Oxford University Press.

Przybylski, A. K., C. S. Rigby & R. M. Ryan 2010. "A Motivational Model of Video Game Engagement". *Review of General Psychology* **14**(2): 154–66.

Putnam, R. D. 2000. *Bowling Alone: The Collapse and Revival of American Community*. New York: Simon & Schuster.

Pyszczynski, T., J. Greenberg, S. Solomon, J. Arndt & J. Schimel 2004. "Why do People need Self-esteem? A Theoretical and Empirical Review". *Psychological Bulletin* **130**: 435–68.

Rachels, J. 1974. "Two Arguments Against Ethical Egoism". *Philosophia* **4**(2–3), 297–314.

Rachels, J. 1986. *The Elements of Moral Philosophy*. New York: Random House.

Raney, A. A. & J. Bryant 2002. "Moral Judgment and Crime Drama: An Integrated Theory of Enjoyment". *Journal of Communication* **52**(2): 402–15.

Rauch, P. 2011. "God of War: What is it Good For? Nietzsche's 'Master Morality' and the Single-Player Action/Adventure Genre". In *Designing Games for Ethics: Models, Techniques and Frameworks*, K. Schrier & D. Gibson (eds), 98–108. New York: Information Science Reference.

Rawls, J. 1971. *A Theory of Justice*. Cambridge, MA: Harvard University Press.

Regis, E., Jr 1980. "What is Ethical Egoism?" *Ethics* **91**(1): 50–62.

Roberts, B. 2009. "Disgusting Baby Shaker iPhone game". *GoMo News* (15 May). www.gomonews.com/disgusting-baby-shaker-iphone-game/ (accessed November 2012).

Rousseau, J. J. [1762] 1973. *The Social Contract and Other Discourses*, G. D. H. Cole (trans.). New York: Dutton.

Royzman, E. B., R. F. Leeman & J. Sabini 2008. "'You Make Me Sick': Moral Dyspepsia as a Reaction to Third-party Sibling Incest". *Motivation and Emotion* **32**: 100–108.

Russell, G. 2008. "Pedophiles in Wonderland: Censoring the Sinful in Cyberspace". *Journal of Criminal Law and Criminology* **98**(4): 1467–99.

Ruthmund, T., M. Gollwitzer & C. Klimmt 2011. "Of Virtual Victims and Victimized Virtues: Differential Effects of Experienced Aggression in Video Games on Social Cooperation". *Personality and Social Psychology Bulletin* **37**(1): 107–19.

Ryan, M.-L. 1991. *Possible Worlds, Artificial Intelligence, and Narrative Theory*. Bloomington, IN: Indiana University Press.

Saltz, D. Z. 1991. "How to Do Things on Stage". *Journal of Aesthetics and Art Criticism* **49**(1): 31–45.

Sando, S. 2010. "Play and Virtuality". *Nordic Journal of Applied Ethics* **4**(2): 41–56.

Scanlon, T. 1998. *What We Owe To Each Other*. Cambridge, MA: Belknap Press.

Schrier, K. & D. Gibson 2010. *Ethics and Game Design: Teaching Values through Play*. New York: Information Science Reference.

Schrier, K. & D. Gibson 2011. *Designing Games for Ethics: Models, Techniques and Frameworks*. New York: Information Science Reference.

Schrödinger, E. 1992. *What is Life? With Mind and Matter and Autobiographical Sketches*. Cambridge: Cambridge University Press.

Schroeder, R. 2006. "Being There Together and the Future of Connected Presence". *Presence* **15**(4): 438–54.

Schulte, P. 2012. "The Difference Between Moral and Rational 'Oughts': An Expressivist Account". *Ethical Theory and Moral Practice* **15**(2): 159–74.

Schulzke, M. 2010. "Defending the Morality of Violent Video Games". *Ethics in Information Technology* **12**(2): 127–38.

Schulzke, M. 2011. "Reflective Play and Morality: Video Games as Thought Experiments". See Poels & Malliet (2011), 51–68.

Searle, J. 1995. *The Construction of Social Reality*. Harmondsworth: Penguin.

Sherry, J. L. 2001. "The Effects of Violent Video Games on Aggression: A Meta-analysis". *Human Communication Research* **27**(3): 409–31.

Shibuya, A., A. Sakamoto, N. Ihori & S. Yukawa 2008. "The Effects of the Presence and Contexts of Video Game Violence on Children: A Longitudinal Study in Japan". *Simulation & Gaming* **39**(4): 528–39.

Shoard, C. 2011. "Human Centipede 2 Director Criticises BBFC Over Rejection". *Guardian* (7June). www.guardian.co.uk/film/2011/jun/07/human-centipede-2-ban-tom-six-spoilers (accessed November 2012).

Sicart, M. 2009. *The Ethics of Computer Games*. Cambridge, MA: MIT Press.

Sicart, M. 2010. "This War is a Lie: Ethical Implications of Massively Multiplayer Online Game Design". See Wankel & Malleck (2010), 177–95.

Simmel, G. 1950. *The Sociology of Georg Simmel*, K. Wolff (trans.). New York: Free Press.

Singer, P. 2007. "Video Crime Peril vs. Virtual Pedophilia". *The Japanese Times* (22 July). http://search.japantimes.co.jp/cgi-bin/eo20070722a1.html (accessed November 2012).

Sky News 2007. "Paedophiles Target Virtual World". *Sky News* (31 October). http://news.sky.com/skynews/Home/Sky-News-Archive/Article/20080641290719 (accessed November 2012).

Skyrms, B. 1996. *Evolution of the Social Contract*. Cambridge: Cambridge University Press.

Šmahel, D., L. Blinka & M. A. Ledabyl 2008. "Playing MMORPGs: Connections Between Addiction and Identifying with a Character". *CyberPsychology & Behavior* **11**(6): 715–18.

Smart, J. J. C. & B. Williams 1973. *Utilitarianism: For and Against*. Cambridge: Cambridge University Press.

Smith, K. K. 2008. "Animals and the Social Contract: A Reply to Nussbaum". *Environmental Ethics* **30**: 195–207.

Soldz, S. 2008. "Healers and Interrogators: Psychology and the United States Torture Regime". *Psychoanalytic Dialogues* **18**: 592–613.

Søraker, J. H. 2010. "The Neglect of Reason: A Plea for Rationalist Accounts of the Effects of Virtual Violence". See Wankel & Malleck (2010), 15–31.

Spicer, A., T. W. Dunfee & W. J. Bailey 2004. "Does National Context Matter in Ethical Decision Making? An Empirical Test of Integrative Social Contracts Theory". *Academy of Management Journal* **47**(4): 610–20.

Spinello, R. A. 2001. "Code and Moral Values in Cyberspace". *Ethics and Information Technology* **3**: 137–50.

Sterba, J. P. 1979. "Ethical Egoism and Beyond". *Canadian Journal of Philosophy* **9**(1): 91–108.

Stock, K. 2005. "Resisting Imaginative Resistance". *Philosophical Quarterly* **55**(221): 607–24.

Strikwerda, L. 2012. "Theft of Virtual Items in Online Multiplayer Computer Games: An Ontological and Moral Analysis". *Ethics and Information Technology* **14**(2): 89–97. DOI: 10.1007/s10676-011-9285-3

Sulkunen, P. 2007. "Re-Inventing the Social Contract". *Acta Sociological* **50**(3): 325–33.

Tamborini, R., A. Eden, N. D. Bowman, M. Grizzard & K. Lachlan 2012. "The Influence of Morality Subcultures on the Acceptance and Appeal of Violence". *Journal of Communication* **62**(1): 136–57.

Tan, T. M. 2007. "Beastiality in Second Life". *Dorks & Losers* (25 July). www.dorksandlosers.com/2007/07/25/beastiality-in-second-life/ (accessed November 2012).

Tavinor, G. 2005. "Videogames and Interactive Fiction". *Philosophy and Literature* **29**(1): 24–40.

Tavinor, G. 2008. "Definition of Videogames". *Contemporary Aesthetics* **6**: 1–17.

The Average Gamer 2010. "What is an Average Gamer?" www.theaveragegamer.com/averagegamers/ (accessed November 2012).

Thomas, L. 1980. "Ethical Egoism and Psychological Disposition". *American Philosophical Quarterly* **17**(1): 73–8.

Thompson, J. A. & D. W. Hart 2006. "Psychological Contracts: A Nano-Level Perspective on Social Contract Theory". *Journal of Business Ethics* **68**: 229–41.

Turkle, S. 1995. *Life on the Screen: Identity in the Age of the Internet.* Cambridge, MA: MIT Press.

Unsworth, G. & G. J. Devilly 2007. "The Effect of Playing Violent Video Games on Adolescents: Should Parents be Quaking in their Boots?" *Psychology, Crime and Law* **13**(4): 383–94.

USA Today 2003. "Take-Two to Edit Haitian Remarks from Video Game". *USA Today* (11 December). www.usatoday.com/tech/news/2003-12-11-taketwo-vs-haiti_x.htm (accessed November 2012).

Vallor, S. 2010. "Social Networking Technology and the Virtues". *Ethics and Information Technology* **12**: 157–70.

Vanacker, B. & D. Heider 2011. "Ethical Harm in Virtual Communities". *Convergence: The International Journal of Research into New Media Technologies* **18**(1): 71–84.

Verweyen, H. 1996. "Social Contract Among Devils". *Idealistic Studies* **26**(2): 189–202.

Waddington, D. I. 2007. "Locating the Wrongness in Ultra-violent Video Games". *Ethics and Information Technology* **9**(2): 121–8.

Walker, A. D. M. 1989. "Virtue and Character". *Philosophy* **64**(249): 349–62.

Walton, K. L. & M. Tanner 1994. "Morals in Fiction and Fictional Morality". *Proceedings of the Aristotelian Society (Supplementary)* **68**: 27–66.

Wankel, C. & S. Malleck (eds) 2010. *Emerging Ethical Issues of Life in Virtual Worlds.* Charlotte, NC: Information Age Publishing.

Weber, R., K.-M. Behr, R. Tamborini, U. Ritterfeld & K. Mathiak 2009. "What Do We Really Know About First-Person-Shooter Games? An Event-Related, High-Resolution Content Analysis". *Journal of Computer-Mediated Communication* **14**: 1016–37.

Weirich, P. 2010. "Exclusion from the Social Contract". *Politics, Philosophy & Economics* **10**(2):148–69.

Whang, L. S. & G. Chang 2004. "Lifestyles of Virtual World Residents: Living in the On-line Game 'Lineage'". *CyberPsychology & Behavior* **7**(5): 592–600.

Whitty, M. T. 2003. "Cyber-flirting: Playing at Love on the Internet". *Theory and Psychology* **13**(3): 339–57.

Whitty, M. T. & A. N. Carr 2003. "Cyberspace as Potential Space: Considering the Web as a Playground to Cyber-flirt". *Human Relations* **56**(7): 861–91.

Whitty, M. T. & A. N. Carr 2005. "Taking the Good with the Bad: Applying Klein's work to Further our Understandings of Cyber-cheating". *Journal of Couple and Relationship Therapy* **4**(2/3), 103–15.

Whitty, M. T. & A. N. Carr 2006. *Cyberspace Romance: The Psychology of Online Relationships.* Basingstoke: Palgrave Macmillan.

Whitty, M. T., G. Young & L. Goodings 2011. "What I Won't do in Pixels: Examining the Limits of Taboo Violation in MMORPGs". *Computers in Human Behavior* **27**(1): 268–75.

Williams, B. 1973. *Problem of the Self.* Cambridge: Cambridge University Press.

Williams, D. & M. Skoric 2005. "Internet Fantasy Violence: A Test of Aggression in an Online Game". *Communication Monographs* **22**(2): 217–33.

Williams, D., M. Consalvo, S. Caplan & N. Yee 2009. "Looking for Gender: Gender Roles and Behaviors Among Online Gamers". *Journal of Communication* **59**: 700–725.

Williams, D., T. L. M. Kennedy & R. J. Moore 2011. "Behind the Avatar: The Patterns, Practices, and Functions of Role Playing in MMOs". *Games and Culture* **6**(2): 171–200.

Williams, K. D. 2011. "The Effects of Homophily, Identification, and Violent Video Games on Players". *Mass Communication and Society* **14**(1): 3–24.

Wissmath, B., D. Weibel & R. Groner 2009. "Dubbing or Subtitling? Effects on Spatial Presence, Transportation, Flow, and Enjoyment". *Journal of Media Psychology* **21**(3): 114–25.

Wittgenstein, L. 1953. *Philosophical Investigations*, G. E. M. Anscombe (trans.). Oxford: Blackwell.

Wolfendale, J. 2007. "My Avatar, My Self: Virtual Harm and Attachment". *Ethics and Information Technology* **9**: 111–19.

Wonderly, M. 2008. "A Humean Approach to Assessing the Moral Significance of Ultra-Violent Video Games". *Ethics in Information Technology* **10**(1): 1–10.

Woodcock, S. 2012. "Horror Films and the Argument from Reactive Attitudes". *Ethical Theory and Moral Practice* (February). http://rd.springer.com/article/10.1007/s10677-012-9338-7 (accessed November 2012).

Worth, S. E. 2004. "Fictional Spaces". *The Philosophical Forum* **35**(4): 439–55.

Yee, N. 2006a. "Motivations for Play in Online Games". *CyberPsychology & Behaviour* **9**(6): 772–5.

Yee, N. 2006b. "The Demographics, Motivations and Derived Experiences of Users of Massively Multiuser Online Graphical Environments". *PRESENCE: Teleoperators and Virtual Environments* **15**: 309–29.

Young, G. 2010. "Virtually Real Emotions and the Paradox of Fiction: Implications for the use of virtual environments in psychological research". *Philosophical Psychology* **23**(1): 1–21.

Young, G. in press. "Enacting Taboos as a Means to an End; But What End? On the Morality of Motivations for Child Murder and Paedophilia within Gamespace". *Ethics and Information Technology*.

Young, G. & M. T. Whitty 2010. "Games Without Frontiers: On the Moral and Psychological Implications of Violating Taboos Within Multi-player Virtual Spaces". *Computers in Human Behavior* **26**(6): 1228–36.

Young, G. & M. T. Whitty 2011a. "Progressive Embodiment Within Cyberspace: Considering the Psychological Impact of the Supermorphic Persona". *Philosophical Psychology* **24**(4): 537–60.

Young, G. & M. T. Whitty 2011b. "Should Gamespace be a Taboo-free Zone? Moral and Psychological Implications for Single-player Video Games". *Theory and Psychology* **21**(6): 802–20.

Young, G. & M. T. Whitty 2012. *Transcending Taboos: A Moral and Psychological Examination of Cyberspace*. London: Routledge.

Zagal, J. P. 2009. "Ethically Notable Videogames: Moral Dilemmas and Gameplay". In *Breaking New Ground: Innovation in Games, Play, Practice and Theory*, Proceedings of the Digital Games Research Association International Conference (DiGRA) 2009, B. Atkins, T. Krzywinska & H. Kennedy (eds), 1–9. London. www.digra.org/dl/db/09287.13336.pdf (accessed November 2012).

Zagal, J. P. 2011. "Heavy Rain: Morality in Quotidian, Inaction, and the Ambiguous". See Poels & Malliet (2011), 267–86.

Zillmann, D. 2000. "Basal Morality in Drama Appreciation". In *Moving Images, Culture, and the Mind*, I. Bondebjerg (ed.), 53–63. Luton: University of Luton.

Zjawinski, S. 2007. "Second Life's Version of My Little Pony Is NSFW". *Wired* (18 September). www.wired.com/underwire/2007/09/second-lifes-ve/ (accessed November 2012).

179

Index